T0398647

PERFORMING PARENTHOOD

Non-Normative Fathers and Mothers
in Spanish Narrative and Film

HEATHER JERÓNIMO

Performing Parenthood

Non-Normative Fathers and Mothers in Spanish Narrative and Film

UNIVERSITY OF TORONTO PRESS
Toronto Buffalo London

© University of Toronto Press 2024
Toronto Buffalo London
utorontopress.com

ISBN 978-1-4875-5421-7 (cloth)
ISBN 978-1-4875-5423-1 (EPUB)
ISBN 978-1-4875-5422-4 (PDF)

Toronto Iberic

Library and Archives Canada Cataloguing in Publication

Title: Performing parenthood : non-normative fathers and mothers in Spanish narrative and film / Heather Jerónimo.
Names: Jerónimo, Heather, author.
Series: Toronto Iberic ; 92.
Description: Series statement: Toronto Iberic ; 92 | Includes bibliographical references and index.
Identifiers: Canadiana (print) 20240316177 | Canadiana (ebook) 20240316207 | ISBN 9781487554217 (cloth) | ISBN 9781487554231 (EPUB) | ISBN 9781487554224 (PDF)
Subjects: LCSH: Spanish literature – 20th century – History and criticism. | LCSH: Spanish literature – 21st century – History and criticism. | LCSH: Motion pictures – Spain. | LCSH: Families in literature. | LCSH: Families in motion pictures. | LCSH: Motherhood in literature. | LCSH: Fatherhood in literature. | LCSH: Motherhood in motion pictures. | LCSH: Fatherhood in motion pictures. | LCSH: Gay people in literature.
Classification: LCC PQ6073.F33 J47 2024 | DDC 860.9/3552–dc23

Cover design: Louise OFarrell

We wish to acknowledge the land on which the University of Toronto Press operates. This land is the traditional territory of the Wendat, the Anishnaabeg, the Haudenosaunee, the Métis, and the Mississaugas of the Credit First Nation.

This book has been published with the assistance of the University of Northern Iowa.

University of Toronto Press acknowledges the financial support of the Government of Canada, the Canada Council for the Arts, and the Ontario Arts Council, an agency of the Government of Ontario, for its publishing activities.

  Canada Council   Conseil des Arts
    for the Arts   du Canada

ONTARIO ARTS COUNCIL
CONSEIL DES ARTS DE L'ONTARIO
an Ontario government agency
un organisme du gouvernement de l'Ontario

To my parents
And to Josh

Contents

List of Illustrations ix
Acknowledgments xi

Introduction 3
1 Writing Fatherhood 28
2 M(other)hood and Disability 61
3 The Shifting Face of Fatherhood 85
4 Lesbian Maternal Community Formation 119
5 Beyond the Biological Family 140
6 A Family in All Senses 175
Conclusion 201

Notes 205
Bibliography 219
Index 233

Illustrations

1.1 Constancito's Album Covers   38
1.2 Newborn Constancito   53
1.3 Underwater boxing match refereed by the Virgin of Montserrat   54
1.4 *Héroes del Cilicio* [*Cilice Heroes*]   55
1.5 Constancito and Heidi on *Titanic*   56
3.1 Marina caring for Daniel in the bathroom   95
3.2 Leo reading a bedtime story to Dafne while wearing Alicia's lipstick   107
6.1 Amador touching Marcela's stomach   185
6.2 Nelson examining the torn-up letter   199

Acknowledgments

This is my first book, so it should come as no surprise that many people have guided and supported me on this journey. I have learned an incredible amount during this process, and I appreciate every person who has positively impacted me along the way. I owe a giant debt of gratitude to Jolene Zigarovich, who has mentored me from the moment I arrived at the University of Northern Iowa, answering all my questions, pushing me to achieve, celebrating every accomplishment, and inspiring me with her passion for research. Jolene and Elizabeth Zwanziger threw me the loveliest book shower to celebrate my contract, and I will always cherish their friendship.

Many people offered feedback at various stages of the book-writing process, giving generously of their time and knowledge when they were under no obligation to do so. Akiko Tsuchiya, Fran Fernández de Alba, and Carmen Granda provided indispensable feedback during the early stages of the publishing process, and their encouraging words gave me the confidence to continue moving ahead.

I have been supported in various ways by my institution, the University of Northern Iowa, during the process of writing and publishing this book. Thank you to the graduate college for awarding me a Professional Development Assignment in the spring of 2021 that allowed me the time to write. Dean Fritch, your enthusiastic support of this book came at exactly the right time, for which I will forever be thankful. I appreciate my home department of Languages & Literatures for their help in funding the book. I also received financial assistance from UNI's Women's and Gender Studies program, made possible by director Danielle Mcgeough. The University of Northern Iowa has top-notch library staff, who have assisted me in countless ways, from contactless book delivery during COVID to answering all my questions to finding resources for me (a special thanks to Amandajean Nolte). While I'm talking about

UNI, I wish to recognize my fantastic students, who supported me and celebrated each step of the process with me. I am moved and humbled to work with students who are genuinely invested in my research and who care about me as a person.

I wish to acknowledge my Spanish colleagues in the Department of Languages & Literatures – Jenny Cooley, Elise DuBord, Juan Carlos Castillo, Gabi Olivares, and Elena Dobrila – with whom I feel a true sense of community and companionship. Several of them read chapters in progress, and I appreciate their valuable feedback, as well as Zak Montgomery and Ana Kogl for their insights on the book. Ana, thank you for allowing me to monopolize large chunks of our Friday afternoons at The Ragged Edge (thanks, Ragged Edge) with conversations about the book. I value your friendship immensely.

Thank you to everyone at the University of Toronto Press for making this incredible experience possible. Mark Thompson, thank you for seeing the potential in this book. It has been an absolute delight to work with you. Bob Davidson, thank you for your enthusiastic support of my work and for making me feel so welcome in this community of scholars. I am grateful beyond words for the time and attention that my two reviewers dedicated to the manuscript. This book would not be what it is without their insightful and gentle guidance.

I am honoured to know author Lluís Maria Todó, who has always been receptive to discussing his brilliant works of literature with me. I am thrilled that Ricardo Cavolo has allowed me to reproduce some of his illustrations from *¿Por qué me comprasteis un walkie talkie si era hijo único?* in this book. Many thanks to Nuria Godón and Michael Horswell for their permission to include part of my chapter "La paternidad periférica y su relación con la crisis de la masculinidad en *Todo lo que tú quieras* de Achero Mañas," which appeared in their 2016 co-edited anthology *Sexualidades periféricas: Consolidaciones literarias y fílmicas en la España de siglo XIX y fin de milenio* in chapter 3 of this book. An earlier iteration of chapter 2 appeared in *Letras Femininas* in 2016 as an article titled "Angels or Monsters? Motherhood in the Dystopian World of Paloma Díaz-Mas's 'La niña sin alas'."

My friends in the Joyous Writing group have been instrumental in answering my questions during the writing and publishing process. Thank you to Hilal Ergül, Sal Attardo, and Elisa Gironzetti. You all inspire me to keep writing.

I'm so glad that graduate school allowed me to meet Chris Carter, Allysha Martin, and Gabby Vidal-Torreira. You have stood by me throughout the numerous ups and downs of academic and personal life. I treasure our various academic collaborations, as well as your friendship.

Acknowledgments

I became interested in the idea of non-normative Spanish families while writing my dissertation at the University of Nebraska-Lincoln, directed by Iker González-Allende. My thanks to him and to my committee members Harriet Turner, Óscar Pereira-Zazo, the late Chantal Kalisa, Margaret Jacobs, and Basuli Deb.

I am fortunate to have a great number of patient friends who have listened to me talk about my book, probably long after they were interested in the topic. Maria Leicy, thank you for thirty-four years of friendship and unwavering belief in me. Melissa Dobosh and Heather Gallivan, I am eternally grateful that I met you during new faculty orientation. Along with that of Sarah Diesburg, your friendship is priceless to me. To my *chicas alicantinas*, I value your friendship and constant encouragement: Maria Smith, Chelsea Rohrer-Dann, Tamara Rhodes, and Hamida Saleh. Thank you, Raquel Medina, for being my friend and mentor, and for always being willing to grab a coffee with me whenever I'm in Barcelona. Kyle Winckler, Joel Robinson, and Jacy Pillitteri, thank you for the many ways in which you have supported me over the years.

Thank you to the grandmas in my life: Grandma Marj for helping to foster my love of books and reading, Grandma Lana for never giving up hope that my book would be published, and Grandma Donna for her love and support.

Finally, I would like to thank my parents, Debra and Roger Hoffart, and my husband, Josh Gregory. My parents have always made me feel like I can accomplish anything, and they raised me in a loving family. Josh, I am incredibly happy that we have chosen each other as family, and I could not have asked for a more encouraging partner. Thank you for always reassuring me when I start to doubt myself. This book is dedicated to Josh and to my parents.

PERFORMING PARENTHOOD

Introduction

Pedro Almodóvar's 2021 film *Madres paralelas* [*Parallel Mothers*] recounts the story of two markedly different single women who share a hospital room as they give birth to their daughters on the same day, embarking on motherhood journeys with some parallels and other divergences due to their personalities and family histories. These women, and the ideological backgrounds their families symbolize, are representative of cultural and political tensions that have categorized two distinct types of familial constructions in Spain throughout much of the twentieth century. Janis (played by Penelope Cruz) is a well-respected photographer nearing forty who, after her hippie mother died of a drug overdose, was raised by her grandmother in a matriarchal family marked by the backlash of their support for Spain's Second Republic. Pregnant as the result of a romantic relationship with a married man, Janis is happy to become a mother and raise her daughter by herself. Ana (played by Milena Smit) is a teenager who has been sent by her wealthy, conservative father in Granada to stay with her mother in Madrid because she is pregnant after being raped by a group of three teenage boys. She is unenthusiastic about motherhood before baby Anita is born. After the birth, Ana dotes on her baby and dedicates herself to caring for her in the luxurious apartment she shares with her mother, an aspiring actress who is rarely home. The hospital accidentally switches Ana's and Janis's babies shortly after birth, leading them to raise each other's daughter. By the time Janis begins to suspect that her baby's features are not a reflection of her own and conducts a DNA test to confirm her fear, the baby that Ana is raising has already died of sudden infant death syndrome. For a time, Janis and Ana live together, raising Cecilia (Ana's biological daughter who was given to Janis) as a couple and engaging in a sexual relationship.

Madres paralelas, a film that begins and ends with a focus on the mass graves of the Spanish Civil War (1936–9), connects the ideas of family and nation on micro- and macrolevels. Ana and Janis form a non-normative family together with baby Cecilia for a time, despite the conflicting political stances they learned from their families, whose trajectories were affected differently during the Spanish Civil War and Francisco Franco's subsequent dictatorship (1939–75). Throughout the film, Janis works diligently to convince the Association for the Recovery of Historical Memory (ARHM) to excavate a mass grave from the Spanish Civil War in her family's small town, so that she can lay her great-grandfather's remains to rest and provide some closure for her family. Ana, much younger than Janis, does not fully grasp how the repercussions of the civil war continue to affect Spanish families generations later. Declaring herself apolitical, Ana tells Janis that her father says it is more important to look toward the future, rather than spending time digging up graves from the past, a statement that reveals her family's fascist leanings. The characters of Janis and Ana demonstrate how Spanish models of the family (that were either lauded or persecuted) during Franco's dictatorship continue to influence contemporary Spanish familial construction.

Madres paralelas demonstrates that families are both personal and political constructions, private and public institutions that function on individual and national levels. The DNA tests that Janis, Ana, and their babies take to clarify their biological connections parallel the cheek swabs that ARHM workers take from surviving family members of Republican families to match with DNA remains of their ancestors found in mass graves. Although Janis and Ana represent only two potential configurations of Spanish families, the political conflicts associated with the Spanish Civil War have shaped Spanish families throughout much of the twentieth century. Throughout Francisco Franco's dictatorship, his conservative and repressive National Catholic ideology promoted the idea of Franco as the father of the Spanish nation, with heteronormative nuclear families attempting to emulate his example. I will establish throughout this book that the model of the traditional family that Franco promoted as ubiquitous was, in fact, far from reality, and no real family was capable of consistently living up to these patriarchal expectations.

Instead, although not the official rhetoric of much of twentieth-century Spain, the realities and lived experiences of Spanish families exist along a diverse spectrum of non-normative configurations. In *Madres paralelas* (as in most of Almodóvar's work), the two featured families are matriarchal, without strong father figures.[1] Janis and Ana are connected to their daughters by emotional ties, not biology; even after learning that their babies were swapped, they continue to love both babies and care for Cecilia together. The two women's construction of family is fluid; at times, they live together and raise baby Cecilia as a couple, but this configuration is not permanent. In addition to addressing changing gender roles within the Spanish family (Janis and Ana provide economically for their children without support from the babies' fathers), *Madres paralelas* touches on the impact of immigration in Spanish familial formations. In this case, the film seems to reveal national anxieties about more culturally diverse families, as Ana's baby was fathered by a South American teenager who raped her. *Madres paralelas* grapples with the concept of the Spanish family, an institution that is reconfiguring its future in response to many social and cultural shifts, while remaining marked by the country's history of dictatorship and National Catholicism. Many of the themes present in *Madres paralelas* are reflected in the literary and cinematic examples of family that I analyze in *Performing Parenthood*, with the goal of highlighting the diversity and complexity of contemporary Spanish families. An examination of non-normative constructions of Spanish family in literature and film reveals many truths about how the society in which these cultural artefacts were produced views the family. Those who observe Spanish families on the page or screen will become more aware of the universally human yet remarkably unique experience of being part of a family by understanding the preoccupations surrounding changing gender roles for mothers and fathers; the challenges and rewards of non-biological parenthood, gay parenthood, and other alternative constructions of parenthood; the ways in which Spanish families adapt to cultural shifts brought on by immigration; and other aspects that affect changing Spanish families.

Defining the Spanish Family

Performing Parenthood evaluates an assortment of enactments of parenthood in twentieth- and twenty-first-century Spain, showing how the family has adapted, or at times failed to do so, within the context of Spain's changing socio-economic reality. By examining a variety of non-normative examples of parenthood in contemporary Spanish literature and film – ranging from gay literary father figures, subversive physical touch between mother and child, fathers who cross-dress, lesbian maternal community building, non-biological parenthood, cross-cultural families, disabled bodies, and the role of domestic help within family identity formation – the book argues that current conceptualizations of parenthood must be amplified to reflect the various existing parental identities in Spain. *Performing Parenthood* contends that parenthood is a performative identity, whose actions and experiences should be acknowledged as part of a spectrum not tied to gender. By releasing individuals from culturally constructed and gendered parental roles, parenthood can be viewed as a fluid performance that adapts over time and due to varying circumstances. Scholars, members of Spanish society, and anyone interested in familial formation can amplify their understanding of the diverse ways in which families function through an examination of the cultural representations of the family in Spanish literature and film.

While the traditional patriarchal family is a central and ubiquitous image within Spanish culture, literature, and film, I assert that no Spanish family has ever been able to fully adhere to all the requirements of this social unit for a sustained period of time. Spanish literature and film often portray the polished exterior of the heteronormative family while exposing or hinting at cracks in the facade, suggesting that the traditional Spanish family is not as unified or universal as we have been led to believe. The portrayal of a cracked or flawed patriarchal traditional family in Spanish literature and film not only critiques familial dysfunction of a "broken institution" (Domingo Amestoy 115) that mirrors larger questions and discomforts about the state of the national ideology, but also pointedly demonstrates that this prized patriarchal family, "a vehicle for the Falange's ideology" (115), has never truly existed in a way that lives up to the expectations imposed upon it. While countless Spanish families have aspired to the principles of the idealized patriarchal family or have consciously or unconsciously upheld aspects of the patriarchal family definition, the reality of Spanish families is plural, allowing for myriad constructions of familial units with a wide range of experiences and enactments of the parenthood role.

As the concept of the patriarchal traditional family is deeply entrenched in the Spanish psyche, it is necessary to understand the characteristics of this symbolic unit in order to measure it against examples of Spanish families from literature, film, and society, despite the lack of actual families who live up to the demands of the definition. The traditional Spanish family is characterized by enforced unity, strict gender roles and expectations for its members, and adherence to patriotic and religious duties. While Franco's dictatorship solidified expectations for the Spanish nuclear family and its members in the early twentieth century, an understanding of the traditional family is firmly situated in Spanish society centuries earlier. The 1732 Spanish *Diccionario de Autoridades* [*Dictionary of Authorities*] described the family as a group led by a patriarchal father figure, the head of the family who holds unquestionable authority and power over the family unit, defined as the "gente que vive en una casa debaxo del mando del señor de ella" ["people who live in a house under the authority of the house's lord"] ("Familia"). The definition described everything within the household as property of the homeowner, including servants and other family members. The gendered nature of family work and roles was perpetuated by strict divisions of space in the nineteenth century, while Franco's National Catholicism calcified rigid gender roles, which "constituted the essence of a unified Spanish identity, the natural moral foundation for family life" (Perriam et al. 10). Within multigenerational nuclear family units, each member had a distinct role to play. The father figure was the authoritative head of the house, presiding over his wife (whose job was to oversee the home life and facilitate the mental, physical, and spiritual well-being of her family) and children, who were (ideally) plentiful gifts from God, although boys were treasured more than girls (Trotman 2). The family's many responsibilities included promulgating and policing religious, sexual, and cultural values, as well as modelling gendered social relationships and physically and mentally nurturing children (Cooper 11).

The Spanish family under the dictatorship was meant to be a microcosm of Spain, the father figure a reflection of Franco as the father of the nation, pressured to embody heterosexual virility, physical and emotional fortitude, economic prowess, and authority. The Álvarez encyclopedia (one of the most widely used during Franco's dictatorship) from 1964 described the father as the "jefe de la familia" ["leader of the family"], whose functions included working outside the home to provide economically for the family and commanding other members of his family, "para que bajo su amorosa autoridad cada cual cumpla su mission" ["so that under his loving authority everyone fulfils their mission"] (Álvarez Pérez 592). Endorsed by National Catholicism, the father figure was to use his authority in the acts of "providing for, protecting, guiding, and disciplining his wife and children" (Perriam et al. 68). Although this privileged role provided the traditional Spanish father figure with much greater autonomy than other family members, he was also limited by gendered expectations that required him to be perpetually unemotional, self-controlled, and disciplined (Aresti 154); provide economically for the family; and display physical strength and sexual virility.

Spanish motherhood in the traditional patriarchal family was characterized by submission to the husband and self-sacrifice for the needs of the family. Shaped by nineteenth-century rhetoric of the woman as the "ángel del hogar" ["angel of the hearth"], this traditional motherhood identity was further solidified by Franco's National Catholic ideology, which elevated mothers to become "the mainstay of the regime on the condition that they restricted their activities to the private sphere" (Brooksbank Jones 40). Under the dictatorship, prolific motherhood was constructed as Spanish women's vocation and patriotic duty, with the Spanish government establishing various financial incentives for those families with many children and discouraging married women and mothers from working outside the home (Perriam et al. 69), which bound them to their husbands through economic and legal dependence. Spanish women were pushed further into a subservient social position, as they could not sign contracts, travel without a father or husband's permission, or receive higher education (Radcliff 504–5), leaving women with few options beyond motherhood. The *Sección Femenina* [*Feminine Section*], the women's branch of the Falange, supported Franco's motherhood mission by teaching classes that transmitted Catholic conservative moral values of self-sacrifice and chastity to women who were expected to convey these ideas to their children and emulate the ideology in their homes (Richmond 4). Mothers were expected to be the moral compass of the family, inhabiting the domestic sphere, giving birth to children, caring for the home, ministering to the family's spiritual and physical needs, and educating the children to be patriotic Catholic citizens, furthering the patriarchal system as a crucial "transmitter of cultural values" (Finnerty 213). While much of the motherhood role was tied to physical touch as part of their caregiver role, sexuality for women was unfathomable outside of the context of reproduction. In all matters, Spanish mothers were to put their needs last, finding fulfilment in caring for their husbands and children.

Although these gendered familial roles have been firmly ingrained in the Spanish psyche, *Performing Parenthood* rejects the concept of the ubiquitous traditional nuclear Spanish family, asserting that normativity is often only surface deep. Rather, Spanish families should be understood as part of a wide and diverse spectrum of relational enactments that, of course, have been impacted by sociohistorical changes, but are not controlled by any one definition of what a family should be. Acknowledging the diversity within familial formation provides a unique lens for reflection on both traditional and alternative family constructions. However, stepping away from traditional definitions of the nuclear family makes it more difficult to establish a single, concise definition of the family or parental roles and expectations. While definitions and lists of characteristics can be helpful, interpreting families as part of a spectrum allows for a variety of possible ways in which we can comprehend the concept of Spanish families. The 2021 *Diccionario de la*

Lengua Española [*Dictionary of the Spanish Language*] defines the family in multiple ways, such as a "grupo de personas emparentadas entre sí que viven juntas" ["group of related people who live together"] ("familia"). While this definition is certainly vaguer than the one provided by the 1964 Álvarez encyclopedia, it is not exclusionary. Although modern definitions of the family may need to sacrifice precision or lose detail, they benefit from allowing space for multiple meanings of the family.

Instead of attempting to define the family, *Performing Parenthood* investigates the multiple functions of the family, questioning expectations for family members and the ways in which they perform familial roles. Families often (but not always) meet the emotional, economic, and physical needs of their members. In many cases, they teach values, gender roles and sexuality, political and religious beliefs, socialization skills, and at times subversion (as Martine Segalen proposes in *Historical Anthropology of the Family*). Not all families fulfil all of these roles, but all of these functions have fallen under the purview of the family at some point, making it easy to see why the familial unit has been of interest as a tool of social or political control. The family holds great power in its potential to shape the ideologies and viewpoints of its members, a mental fashioning that can be beneficial or detrimental for family members. As Sara Cooper elucidates in *The Ties That Bind*, the Spanish family can be a protective nest or stifling prison for its members. Cooper describes the Spanish family's potential to be a "safe haven and refuge," a "[c]aring space where children are nurtured," and a place where women enjoy "a certain amount of power and voice" (6). Alternately, Cooper acknowledges that Spanish "literature has shown family to be a socially constructed prison cell, a set of limitations that chafes and destroys, and a place where unimaginable violence and cruelty are perpetuated" (6). Families are complex, and a family unit that at times supports and uplifts its members may work to oppress them in other ways or in different settings. Furthermore, each family member will have a unique experience within the family unit, making it difficult for members of the same family to arrive at one agreed-upon characterization of the family.

I will not attempt to establish an all-encompassing definition of the family, nor do I believe that such a definition could or should exist. Rather, *Performing Parenthood* offers an examination of enactments of parental roles in Spanish literature and film from the late twentieth and early twenty-first centuries in order to demonstrate that the normative family simply does not exist beyond Franco's fascist propaganda. Instead, the monolithic Spanish family is a concept that can obstruct scholars from acknowledging and analysing the multiple familial formations present in contemporary Spain. Both scholars and members of Spanish society can amplify their understanding of the family by considering it as part of a wide spectrum, wherein parenthood is enacted in a fluid way, motherhoods and fatherhoods understood as performative identities that should not be separated by gendered expectations of the roles. While I argue for a more fluid understanding of parenthood not focused on gender roles, I acknowledge that the chapters in this book do engage in a dialogue about traditional motherhood and fatherhood roles, because this is the current language that we use to discuss parenthood. While I argue that, regardless of gender, a parent should be free to enact their role in the ways they see fit, I cannot ignore the socially constructed gender roles that are attached to traditional understandings of motherhood or fatherhood. While societies may someday move away from gendered understandings of parenthood, this is not currently the case, and I must analyse the films and literary texts within the context in which they were produced. Even within a society that associates parental and gender roles, literary and cinematic examples of Spanish families show diverse enactments of parenthood that at times question and deviate from traditional understandings of gender roles. Everyone, scholars and members of society alike, should be invested in a greater understanding of the Spanish family so as to better understand not only Spanish culture and society but also the multiple meanings associated with belonging to a family as a parent or child, an experience that is both universal and unique, something that everyone participates in, in their own way.

History of the Spanish Family

Spanish society's modernization – which has happened at a staggering pace in recent decades – is an important factor that has contributed to the diverse spectrum of familial enactments within which Spanish families are currently located. The traditional model of the conservative nuclear family, which was promoted by Francisco Franco's dictatorship but existed long before Franco's influence, no longer holds a monolithic cultural presence in Spanish society. The Spanish Transition to democracy (which began after Franco's death in 1975 and continued through much of the 1980s) provided more extensive freedom in familial formation, aided by an influx of women in the workforce, accessible contraception, divorce as a legal option, and a reimagining of maternal and paternal roles. While scholars and society are advancing toward an understanding of more diverse configurations of Spanish families, the family's trajectory is more complicated than a linear path toward acceptance of various iterations of the institution. The tension and opposing ideologies behind the concept of the "dos Españas"[2] ["two Spains"] reverberates within contemporary perceptions of the family, which remain divided between conservative family models and non-traditional constructions. Contemporary gender roles – which establish expectations of fatherhood and motherhood roles – echo the separate spheres rhetoric of the nineteenth century, wherein the family was a project of "collective responsibility" (Labanyi 329), bestowing authority, economic responsibility, and physical mobility on men while confining women to the oppressively limited space of the home as the family's moral compass and angel of the hearth (Mangini 85).

Spain's Second Republic (1931–6) provided some concessions to a restructuring of the Spanish family (mainly through nods to women's agency), but these expanded opportunities were short-lived. Women's rights for suffrage and divorce, as well as greater employment and educational opportunities, were among the rallying points for Spanish women intellectuals of the 1920s, including Victoria Kent, Carmen de Burgos, Margarita Nelken, and Clara Campoamor (Bieder 245). The feminism that developed in Spain during this time was markedly different than its counterpart in North America or other regions of Europe. "El discurso de la domesticidad" ["The discourse of domesticity"] ("Experiencia y Aprendizaje" 160), described by Mary Nash as a gender-based subordination of women, focused on maternity and reproduction as essential elements of women's identity. By maintaining an emphasis on the connection between Spanish motherhood, womanhood, and questions of feminism in Spain, "the notion of true womanhood remained unthinkable without motherhood as its necessary corollary throughout much of the twentieth century" (Jerónimo 58). By accentuating the connection between womanhood and motherhood, the focus of the women's movement in Spain shifted from arguments of gender equality to instead centre the debate on the concept of gender difference (Bieder 244).[3] In addition, the feminist movement in Spain at the beginning of the twentieth century emphasized the connections between social class and women's issues, as many Spanish feminists of the time were interested in bringing more women of all social classes (especially the working class) into civic society, rather than focusing solely on the political endeavours of middle-class women (Johnson and Castro 221).

The Spanish Civil War and Franco's subsequent dictatorship changed the direction of emerging conversations about feminism, women's rights, and their relationship to maternity, returning Spain to "a traditionalist Catholic hierarchy which promoted a model of women as only truly womanly when inside the home or the local church" (Brooksbank

Jones 75), a model that was later examined critically during conversations about Spanish feminism in the 1960s and beyond. Franco's death and *la Movida* – a subversive countercultural movement that emerged to challenge oppressive, phallocentric societal norms and gender roles from the late 1970s through the mid-1980s – created the possibility for a greater number of interpretations of family, motherhoods, fatherhoods, and gender roles in general.[4] The Transition brought about "seismic" (Trotman 4) changes to Spanish culture, questioning traditional gender roles in a way that enabled women to reject restrictive models of motherhood that had constrained women of previous generations. The Transition allowed for more extensive freedom in familial formation, aided by an influx of women in professional and educational settings, accessible contraception, legalized divorce and increased (although far from total) access to abortion[5] (Brooksbank Jones 85), and a reimagining of maternal and paternal roles.

Thanks to women's access to greater economic independence made possible by the Transition, women benefited from increased agency in decisions about marriage and childbirth, leading to alternative configurations of contemporary Spanish families. Couples have begun to have fewer children and frequently choose not to marry, or to do so later in life. While Spain entered the twentieth century with one of the highest birth rates in Europe, the country was on the other end of the spectrum by the end of the century (Ramiro-Fariñas et al. 50). With economic necessity no longer the primary tie holding most families together,[6] the institution prioritizes affective connections more highly. In her 1999 sociological study of the Spanish population, Inés Alberdi argues that for generations, the traditional Spanish family was formed and held together by the concept of sacrifice. In contemporary Spanish society, however, Alberdi asserts that the family strives toward "el derecho individual a la felicidad que atempera el sentido del deber" ["the individual right to happiness that moderates the sense of duty"] (19). This concept of the family concentrates on personal agency, suggesting that individuals' identities are impacted by factors beyond intimate family relationships. Alberdi's study indicates a shift away from economic necessity or survival as the primary link between family members toward an emphasis on affective connection.

In the twenty-first century, a changeable, multitudinous vision of Spanish families stands in stark contrast to the traditional family model stubbornly idealized in the last few years (and exacerbated by Spain's economic crisis [2008–14]) by conservative social factions whose anti-women, anti-immigrant rhetoric works to push the Spanish family back into limited roles. At the same time, the legalization of gay marriage and adoption in Spain (2005), globalization's influence on cultural and gender roles, anxieties and loneliness provoked in part by what sociologists such as Inés Alberdi describe as the Spanish family's increasing individualism, and diversity brought about by immigration are all factors that have expanded the definition of family in contemporary Spain. At a policy level, the current state of parenthood and the family in Spain seems to have improved exponentially.

However, there has been negative backlash against progressive legislation from the Catholic Church and members of the Partido Popular [Popular Party], the main conservative political party in Spain, who have made arguments about the importance of the biological family while evoking the fear that gay parents will raise gay children (Robbins 118). Despite progressive policies, homophobic attacks against queer people are still prevalent in Spain. From 2016 to 2017, hate crimes against the queer community rose by 17.8 per cent, to an officially recorded total of 271 hate crimes in Spain in 2017 (Mar and Aragón 57). Among LGBTQIA+ individuals, the trans population is at greatest risk. One sobering example of transphobic violence in Spain is the 1991 murder of trans woman Sonia Rescalvo in Barcelona's Citadel Park by a group of neo-Nazis. The bandstand where she was murdered has been renamed the "Transsexual Sonia Bandstand," and a Pink Triangle Memorial was unveiled in Barcelona on the twentieth anniversary of her murder (Newton-Jackson 97). Furthermore, the Spanish Catholic group, Hazte Oir [Make Yourself Heard], provoked scandal in 2017 when it covered a bus with anti-trans slogans, such as, "Los niños tienen pene. Las niñas tienen vulva. Que no te engañen" ["Boys have penises. Girls have vulvas. Don't let them fool you"]. The group was planning a cross-country tour until the Madrid City Council confiscated the bus ("Madrid Bans Catholic"). The emergence and popularity of ultra-conservative political parties show that Spain (like many parts of Europe and the world) remains divided between progressive and conservative mindsets, a pattern reflected within the Spanish family throughout the centuries.

The monolithic cultural ideal of the traditional Spanish family has long permeated Spanish culture, although the reality of Spanish families is much more diverse, complicated, and interesting. Contemporary Spanish cinema and literature are beginning to explore non-normative sexualities and non-Spanish ethnicities in relation to family formation. An analysis of the diverse examples of parenthood in individual texts and films uncovers multiple enactments and interpretations of Spanish families. As literature and film begin to create space for more diverse examples of the Spanish family, scholars and society members can use these artefacts to reach a cultural and artistic understanding of the diversity of Spanish families.

Family Studies in Spain

The literature and film analysed in *Performing Parenthood* reflect the impact of Spain's many recent social changes. While each representation of family is unique, these literary and cinematic portrayals of Spanish families share many points of commonality, primarily the institution's potential to support or stymie its members, often doing both to some extent.[7] The book presents diverse versions of the Spanish family, often in competition with one another – the traditional, conservative Spanish family juxtaposed with multicultural families, at times including immigrant members. A modern version of Spanish motherhood, with more economic independence and responsibilities, faces off against Spanish fatherhood and the changing role of masculinity. Many literary and cinematic examples of the family cite instances of incest or loneliness and isolation within the family, crafting the vision of a decaying institution. Another prevalent theme is the parental perspective that frames a relationship with one's children as the answer to longings for immortality, as parents create doppelgängers of themselves in their children, or as parents look to mimesis to understand how to fulfil their parental roles. Throughout this book, examples of diverse families in literature and film contribute to a greater understanding of the messy reality of parenthood, as seen through an artistic lens. These texts and films, although not intended to be completely faithful reflections of lived experiences of families in Spain, provide cultural and artistic interpretations of Spanish families that often capture a wide range of challenges, doubts, joys, and experiences of family units. The texts and films in *Performing Parenthood* touch on themes such as death, changing gender roles, shifting family structures, and sexual and cultural diversity within the family, which are present in contemporary Spanish society and within canonical Spanish literature about the family.

The diverse and non-normative representations of family in the texts and films I analyse in *Performing Parenthood* continue a long literary and cinematic tradition of representations of Spanish families that depart from or critique the traditional model in some way. Many Spanish novels and films from the second half of the twentieth century reveal the disintegration of the family through death and absence of its members.[8] The family is often described as a burden that traps its members (Carmen Laforet's *Nada* [*Nothing*], 1944) or the site of sexual exploitation and incest (Luis Martín-Santos's *Tiempo de silencio* [*Time of Silence*], 1962). In

Juan Benet's *Volverás a Región* [*You Will Return to Region*] (1967), Doctor Sebastián describes the family as

> un organismo con entidad propia, que trasciende a la suma de las criaturas que la forman. Es la verdadera trampa de la razón, un animal rapaz, que vive en un nivel diferente al del hombre y que constituido por una miríada de impulsos fraccionarios, de microseres sin otra forma que una voluntad incipiente, un apetito voraz y un instinto automático para aunar sus fuerzas en torno al sacrificio del hombre. (145)

> [an organism with its own entity, that transcends the sum of the creatures that form it. It is the true trap of reason, a predatory animal, that lives on a different level from man and that, constituted by a myriad of fractional impulses, of micro-beings without another form of incipient will, an insatiable appetite and an automatic instinct to combine its forces around the sacrifice of man.] (145)

This animalistic, voracious depiction of the family reveals the institution's dark underside. Although the family can offer protection to its members, it also requires sacrifice stemming from a sense of collective responsibility that often subsumes the individual.

While Franco's regime worked hard to promote an image of familial unity, many novels published during the dictatorship reveal family structures that barely exist or that contradict or deviate greatly from the official version of the family. Orphans, like the ones found in *Nada* [*Nothing*], Ana María Matute's *Primera memoria* [*First Memory*] (1959), and Juan Marsé's *Si te dicen que caí* [*If They Tell You That I Fell*] (1973), are multitudinous in Spanish literature of the second half of the twentieth century, challenging the patriarchal ideal of the normative family. Literary mother figures during this time are often absent, dead, or "ghostlike" (Schumm 13). When the mother figure is present, such as in Ana María Moix's *Julia* (1969) and Ana María Matute's *La trampa* [*The Trap*] (1969), she is often a tyrant, a symbol of antiquated constructions of motherhood, class stereotypes, and traditional values (Cooper 80) from which "post-Franco daughter[s]" struggle to distance themselves (Barnes 110). In Pilar Miró's films from the 1960s and 1970s, Diana Barnes points out that through their rejection of despotic mothers, a new generation of daughters indicate their disavowal of Franco's regime (110). Father figures are lacking in post-war literature as well, having either died or abandoned their families, such as the father figures in *Volverás a Región* and *La familia de Pascual Duarte* [*The Family of Pascual Duarte*] (1942), the latter a novel (and later film) that reveals the pressures exerted upon the

Spanish heteronormative family, leading in this case to violent consequences and familial destruction.

After the Transition, the elimination of literary and cinematic censorship allowed for increasingly diverse representations of the family, including a more open space in which women could write critically about the experience of motherhood. By the end of the 1990s and the beginning of the new millennium, contemporary Spanish women authors began to reimagine the mother figure in diverse ways that reflected women's changing role in the workplace, at home, and in family planning. Contemporary Spanish authors write about mothers whose roles and identities have changed from those imposed upon the traditional patriarchal family, expanding the social rhetoric of motherhood to become more inclusive of working mothers, single mothers, lesbian mothers, and other representations of motherhoods. Giving literary mothers greater agency and voice, works such as Laura Freixas's collection of stories *Madres e hijas* [*Mothers and Daughters*] (1996) and Lucía Etxebarria's novel *El club de las malas madres* [*The Bad Moms' Club*] (2009) introduce models of motherhood that are less rigid and restrictive. A plethora of authors, including Julia Navarro, Mercedes Abad, Elvira Lindo, Esther Tusquets, and Almudena Grandes, use their writing to analyse motherhood as an imperfect yet rewarding experience, acknowledging the role's challenging aspects. Literary critics highlight the increasing agency of the mother figure (such as Sandra J. Schumm's *Mother & Myth in Spanish Novels: Rewriting the Matriarchal Archetype*), the ways in which mothers must adapt to twenty-first-century demands on the role (as found in Catherine Bourland Ross's *The Changing Face of Motherhood in Spain: The Social Construction of Maternity in the Works of Lucía Etxebarria*), and topics such as lesbian motherhood and the maternal struggle for self-realization outside of the motherhood role (an issue addressed in Tiffany Trotman's *The Changing Spanish Family: Essays on New Views in Literature, Cinema and Theater*).

Shifting gender roles have meant that while Spanish women enjoy more agency in choosing partners and planning their families, many Spanish men are struggling to redefine their roles and responsibilities as men and fathers in a society that prioritizes economic achievement as one defining characteristic of hegemonic masculinity. As Catherine Bourland Ross asserts in her chapter "Why We Are All in the Club: *El club de las malas madres*," "[h]istorically, men have been charged with being the material providers for children; now, however, men and women both provide financially for the child(ren) in many cases. Even if the affective part of childrearing falls on the mother, both parties must deal with the basic needs of the child" (16). Current literary and cinematic depictions of the father figure reflect the anxiety of a generation of men attempting to renegotiate their place within the family. Being dislodged from their place as primary (or often, sole) breadwinner has caused many men to suffer from "feelings of uselessness and marginalization" (Ryan and Corbalán 6) that extend to their paternal identities and familial bonds. In Rodríguez del Pino's 2019 sociological study on masculinity in Spain and Borràs Català et al.'s 2012 study on employment and male hegemony in Spain, many respondents report conflicting attitudes towards more egalitarian households. On the one hand, many men understand the need to make egalitarian changes, but on the other hand, several participants express reluctance to become too deeply involved in childcare and household duties, due to a persistent social stigma that categorizes these tasks as unmanly. While Spanish men may feel unease at the prospect of changing gender roles, masculine and paternal fears of insignificance are reflected in literature and film. For example, while filmmaker Pedro Almodóvar is not known to focus on male protagonists – in fact, the father figures in his films are generally absent – those male characters who do appear in his films are often in crisis. In *Dolor y gloria* [*Pain and Glory*] (2019), protagonist Salvador Mallo is an aging film director seeking out ways to stay relevant. In *Volver* [*To Return*] (2006), the stepfather attempts to rape his stepdaughter Paula (who is a product of rape and incest), leading Paula to murder him. While not all cinematic and literary representations of contemporary Spanish fatherhood centre around masculinity in crisis, it is a prevalent topic that, in real life, too frequently leads to a violent backlash against wives, daughters, and other women.[9] Gender violence is a serious problem in Spain, where over one thousand women have been killed by their partners or ex-partners since 2003, with fifty-five men murdering their women partners in 2019 alone (Álvarez "Spain Sees Worst").[10] International outrage over the light sentencing of members of "La Manada" ["The Wolfpack"] for the 2016 rape they committed during San Fermín celebrations in Pamplona is indicative of a recent increase of sexual assaults in Spain, as reported by Spain's interior ministry ("Spain Sexual Assault"). Spanish women remain vulnerable to sexual assault from strangers or domestic partners, an intimate violence that casts an ominous light on the institution of the family.

The influence of immigration on Spanish culture has also impacted Spanish constructions of fatherhood and masculinity. For Spanish men, anxieties regarding their social place instigated by women's changing economic roles, compounded by the "threatening" presence of immigrant men in the country,[11] may cause contemporary Spanish men to feel disenfranchised and abandoned. Spanish men may then choose domestic violence as a path to regain a sense of control, sentiments frequently reflected in cinematic and literary representations of current Spanish masculinity. The 2015 novel *Natives*, written by Inongo vi Makomè and translated by Michael Ugarte, explores Spanish male sexual anxiety in a text where Spanish women turn to African immigrant men to meet their erotic needs. Other cultural artefacts, such as the 1999 film *Flores de otro mundo* [*Flowers from another World*] directed by Icíar Bollaín, explore the possibilities for creating new, multicultural families by embracing unions between Spanish men and immigrant women. In her article, "Espectros de la paternidad y disolución de fronteras en *Biutiful* de Alejando González Iñárritu," Anna Casas Aguilar argues that this 2010 film maintains a traditional representation of the father figure as bearer of responsibilities, law, authority, and memory, across cultural divides. However, the 2013 film *Ismael*, directed by Marcelo Piñeyro, stirs up further anxieties about parental rights, as Alika, an immigrant to Spain, has kept protagonist Félix from the knowledge that they have a son together. These texts and films exhibit a range of masculine reactions to Spain's immigrant presence, spanning from fear of obsolescence to hopes of incorporation into new constructions of the family.

Literary and cinematic portrayals of immigrant mothers in Spain often serve as a conservative template for Spanish women, urging them to renew their focus on domesticity. Through their idealized, self-sacrificing representations of motherhood, immigrant (especially Latin American) mothers are contrasted with "childless women, often Spaniards, whom they befriend and edify. The guidance and direction offered by the Latin American mother indicates nativist and pronatalist anxieties which aim to get wayward Spanish women back on the motherhood track to boost Spain's low fertility rate" (Flesler and Shepherd 252). Many films dealing with immigration and motherhood in contemporary Spain paint a conservative picture of the role, yet several others consider alternative family formation centred on cross-cultural families, at times foregrounding lesbian mothers. Gema Pérez-Sánchez explores intercultural gay relationships in the films *A mi madre le gustan las mujeres* [*My Mother Likes Women*] (directed by Daniela Fejerman and Inés París, 2002) and *Los novios búlgaros* [*The Bulgarian Lovers*] (directed by Eloy de la Iglesia, 2003), describing the ambiguity of such relationships that allows families and individuals to "play with the appearance of social and political transgression without actually challenging the heteronormative complacency it is required to accommodate" (72). Catherine Bourland Ross's analysis of Najat El Hachmi's 2015 novel *La hija extranjera* [*The Foreign Daughter*] discusses the positive and negative dynamics of the mother/daughter relationship from the perspective of Moroccan immigrants to Spain, adding this intercultural dimension wherein the immigrant mother figure often represents a "threat to national identity" ("Left Behind" 351). The immigrant family in Spain, or the incorporation of immigrants into the Spanish family, is alternately met with hope and trepidation.

The depiction of Spanish families as increasingly diverse is reflected not only in the canonical works described above, but also in the literary texts and films I analyse in *Performing Parenthood*. These texts and films acknowledge the family's negative potential to trap members, as well as its association with death. The texts and films portray a diverse range of parents, with different sexual identities and cultural backgrounds. They question the changing meaning of fatherhood in crisis and motherhood in a more progressive society, as well as the impact of a more globalized world where immigration often changes the structure of Spanish families. Many (but not all) of the texts and films I analyse are not as well-known as those mentioned in this section, but they reiterate the diverse nature of Spanish families found in more canonical works. While not meant to be understood as a realistic recounting of actual Spanish families, these texts and films amplify our understanding of Spanish families from a literary and cinematic perspective.

Performing Parenthood

As the previous overview of diverse literary and cinematic examples of Spanish families demonstrates, scholars and society members need to expand the definitions of Spanish families' realities and potential. Enactments of the parenthood role – which is currently inevitably tied to gender, as certain behaviours or performances of parenthood are labelled as maternal or paternal – are fluid and can be performed in a variety of ways in different circumstances and over time. Parenthood should be conceptualized as a range of experiences and enactments, just as sexuality is accepted as a spectrum wherein one's gender identity, gender performance, and sexual identity can change through time or in given experiences.

My understanding of parenthood as performative is rooted within Judith Butler's work on gender performativity. Scholars have written extensively on the distinction between performance and performativity in Butler's work, and she herself has elaborated on the difference many times. As I perceive the distinction, performance is a necessary action or event that helps to constitute performativity. While it can have subversive potential, Butler states that the performance is always compulsory. Whether individuals are conscious of it or not, they are constantly performing gender in some way, meaning that, as Butler states, it "is not a performance from which I can take radical distance, for this is deep-seated play, psychically entrenched play" ("Imitation and Gender" 311). Heteronormative society views gender performance as a way to maintain the binary, as "the performance renders social laws explicit" (Butler, "Performative Acts" 526). Those who perform their gender in a way that does not align with these norms will be subject to "ostracism, punishment, and violence" (Butler, "Imitation and Gender" 314–15), although Butler does promise "transgressive pleasures" ("Imitation and Gender" 314–15) associated with breaking free from the compulsory performance.

Performativity, then, is what emerges through a series of performances, "a repetition and a ritual, which achieves its effects through its naturalization in the context of a body" (Butler, *Gender Trouble* xv). While consolidating the subject through repetition (Jagose 86), performativity also reveals the thing performed – in this case, gender – to be an empty signifier whose meaning can only be sustained as long as the performances continue. By understanding the performative nature of gender (or parental identity), it becomes evident that "what we take to be an internal essence of gender is manufactured through a sustained set of acts, posited through the gendered stylization of the body" (Butler, *Gender Trouble* xv–xvi). In other words, Butler argues that there is no core identity or meaning behind gender; instead, our enactments or repetitions of what we believe gender to be are, in fact, creating the category of gender, but they are repetitions built on an empty foundation. The fact that identity categories are manufactured through repetitions is both alarming, showing the fragility of those categories, and empowering, as new enactments of identity categories, such as parenthood, lead to new understandings and definitions of these roles.

Performativity can be a way of expressing agency (even though Butler has considered gender performativity as both a way of understanding subject development and a method for contesting the notion of a subject), but Butler cautions that a subject's agency is limited to the circumstances and norms of their world. In Butler's words, "I work within the norms that constitute me. I do something with them. Those norms are the condition of my agency, and they also limit my agency; they are that limit *and* that condition at the same time" (Olson and Worsham 752). Subjects can "rearticulate" the norms that define their lives, finding power in breaking away from the expected binary of gender performance. Like gender, parenthood can benefit from a performativity constituted by "the changeable and revisable reality" (Butler, *Gender*

Trouble xxiv) made possible through repeated non-normative performances of parenthood. Butler points out that identities take time to be established; therefore, the repetition of performances is important. She asserts that one characteristic that distinguishes humans is our constant state of revision and transformation, as human beings are "always about becoming" (Reddy and Butler 116). Applied to parenthood, this notion allows for a wider range of parental identities, as well as ways for parents to interact with their children.

If we can accept, as Judith Butler proposes, that there is no original gender upon which people model their behaviour, then we can also accept that there is no original "parental identity." Butler writes that:

> *gender is a kind of imitation for which there is no original* ... In other words, the naturalistic effects of heterosexualized genders are produced through imitative strategies; what they imitate is a phantasmatic ideal of heterosexual identity, one that is produced by the imitation as its effect ... In other words, heterosexuality is always in the process of imitating and approximating its own phantasmatic idealization of itself – *and failing*. ("Imitation and Gender" 313)

Just as we all constantly perform gender, parents perform parenthood, modelling their behaviour on the examples of parental performances they have witnessed, as well as culturally promoted and traditionally accepted models of motherhood and fatherhood. Butler elucidates the fragility of gender, explaining that it must be repeated in order to exist; yet it constantly fails at reproducing itself, because it is an empty category. Parental identity is much the same; there is no core maternal or paternal identity on which to construct the role, merely a spiral of repetitions. Parental performativity, therefore, does not need to remain static. It should be understood as fluid, a range of possible attitudes and performances that can change given time and circumstances. While parenthood will most likely never be completely separated from the concepts of sex and gender – nor that of mother/father, as society craves binaries – just as sex, gender, and gender performance are constructed and understood independently of one another, so should parental identity be added to that list. While society may someday grow away from describing certain actions and behaviours as "motherly" or "fatherly," for the present, it is helpful to consider that motherly/fatherly attitudes need not be unequivocally tied to gender and sex. For example, a biological man (sex) with a feminized gender expression could perform parenthood in what is traditionally considered to be an extremely maternal or paternal way, or in a way that falls somewhere in any other part of the continuum or changes over time and given new circumstances.

By establishing a non-normative performativity of parenthood, we can expand our understandings of the definition and limitations of parenthood beyond biological and heteronormative constraints, based on the concepts of fluidity embedded within queer theory. I argue that parental performance and identity should be understood as part of a continuum of parental experiences and identities, both positive and negative, that ignores heteronormative restrictions that apply certain characteristics only to mothers or fathers. The novels and films analysed in *Performing Parenthood* show that parental figures are more satisfied and successful in their role (in most cases, with a couple of notable exceptions) when the expression of their parental identity is fluid, allowing parents to freely navigate a parental spectrum (reminiscent of Adrienne Rich's lesbian continuum that proposes an empowering connection between all women) wherein individuals may change given time and circumstances. The spectrum of parental identity creates a common space for discussions of multiple expressions of identity, while appreciating that the gendered ways in which parents perform their roles can change and fluctuate along the lines of the continuum.

Overview of Chapters

In each chapter of the book, I focus on a specific type of non-normative parent/child relationship, examining how characters' performances of identity help or hinder them in their attempts to create meaningful relationships with their children. While characters in these texts and films perform parenthood in non-normative ways that lead to the formation of alternative families, they do not necessarily have a conscious goal of creating non-normative families. Characters are simply living their lives as part of family units that happen to be constructed in ways that facilitate non-normative performances of parental roles. In chapter 1, "Writing Fatherhood," I investigate the interconnection between writing, mimesis, and fatherhood in Lluís Maria Todó's *El mal francés* [*The Bad Frenchman*] (2009) and Santi Balmes's *¿Por qué me comprasteis un walkie talkie si era hijo único?* [*Why Did You Buy Me a Walkie-Talkie if I Was an Only Child?*] (2012). In *El mal francés*, the protagonist is a young man who must simultaneously come to terms with his homosexuality and incipient biological fatherhood. He develops his identity as a gay father by reading various novels written by gay authors, after rejecting the model of fatherhood presented to him by his heterosexual, biological father. In Santi Balmes's novel, the protagonist seeks social validation for his father (who is a failure in the eyes of patriarchal society) by writing his biography. Protagonists use mimesis to imitate various representations of the father figure in an attempt to better understand their identity and place within father/son relationships. When the endless replication and recycling of the patriarchal father figure proves unproductive, they expand their search to non-normative models of identity. Both novels present innovative, identity-forming ways of interacting with the long-standing metaphor of literary paternity, a concept described by Sandra M. Gilbert and Susan Gubar in their seminal work *The Madwoman in the Attic*. Gilbert and Gubar assert that writing has long been considered a masculine domain of creation, wherein the pen is the metaphorical penis, and the author/father creates life in his book/child. By questioning the boundaries of both literature and paternal identity, protagonists embrace the concept of parenthood on a spectrum, wherein they can enact their father/son relationships in the ways that feel most authentic to them, regardless of whether those enactments would be considered failures by the standards of patriarchal society.

Chapter 2, "M(other)hood and Disability," evaluates the non-normative mother/daughter relationship in Paloma Díaz-Mas's futuristic short story "La niña sin alas" (1996), where the relationship between mother and daughter vacillates between supportive and restrictive. The story is set in an advanced civilization where able-bodied people have wings, yet society maintains antiquated prejudices related to mobility and disability. Readers are presented with two "othered" female bodies: a mother who is marginalized through pregnancy, and a daughter who is considered disabled because she is born wingless. Combining Rebecca Kukla's theory on the societal infantilization and control of the pregnant body with disability studies, I propose that mother and daughter reject patriarchal and ableist critiques of their bodies, removing themselves from heteronormative society to pursue a deeper physical and emotional connection. However, with reference to Julia Kristeva's explanation of *jouissance* in "Stabat Mater," I argue that the intensely co-dependent relationship between mother and child raises serious concerns about the daughter's lack of agency. Díaz-Mas's ambivalent portrayal of motherhood outlines a protagonist who is both the self-abnegating mother who sacrifices her identity for the sake of her child and the Oedipal, castrating mother who stymies her daughter's chance for independence. The mother figure's decision to break from society allows her and her child to live free from heteronormative demands on their bodies and relationship, yet the mother begins to constrain her daughter, much as patriarchal society tried to control them both, as her love becomes all-encompassing and obsessive. "La niña sin alas" broadens the conversation about alternate performances of motherhood, demonstrating not only that parental identities exist along a spectrum but that, furthermore, an individual parent may enact their role in diverse ways at different points in time.

In chapter 3, "The Shifting Face of Fatherhood," I examine how father figures in Ricardo Franco's *La buena estrella* [*The Good Star*] (1997) and Achero Mañas's *Todo lo que tú quieras* [*Anything You Want*] (2010) navigate the relationship between hegemonic masculinity and their performances of fatherhood, at times aligning themselves with the concept but ultimately experiencing more personally rewarding relationships with their children through non-normative performances of parenthood that distance them from hegemonic masculinity. In *Todo lo que tú quieras*, Leo cross-dresses as his dead wife to make his four-year-old daughter feel her mother's presence again. In *La buena estrella*, Rafa allows his wife Marina's lover, Daniel, to live with them because Daniel has impregnated Marina with the children that Rafa's impotence would never allow him to father. Father figures cannot successfully comply with the changing norms of hegemonic masculinity, a fragile concept that leads to feelings of masculinity in crisis, but by performing their fatherhoods in alternative ways, they create new models of family. Chapter 3 references masculinity theories by Michael Kimmel, R.W. Connell, and Fintan Walsh, as well as Judith Butler's *Gender Trouble*, to showcase alternative masculinities that cannot or will not always adhere to the dictates of hegemonic masculinity. The films' exploration of impotence, cross-dressing, and father/daughter relationships presents spectators with non-normative performances of paternity in tension with dominant definitions of masculinity and fatherhood.

Continuing the theme of establishing positive relationships through non-normative performances of parenthood, mother/daughter relationships are central to chapter 4, "Lesbian Maternal Community Formation." *Tras la pared* (2010), the second novel in Mila Martínez's trilogy published by Egales, describes an empowered lesbian community of mothering that functions outside of the limitations of patriarchal society. My analysis focuses on Carla and Mel, a lesbian couple who discover that Carla is unexpectedly pregnant after a one-night encounter with a male lover. As Mel struggles to embrace her partner's pregnancy, she realizes that only she can communicate telepathically with the fetus. This discovery both pleases Mel, as it allows her to emotionally invest in the pregnancy, and distresses her, as Mel's relationship with the fetus drives her apart from Carla, who does not believe that the two can communicate telepathically. Although the novel's incorporation of magical realism can arguably be interpreted as manifestations of characters' internalized homophobia, *Tras la pared* creates a primarily positive vision of lesbian motherhood.[12] Through an examination of the legitimization of non-biological motherhood, the sexualization of the pregnant body, and the motherhood community formed between characters, wherein women alternate fluidly between the roles of mother (caregiver) and child (care recipient), the novel establishes a family wherein mother/mother relationships are valued as much as mother/child relationships, leading to the contentment of all family members.

Chapter 5, "Beyond the Biological Family," focuses on representations of non-biological parenthood that critique biologically driven definitions of the family through characters who feel more connected to non-biological parental figures than they do to their biological relatives. In "El amor inútil" ["Useless Love"] (1997) by Luisa Castro, Alberto becomes a non-biological father figure for his friends' infant daughter Fidelia, taking on the primary caregiver role for her. His feelings towards Fidelia turn romantic, so he moves away; the two reconnect when she is eighteen, and this encounter results in the birth of their child. In Esther Tusquets's *Varada tras el último naufragio* [*Stranded after the Last Shipwreck*] (1980), one of the sub-plots focuses on Eva, a character who takes young Clara into her home to save her from a bad living situation, later realizing that she cannot (or does not have the desire to) fulfil the emotional needs of her non-biological daughter figure. Both Alberto and Eva experiment with traditionally gendered parental roles in their enactments of parenthood, as well as obscuring the limits between the roles of parent, friend, and lover. The relationships between parental figures and children are at times supportive and at other times border on incest, while also portraying the parental desire to mould their children into personal doppelgängers. The cyclical nature of these parent/child relationships pushes the limitations of this connection, leading to the complete dissolution of these non-normative families. Nevertheless, the non-normative familial configurations in these texts demonstrate another option along the spectrum of diverse family formation, one that is completely independent of biological connection.

The book concludes with chapter 6, "A Family in All Senses." This chapter examines the role of domestic help in familial formation (hearkening back to medieval concepts of the family and household), arguing that affective ties can be more important than biological ones, while also examining the role of immigration in the 2010 film *Amador*, directed by Fernando León de Aranoa. The film blurs geographic, economic, and social borders while questioning the constructs of family and even happiness itself. The eponymous title character is an elderly, bedridden Spaniard whose family has entrusted his care to Marcela, a young and pregnant undocumented woman from Latin America. Along with Puri, a Spanish sex worker who visits Amador once a week, Marcela cares for Amador and develops an emotional connection to him, while his biological family constructs their dream home across the country. Through a focus on the five senses, Amador and Marcela establish a non-normative family. Taste and touch open the door for a connection between them; cooking and physical assistance are large parts of the caregiver role, which establish a relationship of affection between the two. Sound and sight are symbols of hope for the future and ways for Marcela to find her agency in the film. The smell of rotting flowers functions as a way for Marcela to acknowledge her unhappiness with various aspects of her life. With Marcela's ambivalent attitude toward her pregnancy and her romantic partner, she is an example of an "affect alien," a term coined by Sara Ahmed in *The Promise of Happiness* (2010) to describe someone who does not react "appropriately" to emotional stimuli. Through her rebellion against objects and relationships that are typically understood to cause happiness, Marcela rejects the heteronormative script of pregnancy and romantic relationships as all-fulfilling roles for women. Despite the complexities of their relationship, Marcela and Amador care for each other in ways that members of their established families cannot. Amador and Marcela (and, to some extent, Puri) form a non-normative family through affective ties only possible through a disavowal of traditional family roles thought to bring happiness. Without minimalizing the struggles of women from marginalized groups (undocumented immigrants, sex workers), *Amador* depicts female characters who embrace their otherness, looking beyond superficial happiness to claim emotional support and meaning through non-normative affective ties.

Performing Parenthood explores the multiplicity within non-normative familial construction, and the ways in which literary and cinematic portrayals of the changing Spanish family reflect anxieties and hopes about shifting gender roles, as well as political, economic, and cultural realities. I argue that parenthood should be understood as a performative and fluid identity that exists along a spectrum, whose experiences and enactments change over time and within different circumstances. As Esther Tusquets writes about motherhood in the essay "Ser Madre" ["To Be a Mother"], "No sólo cada mujer la vive de un modo peculiar y distinto, sino que incluso una misma mujer puede vivir de manera muy diferente maternidades sucesivas, según cuál sea su edad, su estado de ánimo, su situación económica y profesional, su relación con los hijos anteriores y con la pareja" ["Not only does each woman live her motherhood in a peculiar and distinct way, but the same woman can even live in her way very different successive maternities, depending on her age, her state of mind, her economic and professional situation, her relationship with previous children, and with her partner"] (84). This spectrum of motherhood experience can also be applied to all forms of parenthood, advocating for such freedom for all parents in their enactments of the role. Given contemporary social changes and the recent wealth of literature and film about Spanish families, *Performing Parenthood* presents a comprehensive and open understanding of the diversity already present within Spanish families through an analysis of aspects of the family that are becoming increasingly socially relevant, such as cross-cultural families, queer families, and non-biological parents. By addressing texts and films that have not received sufficient scholarly attention, I hope to bring visibility to alternative family models and expand the way we discuss and understand the multitudinous realities of Spanish families.

Chapter One

Writing Fatherhood

Writing, fatherhood, and the connection between the two are central themes in Catalan authors[1] Lluís Maria Todó's *El mal francés* [*The Bad Frenchman*] (2006) and Santi Balmes's *¿Por qué me comprasteis un walkie talkie si era hijo único?* [*Why Did You Buy Me a Walkie-Talkie if I Was an Only Child?*] (2012). Lluís and Fernando, the novels' protagonists, rebel against the authoritative image of masculinity and paternity upheld by traditional Spanish society, struggling to see their fathers' or their own identities reflected in the limitations of this patriarchal symbol. Lluís and Fernando's initial mimesis (and rejection) of the patriarchal father figure leads them to imitate various models of fatherhood, driven by a desire to better understand their relationships with their fathers and, in Lluís's case, his imminent fatherhood. Through these mimetic experiences, in addition to an exploration of writing's identity-shaping potential, protagonists come to embrace diverse performances of fatherhood, realizing that parental identities and roles exist along a wide spectrum of realities. Todó's novel, *El mal francés*,[2] follows nineteen-year-old Lluís as he accepts his homosexuality while facing the reality that his girlfriend Margarita will soon give birth to their child. During Margarita's pregnancy, Lluís escapes to France to study, pursue his literary ambitions, and envision his version of fatherhood as a gay man with no literary or societal models of gay fatherhood to guide him. Lluís uses his perspective as a literary scholar to compare the gestation and birth of his baby to the process of writing a book. Literature further impacts Lluís, as it is through reading literature by gay authors that he becomes confident in his sexual identity, allowing him to shape his definition of fatherhood. Questions of identity and fatherhood are central to Balmes's novel, as well. This humorous novel, full of ludicrous situations and characters, recounts the convoluted life of Constancito Obs, a washed-up child star, from the perspective of his son Fernando, who is writing his father's biography in an attempt to combat his internalized judgment of his father as a failure. The writing experience, particularly the ways in which the text itself breaks from literary conventions, allows Fernando to re-evaluate his relationship with his father and reject limiting patriarchal definitions of fatherhood.

Literature and writing become tools for Lluís and Fernando to conceptualize and embrace a diverse range of potential enactments of father/son relationships. Their literary experiments play with the metaphor of literary paternity, wherein authorship is considered a masculine act of creation similar to that of engendering a child. While the metaphor of literary paternity has traditionally supported the rhetoric of the patriarchal father figure by reaffirming his right to authority and power, Lluís and Fernando question the metaphor, finding ways to open it to a more inclusive range of authors and symbolic father figures. In this chapter, I will discuss the symbolic weight of the Spanish patriarchal father figure and the metaphor of literary paternity; demonstrate how Lluís, Fernando, and their fathers fail to live up to the demands of the patriarchal father figure; and argue that, by questioning the boundaries of literary paternity and seeking out alternative models of identity, protagonists discover the innumerable possible iterations of fatherhood, a role that can vary as much as the myriad individuals who perform parenthood.

Franco and the Father Figure

In patriarchal societies, the father figure is the linchpin that assures a continual transition of authority between heterosexual men, while women, children, and men outside of the dominant definition of masculinity remain subjugated and excluded from positions of power. The traditional nuclear family unit is an essential component in preserving patriarchal power, as its existence legitimizes and perpetuates paternal authority. Friedrich Engels's *The Origins of the Family, Private Property and the State* (1884) establishes the family as a patriarchal tool that produces children of undisputed paternity, protects male property interests, and subjugates women. Sigmund Freud's Oedipus complex (*Interpretation of Dreams*, 1899) and Jacques Lacan's *Law of the Father* maintain an emphasis on patriarchy's role in controlling sexual desires and creating a gendered division of work that benefits men. In addition to strict gender roles, women within the family have often been viewed as property. In his alliance theory, Claude Lévi-Strauss argues that the exchanging of women is one of the major functions of patriarchy, equating the goals of the family with those of hegemonic masculinity, wherein women are oppressed by men. Heidi Hartmann describes patriarchy as any social structure (churches, factories, offices, etc.) that allows men to control women's labour. Likewise, in "The Main Enemy," Christine Delphy cites the marriage contract as the main source of patriarchal power that permits men to retain their privileged position. In patriarchal societies, the family holds an institutional role in reaffirming male authority through the father figure and reproducing male authority through the birth of sons.

For twentieth-century Spain, Franco's dictatorship further solidified already traditional expectations and privileges for father figures. Franco enjoyed envisioning himself as the father of the Spanish nation, projecting "an image of self-control and austerity, emphasizing that he didn't smoke or drink alcohol, and that his favourite entertainment was playing with his children" (Aresti 170).[3] As this self-stylized image of Franco demonstrates, the definitions of fatherhood and masculinity were impossible to separate, and individual men were to emulate the dictator in their role as heads of the family. The ideal Spanish man under Franco's regime was heterosexually virile (Begin, "Picking a Fight" 131) but self-controlled, patriotic, and hardworking (Aresti 149), but none of these qualities were as important as fulfilling the role of patriarch and leader of the family.[4] One of the goals of the dictatorship was to populate Spain with an extremely Catholic and patriotic next generation of citizens, best achieved through the traditional nuclear family led by a patriarch. Dominant Spanish masculinity, as described by Franco's regime, was not only about individual enactments of strength, but a willingness to participate in a larger ideology and belong to the "most culturally influential 'families' [which] were the Church and the Falange" (Perriam et al. 6). For Spanish society under Franco, only with great difficulty could the functions of the family be separated from religious or patriotic demands or could individual constructions of masculinity divorce themselves from societal expectations of fatherhood.

Franco wished to produce generations of men who would follow the models of masculinity and fatherhood he proposed (but could not live up to). For the endless replication and recycling of patriarchal authority to continue, mimesis – an imitation of father by son – is crucial. Within a patriarchal society, the transfer of authority as leader of the home is perceived to be the rightful inheritance of male progeny, provided that those sons mould themselves into a reproduction of the father. While it is true that many sons rebel against the model set forth for them by their fathers, the patriarchal privileges established by Franco's dictatorship were only to be passed on to those sons who did their best to imitate the masculine and patriarchal ideal, which provided an assurance, however shaky, about the legacy of patriarchal authority. As Jean Baudrillard states in *Simulacra and Simulation*, "We require a visible past, a visible continuum, a visible myth of origin, which reassures us about our end" (10). The origins of heteronormative society are anchored to the concept of the patriarch, a figure whose authority must continually be reaffirmed. As paternity has long been equated with authority, many male protagonists seeking to understand their place in society start by investigating their relationships with their fathers, examining how their personalities are similar to or diverge from those of their fathers. Consciously or not, they locate themselves within the world of the father, defining themselves in the limited terms of the patriarchal father figure.

Literary Paternity

Literary paternity is a concept that often works alongside or complements the notion of the authoritative patriarchal father figure. Edward Said's definition of authority unequivocally connects the roles of father and author, proposing that an authority figure is "a person who originates or gives existence to something, a begetter, beginner, father, or ancestor, a person also who sets forth written statements" (83). In heteronormative society, father and author are often synonymous titles with overlapping functions. In their seminal work, *The Madwoman in the Attic*, Sandra M. Gilbert and Susan Gubar analyse the many instances of male writers throughout history who have described some variation of the idea that the creation of a literary text is equivalent to the act of engendering a child. A complicated metaphor, literary paternity asserts that "the essence of literary power" comes from male sexuality, that the "poet's pen is in some sense (even more than figuratively) a penis" (Gilbert and Gubar 4). Men, therefore, claim writing as their purview, a creative act in which the pen (when writing a text) is akin to the penis (when creating a child), both acts that demonstrate similarities between men and God, who is often described as the father and creator of the world. This status as creator/father/God imbues the male writer with authority and power, "not just the ability to generate life but the power to create a posterity to which he lays claim" (6). Not only can the literary father claim his son (the book he has written), but this ownership is generational. His ideas live on and are reproduced by future generations of (male) writers; therefore, his influence and power never fully disappear. Literary paternity allows men to claim not only their biological sons but also literary texts as their offspring, bequeathing their authority to successors who will continue the exclusionary tradition of denying women's creative role in the literary world.

The concept of literary paternity can be traced to Greek literature, where the image of the pregnant man was a pervasive metaphor for understanding an author's relationship to his work, "a way to negotiate and indeed perform authorship" (Leitao 127).[5] This metaphor simultaneously acknowledges men's creative power while denying women's literary authority, refuting their claims of ownership to what had previously been interpreted as the exclusively female process of giving birth (176). The conceptualization of literary paternity has shifted from a depiction of the pregnant male to the concept of literature as the result of masculine insemination of the blank page. The pen becomes a metaphorical penis that creates new life by impregnating the paper. Susan Gilbert and Sandra Gubar expound on the corporal elements of literary paternity, asserting:

> Though many of these writers use the metaphor of literary paternity in different ways and for different purposes, all seem overwhelmingly to agree that a literary text is not only speech quite literally embodied, but also power mysteriously made manifest, made flesh. In patriarchal Western culture, therefore, the text's author is a father, a progenitor, a procreator, an aesthetic patriarch whose pen is an instrument of generative power like his penis. (6)

Symbolic sons are those who uphold the patriarchal paradigm, allowing them to enjoy a place of advantage within the masculine legacy of Western literature and patriarchal society. By modelling themselves after the authoritative father figures who have come before them, the next generation of men may partake in the power and privilege passed down to them. The catch, however, lies in the symbolic sons' ability to create something new (within accepted limitations) under the pressure of their literary fathers' legacy. Harold Bloom's term "anxiety of influence" (6) describes this literary relationship wherein sons may draw upon centuries of writing by their symbolic fathers but are also weighed down by the celebrated accomplishments of those writers who have come before them. Bloom describes the anxiety of writers who must draw inspiration from the literary father figures who came before them but also forge a unique place for themselves and their writing, engaging in a masculine "[b]attle between strong equals, father and son as mighty opposites" (11). The privilege of literary inheritance is accompanied by the burden of maintaining tradition, the need to perform an act of mimesis by imitating established literature to reap the rewards of literary paternity while still proving oneself worthy of a place within established traditions.

Emulating the literature of previous patriarchal figures is one way for current male authors to achieve status while gaining a sense of acceptance and even immortality, becoming one more link in the chain of male tradition. However, failure is an ever-present threat for patriarchal fathers and authors. As Baudrillard explains, "To dissimulate is to pretend not to have what one has. To simulate is to feign to have what one doesn't have. One implies a presence, the other an absence" (*Simulacra and Simulation* 3). Once we understand that patriarchal masculine authority is a replication of a model based on an empty original, a system with no legitimate claim to masculine supremacy, the reasons for patriarchal anxiety become clear. Subsequent versions of literary and paternal authority must not waver, lest they draw attention to the lack of original authority vested within these structures. Literary paternity and the patriarchal father figure maintain their authority through convincing repetitions of the system, nothing more. Gilbert and Gubar succinctly link the anxieties of both the author and the father figure, explaining:

> A man cannot verify his fatherhood by either sense or reason, after all; that his child is *his* is in a sense a tale he tells himself to explain the infant's existence. Obviously, the anxiety implicit in such storytelling urgently needs not only the reassurances of male superiority that patriarchal misogyny implies, but also such compensatory fictions of the Word. (5)

Literary paternity's obsession with creating a copy of the father (the original) through the novel is revealed to be a futile process through an understanding of Jean Baudrillard's *Simulacra and Simulation*. In this theoretical treatise, Baudrillard describes simulacra, copies of objects that no longer have an original and therefore are no longer connected to reality. The simulacrum "is never what hides the truth – it is truth that hides the fact that there is none" (Baudrillard, *Simulacra and Simulation*, 1). Simulacrum unmasks the original, in this case the patriarchal father figure, exposing it as an empty signifier. After so many subsequent copies, it becomes impossible to distinguish between real and simulation because the original no longer exists. This notion obfuscates the concept of literary paternity, which is often developed through the lens of mimesis: the act of engendering a child or a novel is akin to the desire to create a new version or copy of oneself. By accepting that the patriarchal father figure does not represent a fundamental societal truth or masculine identity, father figures are liberated to enact their parental roles in the ways that best suit them, a conclusion that protagonists in *El mal francés* and *¿Por qué me comprasteis un walkie talkie si era hijo único?*

reach through their exploration of literary paternity and various models of fatherhood.

Fatherhood as Failure

Lluís Maria Todó's novel *El mal francés* examines the complex nature of fatherhood and its relationship to literary paternity. With many autobiographical elements, the novel tells the story of protagonist Lluís Maria Todó, an author in present-day Barcelona suffering from writer's block while working on his sixth novel. To combat his writer's block, Lluís rereads his diaries from 1969, when he was nineteen years old. Lluís's diaries recount two simultaneous processes of discovery for the young protagonist: an incipient awareness of his homosexuality that he was struggling to reconcile with his upcoming paternity. After impregnating his girlfriend Margarita, seven and a half years his senior (50), reading and writing become tools for Lluís to explore his identity and establish his unique embodiment of paternity. At the end of the novel, the narrator informs readers that the couple gets married and has a second child, living together as a non-normative family for several years before divorcing.

In *El mal francés*, the protagonist has a complicated mimetic relationship with his father. They share the name of Lluís, an element of family heritage passed down through generations as a symbolic reproduction of the father. Lluís Senior embodies the anxiety of generational inheritance, as he has allowed his career to be defined by his own father, accepting his role in the family business despite its discordance with his personal interests. Young Lluís describes his father as "un hombre apasionado por las artes y la cultura, pero sólo cursó los estudios técnicos necesarios para dirigir la pequeña empresa familiar, del sector textil, que heredó de su padre" ["a man passionate about the arts and culture, but who only completed the technical studies necessary to manage the small family business, in the textile sector, that he inherited from his father"] (111). Although he has access to culture and art (his brother is a semi-famous painter), Lluís Senior views his life as a failure due to the economic ruin of the family business and the disappointment of never reaching his professional goals. In Lluís Senior, the facade of the omnipotent patriarchal father figure begins to crack, revealing a dissatisfied and often powerless man. Lluís Senior spends much of his free time reading the newspaper in his chair, perpetually silent and disgruntled. His son recounts, "Allí lo encontrábamos siempre mis hermanos y yo cuando volvíamos del colegio, siempre con un mal humor invariable y amenazante, que podía estallar con la mínima excusa" ["My siblings and

I would always find him there when we returned from school, always in an unchanging and threatening bad mood that could explode with the tiniest excuse"] (204). This image demonstrates Lluís Senior's isolation from his family, his only solace found in reading. His son will later communicate news of Margarita's pregnancy to Lluís Senior through a letter, as the written word is the strongest of the tenuous bonds between father and son. Lluís Senior's isolation reflects sociologist and masculinity scholar Michael Kimmel's findings regarding heteronormative society's emphasis on male successfulness, wherein he notes that men who fall short of these standards often experience loneliness, anxiety, and emptiness, along with the drive to be constantly competitive (*Manhood in America* 202). For someone still invested in the patriarchal system, like Lluís Senior, failure to meet these societal expectations has no freeing or positive attributes, as it will for his son.

Lluís Senior is quietly resigned to a life of disappointments, his relationship with his son one more failure defined primarily by lack of communication and silence. He rarely speaks with his son, exhibiting a greater level of comfort with written correspondence. Although Lluís finds it impossible to confide in his father about his homosexuality, he informs Lluís Senior of Margarita's pregnancy via letter. After receiving the letter, Lluís Senior does not direct more than one sentence to the subject of Margarita's pregnancy, causing his son to realize the futility of changing their relationship. Lluís admits, "[T]uve que acostumbrarme a la idea de aquel silencio paterno, que ya había sufrido durante la infancia y la adolescencia, y que ahora se prolongaba también en aquel inicio tan accidentado, por no decir aquel simulacro, de vida adulta" ["I had to get used to the idea of that paternal silence, which I had already suffered through during infancy and adolescence, and which now also extended to that beginning, so accidental, if not a simulation, of adult life"] (278). Not even the milestone of incipient fatherhood is sufficient to initiate an open, adult relationship between the two men.

Fatherhood is an even more convoluted concept in *¿Por qué me comprasteis un walkie talkie si era hijo único?*, Santi Balmes's first novel, which recounts the history of the Obs family, focusing on three generations of Catalan men. A lengthy novel meant to be humorous, full of bizarrely fantastic elements and elaborate twists, Balmes's work is difficult to summarize. One prominent theme throughout the ever-changing text is that of masculine familial relationships. Protagonist Fernando Obs is obsessed with writing and publishing a biography of his father's life that will redeem his name from its current obscurity as a failed musician. Fernando divides his time between his record label, Dr. Sigmund Floyd's office (a psychiatrist who is helping him write the biography), and a bar where he drinks and consumes copious amounts of drugs. Although Fernando is the novel's first-person narrator, the plot centres on the life of his father, Constancito Obs, who was the incestuous product of a drunken encounter between brother (Joanet) and sister (Angelina). Although he is an "anormal" (165) child, considered ugly with one leg "ligeramente más corta que la otra" ["slightly shorter than the other"] (121) and a large head (166), Constancito is a talented singer exploited by his mother and her lover Manolo Pencas, who is also Constancito's agent. Constancito never becomes a great musical success, but he eventually marries the daughter of a powerful music producer, with whom he has three children, including his firstborn Fernando. Constancito and his wife Heidi conceive Fernando during an acid-induced psychedelic experience. During the same drug-fuelled weekend, Constancito writes, produces, and records the best music of his life. The simultaneous creation of a son and a musical album positions Constancito as an artistic and biological father figure.

Fernando's father, Constancito, has three father figures. Constancito's biological father is Joanet Obs, a man who – like Lluís Senior – endures a life of failure. Even his son's conception can be viewed as a failure, because Constancito is the product of incest between Joanet and his sister Angelina. Although Joanet is in love with Angelina, she has sex with him only because she is intoxicated. After their incestuous copulation, the two are forced to abandon their small village and move to Barcelona as husband and wife.[6] Joanet provides for his family with his meagre earnings from working as a diver, while Angelina spends her time having affairs with other men, eventually abandoning Joanet to go on a musical tour with Constancito and his manager Manolo.

Constancito's conception highlights Joanet's lack of patriarchal authority. While brother and sister are engaged in the taboo sexual act, a ray of lightning strikes Joanet in the anus. Constancito later learns that the lightning bolt was sent by an alien with the purpose of implanting his DNA in Joanet's sperm, an allusion to Freud's analysis of the Schreber case. Dr. Schreber (1842–1911) was a respected judge until he became mentally ill, at which time he began to experience the recurring fantasy of being turned into a woman and impregnated by "divine miracles" or "rays" of sun sent from God (Freud, *The Schreber Case* 9). Freud used Dr. Schreber's memoir about his experiences to diagnose him as suffering from "a regression toward homosexual narcissism, in which the impregnating god is a substitute for the man's father" (Leitao 7). Dr. Schreber's case has been analysed by multiple individuals whose conclusions diverge widely from Freud's. Notably, Lacan interprets Dr. Schreber's fantasy not as a desire for intercourse with his father, but rather as a longing to be incorporated into dominant society as a valued member (Leitao 7–8). An application of either interpretation of Joanet's shocking experience of penetration positions him as an exemplification of a man devoid of paternal power, seeking to regain a place within the dominant group.

Like Joanet, Constancito's alien father reveals the myth of patriarchal power while adding another level of mimesis to the topic of paternity. If Constancito's conception is interpreted with reference to Dr. Schreber's fantasy, then the alien represents God or a higher power, emphasizing yet again the link between masculinity and authority. Both the alien and Joanet are biological fathers to Constancito, meaning that their son's identity should be a copy of both individuals. According to Baudrillard, DNA is an excellent example of mimesis because it is "transmitted by reproduction from one generation to another and furthermore gifted with the capacity of self-reproduction and imitation" (*Simulations* 106). Even though the alien father might be considered a higher power or a more evolved paternal specimen, he is an "alienígena fracasada" ["failed alien"] (214), forced to produce pornographic films on other planets to repay his substantial debts. The alien is never an active father figure in Constancito's life, but when they meet on one of the father's movie sets, he informs his son that aliens from his planet can communicate with the boy through a walkie-talkie that Angelina bought for him. The alien father himself never speaks to Constancito through the walkie-talkie; it is unclear if the alien does not wish to maintain contact with his son or if he is powerless to do so. Either circumstance reflects failure; at best, the alien is an uninvolved father, or at worst, he does not have sufficient authority to access the walkie-talkie. In the end, the alien has authority over no one; he must answer to more powerful patriarchal figures in his society.

Constancito's third father figure is Manolo Pencas, his sleazy musical representative who dislikes the child and exploits his musical talents. Manolo is a father figure who thinks only of himself, exemplifying the negative characteristics of fatherhood that French philosopher Jean-Paul Sartre outlines in his vehement rejection of paternity. Sartre argues that paternity is a harmful relationship for children, differentiating between two types of paternity:

> a biological "making of children" (*faire des enfants*) and a more socioeconomic, one might say, "having" or "possessing of children" (*avoir des enfants*) … in nearly all of its manifestations, the bond of paternity is an appropriation and possession of children rather than a creation that the iniquitous bond rots. (cit. Harvey 33)

Figure 1.1 Constancito's Album Covers

Manolo represents the type of father figure who seeks economic gain from his "adopted" child, due to his personal lack of success. Although he exerts power over Constancito, Manolo is powerless in his own life, controlled by the fascist record label executives in charge of Boltor Records, the label that signed Constancito. Despite his admiration for fascism and fervent support of Francisco Franco – a desire to emulate the dictator so strong that he nicknamed his penis "mi caudillo" ["my commander"] (160) – Manolo's personal powerlessness links the concepts of failure and fascism, resulting in a humorous critique of fascist authority figures. Manolo imposes his fascist ideology on Constancito, whose music becomes increasingly nationalistic. His initial songs are odes to his hometown neighbourhood of Gràcia in Barcelona, the first album labelled *La gracia de ser de Gràcia* [*The Grace of Being from Gràcia*]. With Manolo's influence, the albums become markedly fascist, with images of imperialism of which Franco was particularly fond, including the rising sun and the figure of the *conquistador*.

Manolo enacts one of the worst forms of paternity, one that Constancito does not seek to copy in any way. After Constancito's moderate musical success subsides, Manolo finds positions for mother and son at a circus run by his brother. The circus is full of other mother/son duos who were once represented by Manolo and have now been abandoned. After he has become a member of the circus family, Constancito's talents stagnate, and he realizes that Manolo has been medicating him to stop him from going through puberty. Only after escaping from the circus does Constancito experience happiness, consistent with Sartre's assertion that there are no good fathers, that fathers "bestraddle their sons all their life long" (19), and the only way for sons to gain their freedom is through their fathers' death. Relatively free of all three father figures at last, Constancito must still contend with the weight of the symbolic father figure in Spain, Francisco Franco, and his fascist authoritative regime.

Not only does Constancito live in a fascist country, but his musical world tour includes fascist destinations throughout Latin America. At each stop of his tour, despite Constancito's lack of fascist leanings, he begins to "coleccionar miniuniformes golpistas con los que cada país le obsequiaba a su llegada, junto a un bastoncito bañado en oro cuya empuñadura acostumbraba a ser un águila imperial" ["collect mini-coup uniforms that each country presented to him upon his arrival, together with a little walking stick bathed in gold whose handle tended to be an imperial eagle"] (176). Constancito inadvertently causes the demise of various dictators, who mysteriously die within days of shaking hands with him. Constancito later discovers that aliens from his father's planet are causing these deaths by means of their fantastic connection to Constancito through his walkie-talkie. After his return to Spain, Constancito unwittingly plays a part in the deaths of leading figures in Franco's regime, as well. When he meets Luis Carrero Blanco, Franco's prime minister, Constancito tells him, "Usted llegará muy arriba, Almirante. Me lo han dicho unos amigos" ["You will reach very high, Admiral. Some friends have told me so"] (188). This is yet another example of the (often darkly) humorous aspects of this novel, as Constancito's words can be interpreted as a prediction of success or the upcoming explosion that will mark Carrero Blanco's death in 1973. Days after his encounter with Constancito, Carrero Blanco indeed does "fly high" as he is assassinated by a car bomb placed by members of ETA (Euskadi Ta Askatasuna, or Basque Homeland and Liberty), a Basque separatist group that used terrorism against Franco's dictatorship. Constancito also meets with Josemaría Escrivá, founder of Opus Dei, who dies of a heart attack soon after. In both cases, historical fact is combined with literary fiction to explain the deaths of these important figures within Franco's regime, demonstrating a clear rejection of these father figures and the values they uphold.

Constancito's interaction with and imitation of various dictators both reveal the anxiety hidden within the patriarchal father figure role and subversively reject that image as one worthy of imitation. The fascist leaders Constancito meets are eager to provide him with outfits that turn him into a miniature version of themselves, because they long to see their legacy outlive them. Baudrillard discusses how "charismatic leaders [such as] Hitler, Franco, Mao, having no 'legitimate' heirs, no filiation of power, see themselves forced to perpetuate themselves indefinitely – popular myth never wishes to believe them dead" (*Simulacra and Simulation* 25). Behind the authoritative facade lurks the patriarchal anxiety of being forgotten or replaced. Through his imitation of these patriarchal authority figures, and ultimate rejection of them proved by their deaths, Constancito reveals the authoritative father figures' lack of substance. He demonstrates that simulation "is infinitely more dangerous because it always leaves open to supposition that, above and beyond its object, *law and order themselves might be nothing but simulation*" (20). Although Constancito briefly imitates various patriarchal father figures, this mimesis is not productive for his identity formation.

Mimesis in Identity Formation

In *El mal francés*, mimesis is presented as a way for the protagonist to understand his identity, particularly his sexual identity, which Lluís needs to feel confident in before he can conceptualize his identity as a parent. Many individuals enact their parental role in imitation of those who have parented them, but Lluís shares little more than a name with the man who might provide him with an example of fatherhood within a patriarchal society. Lluís Senior's most convincing vestige of paternal authority, as well as the thing that most clearly connects him to his son, is his relationship to the written word. Lluís's father is "notablemente culto y un lector constante y exigente" ["notably educated and a constant and demanding reader"] (275) despite being "un hombre más bien tímido y poco hábil en la expresión verbal" ["a rather timid man not very skilled in verbal expression"] (275). Lluís Senior buys his son his first typewriter, later used to write novels. Even though they do not have a close relationship, Lluís Senior initiates his son into the literary heritage to which his masculinity makes him an heir.

Before he fully realizes or accepts his homosexuality, Lluís tries to imitate his father and submit to his influence by beginning a romantic relationship with Margarita, the daughter of family friends. He finds that, for quite some time, repressing his homosexuality is fairly easy due to heterosexual society's pressure toward conformity. Lluís knows that his father thinks Margarita is an attractive match for him, so he tries to comply with his father's wishes. Lluís's desire to impress his father by conforming to patriarchal notions of worth aligns with masculinity studies' assertion that, under hegemonic masculinity, men seek personal validation through homosocial competition. This constant competition to be deemed worthy by other males can be exhausting. As Andrew Kimbrell writes, "As competition becomes the male's main avenue of self-validation, fear of losing in competition remains the single greatest anxiety for many men. For boys and men, loss in competition can equal psychic annihilation" (74). In *El mal francés*, Lluís confesses to feeling such pressure, admitting:

> me pareció que me ponía delante de una partitura o de un guión que yo tenía que interpretar, hasta cierto punto obligatoriamente, y en el cual mi papel solo podía ser uno: el de conquistador – recordemos ahora que "yo" (o alguien que actuaba en su nombre) había decidido, por razones terapéuticas, ser lo más parecido a un Don Juan. (115)

> [it seemed to me that they put before me a musical score or a script that I had to perform, up to a certain point obligatorily, and in which my role could only be one: that of the conqueror – let's remember that "I" (or someone who acted in his name) had decided, for therapeutic reasons, to be as similar to a Don Juan as possible.] (115)

Lluís chooses to imitate a heterosexual literary figure, already showing that his creation and understanding of identity centre on literature. Literary father figures are as significant to Lluís's mimetic identity formation as his actual father. Lluís admits that he "tenía una tendencia morbosa a buscarme 'padres suplentes', porque mi relación con el mío natural no había funcionado correctamente – pero nunca nadie me dijo cómo era la buena relación con un padre" ["had a macabre tendency to look for 'substitute fathers,' because my relationship with my natural one hadn't worked correctly – but no one ever told me what a good relationship with a father was like"] (337). As Lluís's relationship with his father has always felt limited or stilted, it is difficult for him to imagine how he might achieve an authentic relationship with his own child through an imitation of his heterosexual father. Ultimately, Lluís will reject heterosexual father figures in favour of those who more truly reflect his identity.

Much like Lluís, Constancito experiences several failed mimetic attempts to replicate aspects of father figures within himself in his journey to self-realization. A strange and unattractive child, Constancito exhibits multiple signs of his incestuous beginnings, from the eyes that are too widely spaced to the mouth that he can never seem to keep closed. He is an extremely mimetic figure, both in personality and physical appearance, completing several fantastic physical transformations in his lifetime. The first transformation occurs as a teenager, when he magically wills himself into becoming attractive. Constancito gazes into a mirror, remembering:

> las palabras de su padre alienígena: "Desea, desea." Y soñó convertirse en aquella imagen que veía reflejada. Fue entonces cuando una especie de cordón umbilical surgió del espejo cóncavo, incrustándose en su vientre, apuñalándole justo por encima de su ombligo. Tras un intenso dolor, vino la calma. Y papá [Constancito] empezó a flotar, en posición fetal, dentro de aquella habitación. El día de Reyes, papá salió de aquella segunda gestación. Su apariencia era justamente la que aquel espejo cóncavo había reflejado. (299)

> [the words of his alien father: "Wish, wish." And he dreamed about converting himself into the image that he saw reflected. It was then that a kind of umbilical cord arose from the concave mirror, embedding itself into his belly, stabbing him just above his belly button. After an intense pain came the calm. And Dad (Constancito) began to float, in the fetal position, in that bedroom. On Three Kings Day, Dad emerged from that second gestation. His appearance was exactly that which the concave mirror had reflected.] (299)

Constancito is transformed into a handsome, strong young man, "como Robert Downey Júnior" ["like Robert Downey Junior"] (298), who reflects the ideal appearance standards of patriarchal society. This rebirth is suggestive of the completion of Lacan's mirror stage, where the individual (normally a baby) recognizes himself in the reflection of the mirror and identifies himself with that image. According to Lacan, as a result of the mirror stage, a child begins to understand his own identity while realizing that there are "others" in the world, particularly that his mother is also an "other." After his transformation, Constancito asks Angelina if she loves him. She tells him that she will never love him, so he leaves their apartment to begin his own life. Angelina's rejection teaches Constancito that his transformation has not really changed him or their relationship; instead, he has created another mimetic version of himself that is more pleasing to patriarchal authority. Constancito no longer resembles a child of incest but rather a handsome teenager, a patriarchal authority insider, although this physical change does not make him feel like less of an outsider.

Constancito's mimesis is nothing more than a copy of a copy, a series of repetitions based on the empty signifier of the patriarch. This empty mimesis occurs once more in Constancito's life after being struck by lightning (an experience similar to Joanet's). Now a married man with three children, Constancito stands on the roof trying to fix the television cable while two storm clouds approach. One cloud resembles James Brown, and the other has the likeness of Elvis Presley. Constancito interprets the lightning bolt that hits him to be a sign that he is the "jodido hijo ... de un matrimonio homosexual e interracial, de dos mitos de la música contemporánea. Universo, fuerzas vivas de la naturaleza o alienígenas, gracias por la señal que me enviáis desde las nubes" ["screwed son ... of a homosexual and interracial marriage, of two contemporary music legends. Universe, living forces of nature or aliens, thank you for the signal that you send me from the clouds"] (347). Magically, Constancito is now Black, the symbolic son of James Brown and Elvis Presley. This mimetic transformation distances Constancito even further from patriarchal power, since Black men have traditionally been excluded from this official type of authority. Constancito, for whom it will be important to have a good relationship with his children, has attempted to recreate himself in the image of various patriarchal father figures, but none of these assumed identities feel authentic to him. Constancito and Lluís are searching for alternative ways to perform their parenthood, as both find that the dominant hegemonic model is not a viable option.

Surpassing Patriarchal Models of Fatherhood

After failed attempts to replicate the patriarchal father figure, Lluís and Fernando search out different models for their mimetic understandings of identity. Lluís realizes that he has been enacting a false mimesis in his imitation of his father and literary figures like don Juan after reading the works of homosexual authors such as André Gide. He is incapable of acknowledging his homosexual identity until he recognizes echoes of himself in works by homosexual authors:

> Fue, pues, en aquel momento, cuando reconocí, asumí, incluso celebré que "yo" también era (¿3ª persona? ¿1ª persona?) homosexual como Gide, como Lorca, como Verlaine y como Rimbaud. Y ahora quiero detenerme en esa palabra "como", ante todo porque, repito una vez más, yo me reconocí como gay por asimilación, por apropiación del deseo que vi representado en otro, en este caso en los personajes de André Gide, o en el personaje "André Gide" tal como se representa a sí mismo en sus memorias. (98)
>
> [It was, then, in that moment, when I recognized, I assumed, I even celebrated that "I" was also (3rd person? 1st person?) homosexual like Gide,

like Lorca, like Verlaine and like Rimbaud. And now I want to pause on that word "like," primarily because, I repeat once more, I recognized myself as gay by assimilation, by appropriation of the desire that I saw represented in others, in this case in André Gide's characters, or in the character "André Gide" as he represented himself in his memoirs.] (98)

Through this realization, Lluís discards the heterosexual father figure by choosing to define himself as a reproduction of homosexual authors. He rejects the patriarchal model presented to him by Lluís Senior and figures like don Juan, who are part of a literary tradition that favours heteronormativity.[7] For Lluís, literature produced by homosexual authors, his "padres suplentes" ["substitute fathers"] (337), allows him to understand his sexual identity and place in the world, affording him "una salvación personal, trascendente y metafísica" ["a personal, transcendent, and metaphysical salvation"] (27).[8] Lluís views this realization of his homosexuality as a "renacimiento" ["rebirth"] (101). The use of the word "rebirth" indicates that Lluís has not simply come to a better understanding of his identity, but rather that he considers himself to be a new creation or newborn son of homosexual authors and their works. In this way, Lluís aligns himself with father figures who are outside of patriarchal domain and control.

Literature and writing inform the father figure role for Lluís, while also helping him to grasp and process his identity as a father. Just as with the process of understanding his sexuality, Lluís first attempts to construct his identity as a father through heterosexual examples before realizing the lack of personal authenticity for him in these models. Lluís tries to find heterosexual desire within himself, wanting to fall in love with Margarita and form a heteronormative family. Because Lluís is studying in France during Margarita's pregnancy, the couple writes letters to each other, providing Lluís an epistolary opportunity to try on different identities. Although the couple converses in Catalan, Lluís writes to Margarita in Spanish, explaining that "esta lengua, para mí, conviene recordarlo, era la de las novelas, y por tanto la que mejor se adaptaba a mi tarea de expresar una vivencia que tenía mucho de libresca" ["this language, for me, it is advisable to remember, was the language of novels, and therefore the one that best adapted to my work of expressing an experience that was very bookish"] (63). By adopting a literary persona, Lluís attempts to change his sexuality, ultimately realizing that a heteronormative model of fatherhood will not be sustainable for him.

Lluís compares the creation of a child with that of a book; he is initially uncertain about his desire to be a biological father but knows that he wants to father a novel. At first, Lluís finds biological paternity to be incompatible with maintaining his goal of writing a novel. He views Margarita's pregnancy as a forewarning of his lost freedom, writing of his fear that becoming a husband and father at nineteen would jeopardize his literary aspirations (105). Throughout the novel, Lluís prepares himself for the "gran sacrificio" ["great sacrifice"] (125) that is fatherhood, later achieving a sense of paternal resignation through his reading of Rimbaud, deciding to "inmolar mis impulsos por el bien de mi hijo, y pensaba que finalmente había llegado a comprender aquel verso tan extraño de Rimbaud: *par délicatesse j'ai perdu ma vie*" ["sacrifice my impulses for the good of my child, and I thought that I had finally begun to understand that strange verse of Rimbaud's: *through weakness I have lost my life*"] (124–5). Lluís equates fatherhood with loss and weakness; after his daughter's birth, his feelings evolve from resignation to happiness. Margarita names their child Guiomar, an homage to poet Antonio Machado (371) and a clear connection between literary and biological paternity.

Throughout Margarita's pregnancy, Lluís's diary serves as a therapeutic resource for exploring his transition into fatherhood. In 1969, Lluís is grappling with two aspects of his identity – his sexuality and his incipient paternity. Writing becomes a way for Lluís to process and develop these identities. As he writes, "Descubrir que eres homosexual cuando tienes diecinueve años y estás esperando un hijo no debe de ser una cosa muy frecuente, y seguro que no es nada fácil, pero resulta que me ha tocado a mí" ["Discovering that you are homosexual when you are nineteen years old and expecting a child must not be a very frequent thing, and it is surely not easy, but it turns out that this is what has happened to me"] (34). When Lluís finally tells his pregnant girlfriend that he is gay, he can do so only through literary references, saying "no puedo renunciar a vivir ... *selon ma nature*" ["I cannot give up living ... *according to my nature*"] (103). Margarita asks, "¿Quieres decir ... como André Gide?" ["Do you mean to say ... like André Gide?"] (103). In this and subsequent conversations, Lluís and Margarita use literary references to explore and create an alternative paternity for Lluís, a homosexual fatherhood for which they have few cultural or literary references. In his letters, Lluís tries to create a paternal image of himself, saying, "En las cartas que le escriba a partir de ahora, tengo que procurar ser, como mínimo, atento y afectuoso: es una mujer embarazada, está sola en París, y resulta que el padre de su hijo soy yo" ["In the letters that I write her from here on, I have to make sure to be, at a minimum, attentive and affectionate: she is a pregnant woman, she is alone in Paris, and it turns out that I am the father of her child"] (121). Just as writing permits Lluís to conceptualize his role as a father, one might argue that the author Lluís Maria Todó explored his own paternity through writing *El mal francés*. The novel is dedicated to his children, Guiomar and Pau, who "aparecen en este libro en estados diversamente embrionarios. Este relato les quiere decir, entre otras cosas, que nacieron de un amor complicado y difícil, pero firme y real" ["appear in this book in diversely embryonic states. This story wishes to tell them, among other things, that they were born from a complicated and difficult, but strong and real, love"] (1). In *El mal francés*, Todó has created a mimetic version of his biological children, albeit in embryonic form.

When Lluís travels by train from France to Barcelona to meet his newborn daughter, his identity as a gay father figure is tested and solidified. Lluís's physical journey back to his family is mirrored by a symbolic journey. At the beginning of the trip, he considers the idea of constructing a false heterosexual identity, alluring in its ability to provide him with heteronormative acceptance and status. Lluís catches the eye of an attractive woman on the train who looks at him with what he interprets as a lustful gaze. Although filled with "la satisfacción narcisista" ["the narcissistic satisfaction"] (394) of being desired, Lluís quickly discards the notion of flirting with her as he begins to read a work by Proust, the only book he has chosen to bring along for his trip. Throughout the novel, Lluís mentions the importance of several gay authors such as Proust and Gide in his identity formation, admitting, "[M]e dedicaba básicamente a ejercer mis grandes dotes para el camaleonismo y la mimesis [...] por escrito gracias a los libros" ["I dedicated myself basically to apply my great talents for chameleonism and mimesis (...) through writing, thanks to books"] (56). Lluís's homosexuality is affirmed as he reads Proust. He realizes that he cannot be heterosexual; rather, his vacillation regarding sexual identity formation has in part been due to a lack of mimetic models. Lluís writes:

> Yo estaba construyendo mi identidad homosexual, y tuve la seguridad de que aquel libro, después de los de Gide que había leído unos meses antes, sería una pieza importante en este largo proceso de elaboración simbólica. Eso mismo también se podría decir de una manera menos alambicada: en aquellos momentos, yo estaba ávido de representaciones de homosexuales, necesitaba que me mostraran ejemplos interesantes, quería que se me dijera y repitiera que no todos los homosexuales son como las peluqueras y flamencas que inspiraban el desdén unánime de la gente de mi entorno. (374)
>
> [I was building my homosexual identity, and I had the certainty that that book, after the books by Gide that I had read some months before, would

be an important piece in this long process of symbolic elaboration. That could be said in a less complicated way: in those moments, I was eager for homosexual representations, I needed to be shown interesting examples, I wanted to be told and to have it repeated that not all homosexuals are like the hairdressers and flamenco dancers that inspired the unanimous disdain of the people I was surrounded by.] (374)

Lluís's reflection highlights the importance of representation. In the limited literary offerings written by gay men to which he has access, many portrayals of gay men do not match with the identity that Lluís would like to build for himself. Lluís therefore begins the process of forging a homosexual identity that will inform his fatherhood, using literary references when possible and inventing the rest.

After considering and discarding ubiquitous examples of the patriarchal father figure, Fernando and Constancito also come to reject the patriarchal father figure as corrupt and unworthy of imitation. Constancito is not like his agent and stepfather Manolo Pencas, the Latin American dictators, or the leaders of Franco's regime, a fact that initially upsets Fernando, as he considers his father to be an embodiment of failure, experiencing "la incómoda sensación de ser hijo de un famoso don nadie" ["the uncomfortable sensation of being the son of a famous Mr. Nobody"] (26). At the beginning of the novel, Fernando craves patriarchal society's acknowledgment of his father so that he himself can feel like a legitimate receiver and bearer of paternal authority. Fernando feels that he will never be a worthy patriarchal figure if his own father (the source for Fernando's mimetic replication) is devalued by heteronormative society. As a solution, Fernando wants to write a biography of his father; in other words, he wishes to create a powerful myth of origin that will be respected by society and change his current social status. Fernando laments his lack of societal authority and acceptance, saying:

[N]o soy nada más que el hijo del protagonista, algo así como el cicerone de este libro que ustedes tienen en sus manos, abierto de piernas, frente a sus ojos libidinosos. Ni siquiera me considero una persona, sino una caricatura dibujada por un Dios menor, hasta hace un año sin rumbo consciente, un náufrago resignado a no ver tierra firme, dejándose llevar por las olas como una sepia que únicamente pretende pasar por la vida sin que nadie le moleste demasiado. (40–1)

[I am nothing more than the protagonist's son, something like the guide of the book that you have in your hands, legs open, in front of your libidinous eyes. I don't even consider myself a person, but a caricature drawn by a minor god, until a year ago without a clear path, a shipwreck resigned to not see solid ground, letting myself be taken by the waves like a cuttlefish that only hopes to go through life without being bothered too much.] (40–1)

Through the words that he uses to describe himself, Fernando further reveals his insecurity and lack of authority. He creates a feminized version of himself, connected to his father's biography and open to male objectification, the vulnerability of the book's content making him feel as if his legs were open and exposed to the male gaze. With this comparison, Fernando shares his sentiments of weakness.

Patriarchal society would categorize the inheritance of the Obs men as one of failure, rather than authority or power. During Fernando's childhood, Constancito suffers from "Menguismo Mediático" (335), a fantastic condition that causes him to shrink in stature. Fernando believes that this condition stems from his father's lack of paternal authority, non-existent confidence in himself as a musician, and the obscurity of his name as a performer. In this novel and in real life, Santi Balmes presents an irreverent representation of masculinity, failure, physical inadequacies, and social expectations. In an interview with *Rolling Stone*, Balmes responded to the question of whether or not his band had groupies by saying, "Yo tengo problemas de erección … Si el éxito nos hubiera llegado diez años antes, sería distinto. Ahora solo podemos mirar" ["I have erection problems … If success would have reached us ten years earlier, it would be different. Now we can only look"] (Portela Jordi Antón, "¿Tienen *groupies*"). While Balmes made light of masculine failure to perform in this interview, he later requested that *Rolling Stone* remove the interview from their site, as it had become "embarazoso" ["embarrassing"] for him (Portela Jordi Antón, "Santi Balmes"), a request that was ignored. Balmes and his characters engage with the concept of masculine failure, something with which Constancito is comfortable.

Just as Constancito is not concerned that his identity does not meet patriarchal standards for masculinity or fatherhood, he advises his children to pursue a literary and identity creation that does not privilege patriarchal power, saying:

El amor de verdad tiene que alimentar tus sueños, y viceversa … Y una última cosa: no permitáis que nadie decida por vosotros, como a mí me ha pasado. Tenéis que hacer de vuestra vida un libro escrito por vosotros mismos. Tendrá faltas de ortografía, pero al releerlo, como mínimo, os sentiréis identificados con el personaje. No tengo nada más que decir. Yo no planté cara a la vida y sucumbí. (387)

[True love has to nourish your dreams, and vice versa ... And one last thing: don't allow anyone to decide for you, as has happened to me. You have to make your lives a book written by yourselves. It will have spelling errors, but upon rereading it, at a minimum, you will identify with the character. I don't have anything else to say. I did not face up to life and I gave in.] (387)

Fernando chooses to immortalize his father, who is a clear symbol of rejection of patriarchal power and authority, through literature. Readers can assume that *¿Por qué me comprasteis un walkie talkie si era hijo único?* is in fact Fernando's biography of his father's life. This book does not shy away from Constancito's many failings; rather, they are continually exposed for the readers. By choosing to tell his father's story in this way, Fernando embraces his father's failings and presents him as the hero of the story, in contrast to the evil patriarchal father figures. Although heteronormative gender roles view masculine emotion as weakness, Constancito's unfettered love for his children becomes his greatest strength and a bonding force between himself and his son. Todó's and Balmes's characters ultimately use their exploration of mimesis to arrive at enactments of fatherhood that do not follow the strict guidelines laid out by Franco's regime, allowing them to perform parenthood as part of a wide spectrum of possible performances of the role, rather than limiting themselves to patriarchal society's strict expectations.

Breaking Literary Boundaries

Just as Todó's and Balmes's characters employ mimesis in their search for a greater understanding of their identity and connections to fatherhood, the use of literary techniques that break free from established literary conventions help elaborate a wider definition of literary paternity. One such technique is the inclusion of multiple narrative voices. In *El mal francés*, the narrative voice is complicated by several mimetic versions of real-life author Lluís Maria Todó. The novel begins with an anonymous third-person narrator who describes the adult Todó sitting before his computer, reviewing various files that contain segments of a future novel. After this brief section, the narrator declares, "Y ahora le cedemos la palabra" ["And now we give the floor"] (37) to a present-day version of Lluís Maria Todó, who narrates his thoughts in first person about his nineteen-year-old self's life. The narration is heavily interspersed with Lluís's diary entries from 1969, wherein a younger narrator shares his perspective. The use of multiple narrators reflects a widening of the spectrum of identity. What is the identity of the first narrator? Can he be anyone other than another mimetic representation of Lluís Maria Todó? Which Todó is the authentic Todó? Does a real representation of Todó exist, or are all the representations real? The multiple narrative voices in *El mal francés* play with mimesis in order to reflect on the limitless ways of experiencing identity, fatherhood, and writing.

Multiple narrative voices are present in Balmes's novel, as well. While Fernando is the novel's first-person narrator, his voice exists in juxtaposition with the editor, who frequently interjects his opinion in the novel's footnotes, which are written in a conversational tone and do not add informational value to the text.[9] It can be assumed that *¿Por qué me comprastéis un walkie talkie si era hijo único?* is, in fact, the finished biography of Constancito Obs, with footnotes written either by the editor of the publishing house that has agreed to produce Fernando's work, or perhaps written by Dr. Floyd, who agreed to work on the text with Fernando. While footnotes generally lend additional authority or knowledge to a text, Balmes's footnotes provide inaccurate or irrelevant information, thereby playing with the notion of authority and broadening the potential function of footnotes within a literary text. The editor's first footnote reads, "Ahora se acostumbra a pasar a la siguiente página. Lo digo por los primerizos" ["Now one usually goes to the next page. I say this for the first-timers"] (33). With the humorous tone of the footnotes, the editor diminishes the austerity and importance attributed to canonical literature and traditional understandings of literary paternity. In many of the footnotes, the editor expresses his exasperation with the author or his disapproval of what is being written in the novel. One footnote makes a tongue-in-cheek statement about the veracity of footnotes, stating that the editor tried to contact one of the characters to verify whether the story the author writes about him is true (188). Among all the fantastic and unverifiable elements of the novel, it is absurd that the editor would try to fact-check this particular story to convince readers of its believability. Other footnotes break the facade of the text's literary authenticity more directly, to ask, in one case, how the readers are enjoying the text so far. A small survey is provided in the footnote with boxes that readers can check, depending on their evaluation of the novel. These options range from, "Ovra de harte, a la altura del *Ulises* del Jeims Jois [sic]" ["Work of art, on the level of *Ulysses* by James Joyce"] to "Soy enanito y he podido cambiar una bombilla encaramándome sobre este tocho" ["I am a dwarf, and I was able to change a lightbulb by climbing up on this tome"] (143). Through their humorous, ridiculous tone, the footnotes in Balmes's novel question the authority imbued in the process of literary paternity, demonstrating a space of opportunity for other types of texts and authors. By extension, the concept of a widening spectrum of literary creation can be applied to an acceptance of diverse performances of fatherhood.

Another intertextual element in both novels that addresses issues of identity and mimesis is the inclusion of letters and diary entries in the text. In *El mal francés*, the letters and diary entries are mechanisms for Lluís to understand his sexuality and paternity. As a homosexual man living in a heterosexual society, Lluís narrates the importance not only of what his nineteen-year-old self's letters to Margarita say, but also what they do not or cannot say. Before he shared his sexual identity with Margarita, his letters could not fully convey the complexity of his emotions about her pregnancy, nor could he share the motivations behind his actions. Even though teenage Lluís uses letters and writing to reach a greater level of self-comprehension, the adult Lluís realizes that his younger self intuitively wrote about his homosexuality in veiled terms. Just as any other autobiographical text, his letters did not necessarily reveal his true or entire self, but rather one of many possible selves. Lluís reflects:

> Sin ser consciente de ello, estaba empezando a practicar, de una forma muy poco hábil, por cierto, una modalidad de discurso que los gays hemos tenido que adoptar muchas veces, con mayor o menor fortuna, con más o menos humor, más o menos obligados por la presión social: me refiero a ese discurso lleno de medias palabras, alusiones y sobreentendidos, que a veces sólo unos pocos saben descifrar, y otras veces, en cambio, son tan fácilmente accesibles que se vuelven ridículos por innecesarios. (106)

> [Without being conscious of it, I was beginning to practise, in a very unskilled way indeed, a method of discourse that we gays have had to adopt many times, with more or less success, with more or less humour, more or less obligated by social pressure: I refer to this discourse full of half-words, allusions, and implications, that sometimes only a few know how to decipher, whereas other times, they are so easily accessible that they become ridiculous because they are unnecessary.] (106)

In Lluís's early letters and diary entries, then, one could assert that the mimetic self-image he created was false or incomplete, based on his inability to use words in a fully truthful manner. Since Lluís's discovery of his homosexuality takes place in the 1960s, the process presents linguistic challenges to identity formation, based on the absence of terms to describe homosexuality. The term "gay" was not yet in popular use, and Todó writes that "homosexual" seemed too dry and clinical a term to describe a part of his identity. For an individual who processes his subjectivity through the lens of words, a lack of words is equivalent to a lack of identity. Eve Kosofsky Sedgwick writes about the damaging gaps within language's ability to describe human difference, particularly regarding sexuality, asserting that to

> alienate conclusively, *definitionally*, from anyone on any theoretical ground the authority to describe and name their own sexual desire is a terribly consequential seizure. In this century, in which sexuality has been made expressive of the essence of both identity and knowledge, it may represent the most intimate violence possible. (26)

Before Lluís can begin to conceptualize himself as a father, he must first understand his sexuality and identity, a difficult task given the limited patriarchal language of the 1960s. It is not until Lluís receives clarity about his homosexuality through reading the work of several gay authors that he decides to return to Spain and commit to raising his child with Margarita. This decision is a direct result of his reading, which provides him a better grasp on his sexual identity and how he, as a gay man, might perform parenthood.

In Balmes's novel, the written word similarly provides opportunities for breaking personal and literary boundaries. Constancito's diary, which is the basis for the anecdotes Fernando shares with Dr. Sigmund Floyd, has most likely been expanded upon by Fernando. Dr. Floyd does not believe a majority of what Fernando tells him, accusing Fernando of having written Constancito's diary himself, asserting, "Estoy seguro de que esa es su caligrafía. Fingir que es de su padre me parece demasiado" ["I am sure that this is your handwriting. To pretend that it is your father's is too much"] (216). The probable combination of father's and son's words in the diary creates a new genre of text that does not respect traditional literary limitations: part autobiography, part biography, and part fiction. Autobiography on its own can be considered "a threshold genre. It traces and crosses boundaries between fact and fiction, memory and history, selves and others, images and texts – sometimes drawing these distinctions, but more often blurring them" (Döring 72). Fernando's literary boundary crossing reflects the approach he will ultimately adopt toward identity formation and father/son relationships, that of crossing beyond the boundaries of patriarchal expectations of the fatherhood role.

Figure 1.2 Newborn Constancito

Ricardo Cavolo's illustrations for *¿Por qué me comprasteis un walkie talkie si era hijo único?*, humorous and at times shocking, are another example of breaking literary boundaries, as the images question the concept of the traditional Spanish family while constructing alternative and at times polemic representations of family and religion. Speaking of his illustrations, Cavolo asserts, "Normalmente prestamos atención a la parte oficial de la vida, pero la cara B, la de lo *outsider*, aunque sabemos de su existencia, muchos no la quieren vivir. En el libro lo que hacemos ver es que en esa parte también hay cosas interesantes" ["Normally

Figure 1.3 Underwater boxing match refereed by the Virgin of Montserrat

we pay attention to the official part of life, but the Side B, that of the *outsider*, although we know of its existence, many people do not want to live that life"] ("El líder"). Among the explicit illustrations is an image of newborn Constancito, covered in blood, showing the messy reality of childbirth (119). This is an early indication that Cavolo will not shy away from negative or distasteful aspects of the family.

Another image depicts an underwater boxing match between Constancito's father Joanet and an assassin sent by Boltor Records to kill or incapacitate Joanet so that he cannot negotiate Constancito's contract on his son's behalf (172). The Virgin of Montserrat referees the boxing match, while holding baby Jesus (the announcer) in her arms. One of the many nods to Catalan culture,[10] Montserrat is an important religious and regional figure whose participation in such a violent activity could be construed as disrespectful or sacrilegious. The bizarrely humorous image challenges the authority of the Holy Family and, by association, the institution of the heteronormative family.

Joanet does not die in this encounter, but he loses the match and is unable to defend his son's contract, another moment in which he embodies failure in the eyes of patriarchal society. Here the novel explores the possibility of the generational inheritance of failure, the notion that literary paternity and patriarchal power are not the only legacies that can

Figure 1.4 *Héroes del Cilicio* [*Cilice Heroes*]

be passed from father to son. Joanet's failure to live up to heteronormative society's standards for authority figures is passed on to Constancito, who exhibits a similar lack of desire or ability to conform.

In an explicit image that combines religion and sexuality, a music album cover appears with an image of genitalia, with the phallus replaced by the figure of the Virgin Mary (208). Here, Cavolo's irreverent image questions religion, sexuality, and family by replacing male genitalia with the Virgin Mary, the quintessential maternal figure. The title of the record, *Héroes del Cilicio* [*Cilice Heroes*], references religious flagellation and possibly Opus Dei, linking religious pain and guilt to similar emotions experienced as part of a family unit.[11]

Finally, an illustration of Constancito and Heidi parallels the scene from the movie *Titanic* where Jack and Rose are standing on the bow of the ship. In Cavolo's version, only Constancito has his arms outstretched because Heidi is performing oral sex on him (319). These illustrations provide a satirical perspective on societal institutions that are generally held in great esteem, such as heterosexual relationships, religion, and the family.

Figure 1.5 Constancito and Heidi on *Titanic*

While many of the literary techniques in Balmes's novel have humorous elements, they – along with the focus on writing in *El mal francés* – raise the serious point of who is allowed to participate in the intergenerational transmission of literary paternity. By questioning or breaking the boundaries of literary conventions, these novels express the necessity of creating space for a variety of literary voices, an argument that transfers to the widening spectrum of paternal identity.

A Spectrum of Fatherhood

Lluís's and Fernando's relationship to writing allows them to explore a more comprehensive definition of literature and its functions, which assists them in expanding their definitions of the father/son relationship and how those roles can be enacted. Realizing that the authoritative, patriarchal father figure holds little relevance in their personal lives, they instead gravitate toward definitions of fatherhood that would likely be considered failures by heteronormative society. Within concepts or identities that dominant society considers to be failures, there exists the potential for a different type of authority or power. J. Halberstam proposes the theory of failure as a queer art, stating that "[u]nder certain circumstances failing, losing, forgetting, unmaking, undoing, unbecoming, not knowing may in fact offer more creative, more cooperative, more surprising ways of being in the world" (2–3). According to Halberstam's theory, failure can be a site of personal growth or positive resistance, proffering a critique of dominant ideologies and powers while offering individuals alternative ways of living that would not be compatible with the lifestyle of someone pursuing heteronormative success. Lluís and Fernando, then, discover that there are many ways of experiencing the father/son relationship, a wide spectrum of existence that needs not adhere to patriarchal pronouncements of success or failure.

Although Lluís and Margarita are satisfied with Lluís's construction and enactment of his paternity, it is a type of fatherhood that can be considered a failure by the standards of patriarchal society. An openly homosexual man married to a heterosexual woman, happily raising a family, is a relationship that does not conform to the definitions of the family and fatherhood laid out by Franco's regime. Lluís's failure or refusal to mimic heteronormative parental guidelines allows him to embrace his identity as a gay man, which drives his understanding of fatherhood. As parental examples in other chapters will reaffirm, those parents who are willing to step outside of the limited definitions of parenthood proposed by patriarchal, heteronormative standards have the opportunity to "escape the punishing norms that discipline behaviour and manage human development with the goal of delivering us from unruly childhoods to orderly and predictable adulthoods" (Halberstam 3). By refusing to follow heteronormative guidelines for paternity, Lluís breaks away from predictable patterns and develops a parental identity unique to himself, while staying true to his sexual identity.

El mal francés presents a family that subverts patriarchal binaries, because it consists of an openly homosexual father figure who is married to a heterosexual woman. Although Margarita does not know that Lluís is gay when they conceive their first child, she marries him with this knowledge, and the couple later has a second child. Lluís and Margarita do not avoid the traditional family structure altogether, but instead they subvert it from within, creating a plurality of the definition of fatherhood. Perhaps Lluís is heeding the words of one of his literary father figures, André Gide, who argued in *Nourritures terrestres* [*The Fruits of the Earth*] "that the morally spent institution of the family only served to impede one's freedom" (Harvey 175). From within the existing structure of the family, Lluís and Margarita create new morals and identities for their children, as well as for themselves. At the end of the novel, Lluís describes his hopes and desires, some of which are incongruent with the heteronormative father figure role. He writes, "Tengo ganas de pasar los próximos meses con Margarita y Guiomar, y tengo ganas de tener un amante masculino. Tengo ganas de formar una familia, y tengo ganas de vivir en una sociedad sin familias" ["I feel like spending the next few months with Margarita and Guiomar, and I feel like having a male lover. I feel like forming a family, and I feel like living in a society without families"] (406). Lluís expresses desires that patriarchal society would deem contradictory and impossible. Through the creation of this "familia poco convencional" ["unconventional family"] (422), Lluís experiences the best of what paternity has to offer without relegating himself to what would be, for him, the falseness of a heterosexual lifestyle. He can have a family with biological children while simultaneously exploring his homosexual desire. In a personal interview in July 2012, Todó spoke about the alternative nature of the family he formed with Margarita, affirming, "Pensábamos, pues, que era una manera de romper los límites de la familia tradicional, convencional. Esto para los dos era un estipulo. Era una cosa bonita y eufórica, lo de romper los límites de la familia tradicional" ["Well, we thought that it was a way of breaking the limits of the traditional, conventional family. For us, this was a stipulation. It was a beautiful and euphoric thing, breaking the limits of the traditional family"] (Jerónimo and Todó 128). *El mal francés* speaks out against oppressive gender binaries that affect all members of society who are not heterosexual males.

Similarly, Fernando comes to embrace and value those aspects of his father that patriarchal, heteronormative society would view as failures. Despite Constancito's legacy of a long line of paternal lack of authority, he does not feel the desire to seek patriarchal justification of his fatherly identity. After a childhood of absent or selfish father figures and a mother who refused to love him, Constancito's only wish is to be loved by his wife and children. When his wife Heidi asks him what his life goals are, Constancito replies, "A que me quieras. A que este niño me quiera. A poder mantenernos como una persona normal, como hacía mi padre. No necesito gran cosa en realidad" ["That you love me. That this child loves me. To be able to provide for you all like a normal person, like my father did. In reality, I don't need grand things"] (334). Constancito's enactment of fatherhood receives its authority or authenticity through Constancito's focus on love, offering readers one more example of a different way in which to enact fatherhood. Halberstam discusses the concept of "weapons of the weak" (88), the idea that behaviours that could be construed as examples of "inaction [or] passivity" (88) can be tools for subverting dominant culture. Constancito's apparent failure to become an authoritative father figure can be interpreted as an alternative lifestyle made possible through the freedom of failure, "embedded already in the dominant ... indeed failure can exploit the unpredictability of ideology and its indeterminate qualities" (88). Constancito is self-assured in his enactment of fatherhood, desiring to spend time with his children above all else.

¿Por qué me comprasteis un walkie talkie si era hijo único? is a parody and criticism of heteronormative society's drive for all men to be viewed as powerful, successful authority figures. In an interview with *20 minutos* [20 Minutes], Balmes said that his novel represents a revenge against "la aparente normalidad post-burguesa que desprendemos todos y que en realidad es un miedo a no ser aceptado" ["the apparent post-bourgeois normality that emits from all of us and that, in reality, is a fear of not being accepted"] ("El líder"). In his depictions of the father figure, Balmes elucidates the process of surpassing patriarchal power while exposing the myth of the father's authority by revealing the failure of multiple generations of fathers. Constancito is undoubtedly a character who debunks the myth of the all-powerful father figure, as he has no desire to have his talent recognized or have paternal authority bestowed upon him. As an adult, Constancito marries Heidi Ausdenmeyer, daughter of Gustav Ausdenmeyer, a Nazi and powerful music producer who despises his son-in-law and effectively ends his musical career. Fernando hates his maternal grandfather, ultimately fighting against larger representations of patriarchy by defying his grandfather and attempting to take down his corrupt record label. At the same time, Fernando realizes that, despite his best intentions, he cannot erase all traces of his grandfather's identity from his own. Just as Fernando is a reproduction of Constancito, he is also partially a repetition of Gustav. Fernando laments, "El abuelo, ah, maldita sea. Me miro en el espejo de la barra, tengo su misma altura y probablemente, cuando tenga su edad, tendré su misma complexión. Compréndanme, cuando alguien se avergüenza de uno de sus antecesores también detesta encontrar algún rasgo en común" ["My grandfather, ah, damn it. I look at myself in the mirror at the bar, I have his same height and probably, when I am his age, I will have his same complexion. Understand me, when

someone is ashamed of one of their ancestors, they also detest finding any character trait in common with them"] (388). By vowing to take on his grandfather's record label and ruining him financially, Fernando seeks to reject patriarchal authority, even those elements within himself.

El mal francés and *¿Por qué me comprasteis un walkie talkie si era hijo único?* are two contemporary Spanish novels that explore the expansion of both the concept of literary paternity and the spectrum of possible performances of fatherhood. Although patriarchal society seeks to uphold the myth of the omnipotent father figure through representations of literary paternity – a metaphor for heteronormative male power and privilege – Todó and Balmes challenge and surpass this theory through an investigation of how mimesis and authenticity relate to fatherhood and writing. The mimetic processes that characters in these novels pass through, then, do not create a vindication of the father figure but rather are bereft of any contribution to patriarchal society. Each novel finds a creative method of challenging dominant and accepted ideas of fatherhood, suggesting the multiplicity of ways in which a father may experience his paternal identity and establish a relationship with his child. Forging new paths for fatherhood through failure, Todó's and Balmes's characters reject the authoritative patriarchal father figure in favour of non-normative enactments of parenthood. With their revolutionary reconfigurations of fatherhood, these novels initiate a dialogue about fatherhood in the twenty-first century that is not centred on patriarchal privilege; rather, father figures embrace their authentic identities through alternative ways of enacting the fatherhood role.

Chapter Two

M(other)hood and Disability

Whether she is portrayed as self-abnegating or castrating, the mother figure in Spanish literature has always been a forceful presence. She has been alternately vilified as an emotionally coercive enforcer of patriarchal norms and lauded as the woman who sacrifices her own needs and identity for her children, yet she is rarely presented as a fully actualized person in her own right with a personality separate from her maternal role. Díaz-Mas's futuristic "La niña sin alas" ["The Girl without Wings"] depicts a complex portrayal of the maternal experience, describing a relationship that alternately supports and confines mother and daughter. The short story tells of an anonymous woman who finds herself unexpectedly pregnant for the first time at the age of forty after first disdaining, then becoming indifferent to, the possibility of bearing children. In the world of the story, humans can fly by virtue of their own wings and only remember a time prior to wings as ancient history, or even myth. Wings have become hereditary, so every normal child born into their world has them. Wingless individuals are considered physically handicapped, "hombres mutilados" ["mutilated people"] (Díaz-Mas 161). Through an ultrasound, the story's protagonist learns that her fetus has no wings. Although she is given the option to terminate the pregnancy and realizes her child will be seen as seriously handicapped, she refuses to do so, claiming a deep attachment to her unborn child. In the grips of the intense emotional bond the protagonist feels with the infant, she transforms herself by refusing to use her wings (essentially disabling herself in society's eyes) so as to better adapt to her child's physical and emotional needs. The child's winglessness and the protagonist's acceptance of her daughter's disability provoke various degrees of rejection, from the infant's father, members of the protagonist's social circle, and society at large. Shortly before turning two, however, the child begins to grow wings (apparently they were there all along, so her abnormality was a matter of delayed development rather than fetal deformity). At this point, the mother does everything in her power to prevent the growth of the organs that would correct the child's handicap. First, she bandages the tiny wings to inhibit their growth, then bites them off when the wings persist in growing through the bandages. The story leaves readers with an ambivalent message about the mother/child bond, particularly where supportive emotional connection crosses the line into unhealthy dependency.

"La niña sin alas" presents two seemingly antithetical models of motherhood. On the one hand, the protagonist's willingness to de-evolve into a more prehistoric being in order to nurture her daughter signals the kind of mother/daughter intimacy that one associates with the mother who is willing to sacrifice herself for the sake of the child. On the other hand, the protagonist's act of mutilation casts her as the kind of castrating woman who appears frequently in Oedipal theorizations of the mother figure. This chapter examines the two models of motherhood that Díaz-Mas proffers in this story, drawing upon Julia Kristeva's "Stabat Mater" and a well-developed canon of motherhood research to reveal how the protagonist's self-sacrifice turns to castration and oppression when the threat or the possibility of the child's eventual independence provokes anxiety in the mother. In "La niña sin alas," mother and daughter isolate themselves from male-dominated society to create a co-dependent relationship; however, exclusion from patriarchal society does not guarantee a freer or healthier relationship between mother and daughter. The protagonist's attitude towards motherhood changes from indifferent to devoted, but when she bites off her daughter's wings, the story ends with a restrictive relationship that repeats tired motherhood tropes. In this chapter, I will argue that the patriarchal, ableist society in which the characters live relegate mother and daughter to a disabled status as monstrous others due to the mother's pregnancy and the daughter's physical handicap; explain how the pair breaks free from the constraints of their society to create an alternate iteration of physical and emotional intimacy that is just as identity-forming for the mother as for the child; and reflect on the mother's capacity to be both nurturing and self-serving in her relationship with her child. The ambiguous representation of motherhood throughout the story reveals the complexities of the role, which can be enacted in a variety of ways along a diverse spectrum of parental performance that varies not only from parent to parent but also in relation to how one individual performs their parenthood given different moments in time and various societal and personal circumstances.

Models of Motherhood in Spain

Although Díaz-Mas's story is set in an unknown future society, her commentary on the relationship between maternity and womanhood is worth examining within a Spanish context. Spanish society and literature have long promoted the image of the Spanish woman as the self-sacrificing mother figure who reflects nineteenth-century ideals of the "angel of the hearth," serving as the moral compass of the family, "the comforter, the womb, absent of mind and spirit" (Mangini 85). This concept of motherhood as religious sacrifice and patriotic duty was further strengthened under the National Catholicism of Franco's dictatorship, which asserted that it was women's patriotic duty to produce as many children as possible, "virtually up to the menopause" (Brooksbank Jones 53), children to whom mothers would transmit the cultural values of the regime. The ideal Spanish mother was characterized by her chastity, caring nature, dedication to the home and moral guidance of the family, and above all else, her capacity to disregard her own needs while sacrificing everything for her husband and children (Ryan, "All Turbulent on" 47).

Franco's dictatorship characterized this model of motherhood as "good," while any enactment of motherhood that deviated from these stipulations was socially condemned as "bad" mothering. The dichotomy of the good or bad woman (and mother) is not new. From the beginning of Judaeo-Christian mythology, Eve has been criticized as the guilty temptress and sinner, while being recognized as the quintessential mother figure. The Spanish version of the "bad" mother has evolved throughout history to target different groups of women, from the Republican mother in need of punishment during Franco's dictatorship (Finnerty 213) to the "liberal, Transitional woman" (Ryan, "All Turbulent on" 40) in contemporary Spain. In *The Changing Face of Motherhood*, Catherine Bourland Ross reflects on the value judgments behind Spanish social constructions of motherhood, explaining that "society creates and defines the way in which women should perform mothering in order to be a *good* mother. Sacrifice, patience, love, support – those are some of the characteristics of a good mother. However, the lived experience of mothering does not always follow those descriptions" (1). The rigid requirements described here indicate a very traditional idea of Spanish motherhood, impossible to fully live up to even for those women who wish to do so. Bourland Ross goes on to argue that, as Spanish society changes, motherhood cannot be judged by the same antiquated standards, as society needs to recognize the multiplicity of ways in which motherhood is performed.

The Pregnant Body and Disability

Motherhood had never been a serious consideration or desire for Díaz-Mas's character. As a young woman, the protagonist felt isolated from her peers because she was unable to grasp the appeal of maternity. She recalls how many of her childhood friends constantly talked about becoming mothers, saying, "[Y]o no sabía si emprenderla a bofetadas con ellas, por bobas y pánfilas, o conmigo misma, por despegada e insensible. Verlas tan ilusionadas por algo que a mí me dejaba fría me hacía sentir mal" ["I didn't know whether to slap them, for being silly fools, or to slap myself, for being cold and insensitive. Seeing them so excited about something that left me cold made me feel bad"] (162). When she unintentionally becomes pregnant many years later, her perspective immediately changes. Despite the fact that her baby will face social challenges due to her disability, the mother will not consider the possibility of abortion, affirming that, "Yo, que nunca me había sentido atraída por la idea de ser madre, amaba ya a aquella niña desconocida, aun a sabiendas de que sería un lastre para toda mi vida" ["I, who had never felt drawn to the idea of being a mother, already loved that unknown girl, even knowing that she would be a burden for my whole life"] (162). Marking her disinterest in motherhood is important to the story, because it lets readers know that this is not a woman so desperate to be a mother that she would rather have a deformed (wingless) child than no child at all. She is not deluded by an unrealistic illusion of motherhood, but she feels strongly committed to carrying her pregnancy to term. The text does not romanticize pregnancy as a woman's natural calling, nor does it vilify motherhood as an unmanageable burden. The narrative acknowledges the protagonist's right to opt out of motherhood if she so desires, while demonstrating that a woman's feelings towards motherhood can change over time.

The protagonist lives in a society where she may choose the best course of action for herself and her pregnant body.[1] Pregnant individuals may struggle to maintain agency over their bodies, as patriarchal rhetoric often constructs the pregnant body as infantilized and desexualized.[2] This fosters a sense of entitlement within heteronormative society to invade pregnant individuals' physical space, offer unsolicited advice, and even make legal decisions on behalf of the pregnant body. Beginning in the late eighteenth century in Europe and North America, with the advent of nationalism and nationhood, advances in science transformed the pregnant body into a public space. Rebecca Kukla argues that society established two images of the pregnant body, one positive (the Fetish Mother) and one negative (the Unruly Mother), neither accurate. According to Kukla, the Fetish Mother is an individual who successfully connects with her fetus or infant, is capable of breastfeeding, and births children without deformities or flaws (82). Representing the regulatory ideal, this fetishized version of motherhood can never be fully embodied by any real mother figure. The Unruly Mother must be regulated and disciplined by society, particularly the medical community, as she is "volatile, fragile ... governed not by orderly principles" (83) and most likely to reproduce her own disorder through a deformed fetus. Both categorizations of pregnant bodies – which Kukla asserts do not represent real maternal bodies but rather imaginary ones that society can use to define, judge, and control real maternal bodies – require societal control to assure the production of "acceptable" babies. This eighteenth-century legacy of public intervention in pregnancy and societal distrust in pregnant individuals lives on in contemporary societies, further reflected in the medical community's treatment of Díaz-Mas's mother figure.

The protagonist in "La niña sin alas" can be classified as an Unruly Mother because she wilfully chooses to carry out her pregnancy with the knowledge that her baby will be socially stigmatized because society considers the fetus disabled or deformed. Medical professionals, acquaintances, and her husband recognize her behaviour as nonstandard, fitting into the category of Unruly Mother. Throughout "La niña sin alas," individuals attempt to control her disorderly pregnancy through "public discipline and surveillance" (Kukla 84), as the protagonist is submitted to various exams that aim to assess her fetus's development and search for any abnormality. The protagonist recounts how, "a mi marido y a mí nos extrañó la solícita preocupación del médico, su insistencia en someterme a pruebas y análisis, en repetir algunos de ellos alegando que no veía claros los resultados" ["my husband and I were surprised by the doctor's attentive concern, his insistence in subjecting me to tests and analyses, in repeating some of them alleging that he could not see the results clearly"] (162). The mother in "La niña sin alas" is unfazed by the test results that attempt to prove her fetus's social unacceptability. She describes the moment in which she and her husband learn about the fetus's disability, recalling that it was, "ya en el inicio del tercer mes de embarazo cuando el doctor nos convocó en su despacho y nos dio las dos noticias. La primera, que el bebé era una niña; la segunda, que con toda probabilidad nacería sin alas" ["already in the beginning of the third month of pregnancy when the doctor called us to his office and gave us the news. First, that the baby was a girl; second, that with all likelihood she would be born without wings"] (162). Told together in this way, this statement reads as a tongue-in-cheek comment on the status of femaleness, disability, and social standing in patriarchal society. Not only will the protagonist's daughter face challenges due to her disability, but she will also suffer because of her gender. Immediately after learning these two facts about her fetus, the protagonist asserts for the first time that she "amaba ya a aquella niña desconocida" ["already loved that unknown girl"] (162). She chooses to use the gendered word "niña" ["girl"] instead of a more gender-neutral term like infant or baby, indicating that the baby's gender is important to and valued by her. Although not explicitly stated, her admission of love for the fetus after learning about its wingless state indicates an act of resistance, a decision to love a fetus that patriarchal, ableist society would sooner see eliminated.

Hospital staff and society at large pressure the protagonist to terminate her pregnancy, judging her for decisions she makes about her own body. The ownership and subjectivity of her pregnant body seems up for debate. To whom does the pregnant body belong, the mother or the fetus? What level of input or control should the biological father, medical professionals, or societal conventions retain over decisions related to the pregnant body? With society's growing access to medical technology, including ultrasounds and prenatal testing, it is possible to know more about each fetus and its characteristics. This information facilitates a tendency to bestow increasing agency upon the fetus, and allows doctors, nurses, and politicians to feel justified in intervening in decisions about the pregnant body, even though that pregnant body belongs to the mother. Susan Bordo explains in *Unbearable Weight* that, as technology allows for a more complete depiction of the fetus, some doctors have shifted their perspective to view the fetus as their patient rather than the pregnant individual:

> Because of such changes in the perception of the fetus's status, combined with the advancing technologies that enable the doctor to treat the fetus directly, as an autonomous patient, doctors have come to feel confused, angry, and, perhaps, morally outraged when mothers refuse a recommended treatment ... But the disturbing fact remains that increased empathy for the fetus has often gone hand in hand with decreased respect for the autonomy of the mother. (Bordo 86)

While the fetus seems to be gaining rights and support, individuals inhabiting pregnant bodies find their autonomy increasingly under attack. With greater technology and advances in prenatal testing, "women in contemporary Western society are encouraged to imagine their pregnancies as processes that can be perfected, indeed that they have a responsibility to perfect" (Karpin and Savell 3). In *Perfecting Pregnancy: Law, Disability, and the Future of Reproduction*, Karpin and Savell argue that, while prenatal testing may appear to give pregnant individuals more choices when it comes to their fetus, those choices are an illusion, as society has delineated clear responses as to which types of fetuses may appropriately be carried to term. Not only are pregnant individuals' personal choices about the health of their own bodies and their fetuses heavily scrutinized by public figures like doctors, but in many countries, the relationship between pregnancy and workers' rights is framed within the discourse of disability.[3] This construction of the pregnant body as a disabled body is another way in which the mother in "La niña sin alas" may feel connected to her daughter, who is socially stigmatized in similar ways. It is not much of a leap, then, for society to label these non-conforming and disabled bodies as monstrous, as well.

Monstrous (M)others and Daughters

The maternal body has long been an object of misogynistic manipulation that seeks to maintain the mother within a subjected space by constructing her as a horrifying or monstrous figure. Freud, the quintessential theorist to connect motherhood and monstrosity, linked the mother figure to death, castration, and the frightful yet familiar unknown space (the uncanny) of the womb. In "Medusa's Head," Freud argues that this mythological female monster represents female genitalia, horrifying due to its lack of a penis, reminding those who gaze upon it of the fear of castration. Freud argues that just as Medusa's face paralyzes victims in fright, a male child who "catches sight of the female genitals, probably those of an adult, surrounded by hair, and essentially those of his mother" ("Medusa's Head" 273) will be shocked by her lack of a penis. The mother and her reproductive organs are construed as monstrous, a castrating, threatening "other" from whom her children must flee. Patriarchal society uses the monstrous construction of motherhood to keep mother and child in their "correct" (subjugated) social spaces, creating a multitude of uncanny identities for the (m)other figure:

> Precisely this "other" constitutes an important and complex fantasy of gender that can be broken down into a number of subconsciously present figures: a monstrous womb, vampire, hysterical, possessed body, femme fatale, witch, oracle, castrating mother. Of a particular importance is the phrase "monstrous-feminine" ... emphasizing the importance of gender in the construction of monstrosity. (Sempruch 65)

By this definition, the protagonist in "La niña sin alas" is doubly monstrous: first, by her insistence on carrying a disabled fetus to term, and second, through the castrating action of biting off her daughter's wings, which guarantees her daughter will remain in a state of otherness.

Womanhood is often the main requirement for being considered monstrous in patriarchal society. Mother and daughter in "La niña sin alas" experience a monstrosity further "othered" by its connection to disability. The daughter in "La niña sin alas" joins her mother as a marginalized subject, a monster in the eyes of male-dominated society that would rather have seen her aborted than born outside the confines of what constitutes the acceptable female body. Rosemarie Garland Thomson discusses the intersections between these identity categories, asserting, "Both the female and the disabled body are cast as deviant and inferior; both are excluded from full participation in public as well as economic life; both are defined in opposition to a norm that is assumed to possess natural physical superiority" (19). Perhaps this explains the ease with which mother and daughter embrace their deviant otherness; the protagonist has lived her life as a woman, already familiar with exclusion and otherness. Because they are seen as lesser and weaker, society wishes for marginalized groups – women, individuals with disabilities, etc. – to either conform or disappear. When the protagonist chooses to carry her pregnancy to term, despite adamant disapproval from everyone in her life, she is failing to fulfil the social contract promised by reproductive technologies, thereby challenging the heteronormative family. As Alison Kafer explains in *Feminist, Queer, Crip*, ableist society assumes that potential parents will use assistive reproductive technologies as a gate-keeping mechanism, regulating birth through the ability to "deselect or prevent disability; doing otherwise – such as selecting for disability – means failing to properly reproduce the family" (69). After the child's birth, society in "La niña sin alas" continues to disapprove of the protagonist's physical relationship with her daughter and attempts to "correct" their behaviour and interactions by suggesting that she purchase orthopaedic wings for her daughter (164), demonstrating their belief that disability "is the attribution of corporeal deviance – not so much a property of bodies as a product of cultural rules about what bodies should be or do" (Garland Thomson 6). The mother ignores those who believe they are entitled to instruct her on how to raise and interact with her daughter, leading to an even harsher backlash from the community, wherein the "enfrentamientos se hicieron progresivamente más violentos con todo el mundo: con mi marido, con los familiares, con los amigos" ["confrontations with everyone became progressively more violent: with my husband, with family, with friends"] (164). The mother rejects society's patriarchal and ableist wisdom about the definition of an acceptable fetus and the way in which one must physically interact with a child, eventually withdrawing from society completely to live her relationship with her daughter as she chooses.

Instead of seeking to conform or change their monstrousness, the mother embraces and reconfigures her and her daughter's roles as monstrous "others." Even though the protagonist has wings and can "pass" as an able-bodied member of society, she chooses to act as if her wings did not exist. She moves as her daughter does, even though this provokes disgust and discomfort in others. The protagonist discovers a painting from an ancient time before humans developed wings that depicts a woman carrying her baby in her arms, "en vez de acogerlos entre las escápulas y las plumas remeras, como hacemos hoy" ["instead of holding them between the shoulder blades and the flight feathers, as we do today"] (164). At first, the protagonist only holds her daughter in her arms in secret, as the posture would seem grotesque to a winged observer. She gradually gains confidence to interact physically with her daughter in ways that society would view as disabled because she feels a deeper physical and emotional connection to her child in this way. Although the protagonist could perform the physical acts of motherhood in "normal" ways, she prefers the "monstrous" alternative.

While her daughter was afforded no choice regarding her handicapped status, the mother's rejection of society's ableist standards and decision to live as disabled is a monstrous rebellion, as ableist society cannot fathom such a preference. According to McRuer's seminal concept of compulsory able-bodiedness – which argues that the societal assumption of able-bodiedness is normalized as the standard and desired way of existing – individuals with disabilities are just as crucial as able-bodied individuals in upholding the system. Compulsory able-bodiedness "demands that people with disabilities embody for others an affirmative answer to the unspoken question, Yes, but in the end, wouldn't you rather be more like me?" (372). Individuals living satisfied lives while disabled, or those who do not assert unhappiness with their otherness, are threatening to a society so deeply invested in ableism. As Eli Clare affirms in *Exile and Pride*, the "dominant story about disability should be about ableism" (3), demonstrating that the social narrative about disability would not exist in its current form without the shaping provided by able-bodiedness. In "La niña sin alas," society finds the mother/daughter pair so alarming because they do not affirm the discourse of able-bodiedness. Instead, the mother finds fulfilment through renouncing her able-bodied privilege and dedicating herself to her relationship with her disabled daughter, implicitly questioning the superior social standing of able-bodiedness. This rejection of ableist, patriarchal society reveals itself primarily in two ways: a withdrawal from the society that disapproves of her relationship with her child and the development of an alternate way of physically interacting with her child that does not include flying.

Breaking with Patriarchy to Redefine Mother/Daughter Relationships

To find fulfilment in her bond with her child, the protagonist must remove herself from relationships that uphold patriarchal and ableist standards, particularly her relationship with her husband. Although the story does not reveal whether the protagonist's husband urges her to abort the fetus, he is uncomfortable with, or even disgusted by, the baby's disability. The husband clearly wishes his family to conform to heteronormative, ableist standards. He becomes upset when he sees his wife lying on the floor (instead of flying) as she plays with their daughter. When her husband sees their daughter crawling, he "se ponía enfermo" ["became sick"] (163) and "decía que parecía un animal" ["said that she looked like an animal"] (164). As time passes and the mother's behaviour becomes more non-normative to match her daughter's, the husband distances himself further from his family. As the mother asserts, "Mi marido pasó por varias fases, de la indignación al aburrimiento. Cuando la niña cumplió dos años apenas nos hablábamos, casi ni coincidíamos en casa" ["My husband went through various phases, from indignation to boredom. When the girl turned two, we barely spoke to each other, we were almost never home at the same time"] (166). The husband begins to take overnight work trips and have affairs, actions that do not bother his wife because she has completely submerged herself in the relationship with her daughter. Whether he could verbalize it or not, the husband clearly wishes to have a normative family, understanding that a different body is considered a lesser body, "those bodies deemed inferior become spectacles of otherness while the unmarked are sheltered in the neutral space of normalcy" (Garland Thomson 8). As long as he inhabits a normative body, the husband can pass through life without scrutiny, protected. His daughter's disabled body brings attention to his family, an example of "[c]orporeal departures from dominant expectations [which] never go uninterpreted or unpunished" (Garland Thomson 7). Such close proximity to those who are socially othered puts the husband in danger of becoming an "other" as well.

The father figure is physically present in Díaz-Mas's story, but emotionally he offers nothing to his wife and daughter. A traditional understanding of parenthood posits that a father figure is necessary in child-raising, proffering the idea that "mothering, then, is informed by [the mother's] relationship to her husband, her experience of financial dependence, her expectations of marital inequality, and her expectations about gender roles" (Chodorow 86). This definition of mothering explains the role within a patriarchal, heteronormative context with rigidly defined and distinct social spaces and expectations for fathers and mothers. In such societies, including Spain throughout most of the twentieth century, motherhood has historically been dependent (at the very least in an economic sense) on a father figure. Díaz-Mas's protagonist, despite her willingness to reframe her relationship with her daughter outside of patriarchal dictates, retains the traditional belief that the ideal iteration of family includes a father figure, affirming that she "no estaba dispuesta a que mi hija se criase sin la figura de un padre, aunque fuese meramente simbólica. Una niña así necesita toda la protección que se le pueda dar" ["was not willing for her daughter to be raised without a father figure, even if he were merely symbolic. A girl like that needs all the protection that she can get"] (166). While Díaz-Mas's protagonist stays with her husband and ignores his infidelity for the economic security that he can provide her daughter, her experience of mothering is not influenced in the least by his presence or lack thereof. Beyond the assurance that he has not left the family, her husband's existence barely registers in her mind, as she devotes all her energy and derives all her emotional support from her daughter.

Unfazed by her husband's rejection of her as a mother and wife, the protagonist's relationship with her daughter becomes all-important, granting fulfilment to the mother through the ways in which her body physically relates to her daughter's. She must remove herself from society to establish this relationship, as society urges the mother to train her daughter how to assimilate as closely as she can to normative behaviour, with advice from others ranging from the suggestion of orthopaedic wings to restraining her daughter when she attempts to crawl (as winged babies fly instead of crawling). Various individuals who meet the wingless child are of the opinion that if the baby "era distinta no podíamos fomentar que lo fuese cada vez más" ["was different, we could not encourage her to continue to become more different"] (164). Those members of society who offer advice to the protagonist likely have a wide range of motivations, from those who are uncomfortable with societal non-conformity to other well-meaning (even if misguided) individuals who view societal conformity as the best form of protection.

The protagonist must remove herself from society to connect with her child because social pressure towards conformity is pervasive. "La niña sin alas" begins by recounting the myth of Icarus, the young boy who flies too close to the sun and falls to his death after disobeying his father, an aptly chosen example that can be interpreted as a tool of social conformity in this society.[4] Beginning with the seemingly innocuous phrase, "Había una vez un tiempo en que los hombres no tenían alas" ["Once upon a time when humans did not have wings"] (161), the story positions the state of humanity prior to the evolution of wings as such a distant memory that it is only remembered as myth or ancient history. The myth of Icarus illustrates the lengths to which ancient humans would go in order to fly, showing that, throughout history, or pre-history, humans were willing to die in the attempt to achieve flight. The human desire for wings expressed in these myths or fairy tales at the beginning of Díaz-Mas's story frame and explain the reaction of everyone but the protagonist upon being told her fetus is missing her wings. The child's deformity, which would be comparable, in our world, to an infant being born without legs, makes the mother's choice to keep her child not only puzzling but – to the woman's husband and some of her friends – irresponsible.

The meaning of the myth of Icarus in "La niña sin alas" is multi-layered. The narration begins with a reference to the myth of Icarus, "aquel héroe desalado que, a falta de alas propias, se construyó unas de cera y plumas de aves" ["that impetuous hero, who, for lack of his own wings, built some from wax and bird feathers"] (161), only to tragically fly too close to the sun, which melted his wings. The protagonist explains that her mother used to tell her this story about when, in "una época antigua y tal vez mítica" ["an ancient and perhaps mythical age"] (161), humans had neither wings nor the capacity to fly. For Díaz-Mas's readers, those of us who do not live in a winged society, the story of Icarus is a reminder of what can happen to individuals who dare too much. For Díaz-Mas's characters, who live in a winged society, the story could easily be interpreted as a mechanism to reinforce patriarchal norms, since the purpose of relating this myth to the protagonist was most likely to teach her about social conformity and the value placed on able-bodiedness. For the protagonist, the myth of Icarus enforces the dominant view of what a human body should look like (winged), as well as the consequences of disobeying the patriarchal father figure, since Icarus flew to his death after disobeying his father Daedalus. This reference at the beginning of "La niña sin alas" serves as a marker of the protagonist's adherence to patriarchal society before becoming pregnant. During her pregnancy and after she became a mother, social conformity is clearly no longer of any concern to the protagonist.

Instead, the mother experiences non-conforming pride and love for her child. She allows her daughter to be different, finding it logical that she does not behave like everyone else, explaining, "Nadie quería entender que si la niña era diferente, resultaba lógico que lo hiciera todo de diferente manera" ["No one wanted to understand that if the girl were different, it was logical that she would do everything in a different way"] (164). While acknowledging the differences that mark her child as monstrous within larger society, the mother rejoices in her daughter's accomplishments, areas where she excels beyond her able-bodied peers. The protagonist exhibits a concept that Rosemarie Garland-Thomson describes as "extraordinary bodies," an alternate way of thinking about disability, or rather, "a tendency to claim physical difference as exceptional rather than inferior" (Gallop, *Sexuality, Disability* 2). The mother sees not what her daughter is lacking, but rather, all the exceptional abilities she possesses, which other children lack. At two years old, the young girl "casi hablaba de corrido; era una niña extraordinariamente despierta y yo me sentía orgullosa de ella" ["almost spoke without stopping; she was an extraordinarily bright girl and I felt proud of her"] (166). Her daughter's limbs are stronger than those of infants who depend on wings; her mobility may be different, but the mother does not consider it inferior. Comfortable with their monstrous otherness, the mother appreciates her daughter's strengths and capabilities.

Alternative Physical and Emotional Intimacy

The strong societal backlash the protagonist receives in response to her alternative physical relationship with her daughter is unsurprising, as heteronormative, ableist society has always worked to monitor and channel the bodily reactions of its members, creating an implicit model of behaviour. As Douglas Robinson asserts, the behaviours and language that parents teach their children are never random but rather a set of beliefs that follow "collective norms: somatically inscribed ideology. Actions that the infant's parents consider wrong are 'wrong' because they *feel* wrong to the parents – because the proscriptions that they inscribe on their child's body were once inscribed on theirs" (12). The protagonist's friends, husband, and medical professionals with whom she comes into contact all attempt to condition the mother/daughter connection to align it with social norms and impose bodily prohibitions on their connection. The mother refuses to perform her relationship with her daughter in a more normative way, as their alternate forms of physical touch bring the protagonist a sense of well-being and emotional connection to her daughter.

Díaz-Mas's protagonist forgoes social conventions concerning appropriate types of physicality between parent and child, with the goal of creating a more valuable or authentic familial connection. In doing so, she embraces the physical connection between maternal and infant bodies, which can be sensual or even erotic for mothers. An important aspect of the emotional, joyful connection between mother and child, as outlined in Kristeva's "Stabat Mater" is the role of eroticism in this link. Kristeva proposes the theory of herethics, a discourse about pregnancy and mothering that embraces the sensual nature of these aspects of women's lives. She describes the joy that connects mothers and children as *jouissance*, a deep pleasure, bordering on pain, with sexual undertones.[5] For Kristeva, in contrast to Freud, this *jouissance* draws from "femininity and maternity itself" (*The Portable Kristeva* 296), ignoring any relationship between female and male bodies and sexuality. The text in "Stabat Mater" is divided into columns whose organization embraces the multifaceted nature of the motherhood role. On the left side of the page, Kristeva describes how religion and science have historically constructed the maternal figure, while the right-side column details her personal experience of motherhood through a prioritization of both physical and emotional connections with her child. While Kristeva asserts that the relationship between mother and child can have a sexually erotic nature, I find Audre Lorde's definition of the erotic in "Use of the Erotic: The Erotic as Power" to provide a helpful context in understanding the mother/daughter relationship in "La niña sin alas." For Lorde, the erotic is a form of power that women have been taught to ignore by patriarchal society, which fears its potential for empowerment. Lorde describes the erotic as physical, but not sexual. Rather, the erotic is the joy to be found in sharing any deep experience with another individual. Lorde explains that the "sharing of joy, whether physical, emotional, psychic, or intellectual, forms a bridge between the sharers which can be the basis for understanding much of what is not shared between them, and lessens the threat of their difference" (*Sister Outsider* 56). For both Lorde and Kristeva, the erotic implies an intense physical bond, the power of the connection bringing joy and fulfilment to those who share it.

While the protagonist in "La niña sin alas" does not indicate that she receives sexual pleasure from her relationship with her daughter, the physical contact between them is pleasurable for her. In the protagonist's society, mothers cradle their babies behind them in their wings, which does not allow for the face-to-face interaction that the protagonist achieves by holding her daughter in her arms. In this posture, the protagonist experiences a "ternura para nosotros inexplicable" ["tenderness unexplainable for us"] (165), the "us" referring to a society that has normalized skin-to-wing contact while characterizing the skin-to-skin contact created by holding a baby in one's arms as improper. When the protagonist attempts to explain the emotional connection provoked by this alternate and pleasurable physical touch, others listen in a silence that communicates "rechazo" ["rejection"] and "lástima por una desgracia ajena" ["shame for another's troubles"] (165). The protagonist's alternative relationship with her daughter is an example of what Kristeva calls herethics, because it provides a space wherein mother and daughter can explore physical pleasure outside of the limitations of (and therefore, threatening to) patriarchal society. Power and pleasure are linked, so expressions of maternal or childhood physical pleasure that circumvent masculine influence and create spaces of connection removed from the father figure's control therefore establish a source of power inaccessible to him.[6]

While the protagonist in "La niña sin alas" does not state that she receives sexual pleasure from this relationship, a possibility suggested by Kristeva, she does experience a visceral physical pleasure that links her to the child, an element of the mother/child relationship that is "a natural given, an otherwise unproblematic joyous connection between mothers and children which patriarchy and compulsory heterosexuality represses" (Ferguson 10). The first time that the mother holds her daughter is a life-changing moment that redefines her identity completely outside the confines of patriarchy. The mother describes their first embrace, saying, "No puedo explicar la dulzura que me invadió entonces: tenía a mi hija en el hueco de mi regazo y mis brazos la enlazaban por la derecha y por la izquierda; ... cuerpo contra cuerpo ... unidas únicamente por nuestros brazos entrecruzados" ["I can't explain the sweetness that overwhelmed me then: I had my daughter in the space of my lap and my arms linked around her to the right and to the left ... body against body ... united only through our linked arms"] (164). The power of the physical relationship between mother and daughter stems from the vulnerability in their touch, a "desnudez" ["nakedness"] (163) that she has never experienced before. Society may judge her, but the protagonist finds her life enriched by this physical relationship with her child, musing, "Y quién sabe si al ganar alas no hemos perdido otras muchas cosas, dulces y suaves como la piel desprotegida" ["And who knows if, by gaining wings, we haven't lost many other things, sweet and smooth like defenceless skin"] (163). Luce Irigaray writes about the pleasure of physical contact between mother and child that male-dominated society attempts to shame into silence:

> It is true that she still has the child, in relation to whom her appetite for touch, for contact, has free rein, unless it is already lost, alienated by the taboo against touching of a highly obsessive civilization. Otherwise her pleasure will find, in the child, compensations for and diversions from the frustrations that she too often encounters in sexual relations per se. Thus maternity fills the gaps in a repressed female sexuality. (27)

While Irigaray explains how the physical touch between any mother and child contains taboo elements by providing physical pleasure that does not originate from a heterosexual romantic relationship, the protagonist in "La niña sin alas" takes this taboo relationship one step further, as she is physically interacting with her daughter in a way that her society finds unacceptable or shameful due to its boundary-breaking nature. By focusing on the joy she finds in an alternate physical and emotional relationship with her daughter, the protagonist performs her parenthood outside of limiting social norms.

Motherhood's Role in Identity Formation

In "La niña sin alas," the alternative physical relationship the mother shares with her daughter brings her joy and physical pleasure, while creating drastic changes within her that help the protagonist further develop and understand her identity. Instead of urging her child to assimilate to heteronormative society, the mother adapts to be more like her non-normative child, changing her movements and perception of the world. In her interactions with her daughter, she stops using her wings, finding the physical touch produced by her non-normative relationship with her baby to be uniquely gratifying. Since she holds her daughter in her arms, instead of in her wings, she soon notices a new strength to her arms. Whereas most women would not have well-developed arm muscles, the protagonist's arms "se fueron fortaleciendo a fuerza de repetir ese movimiento, e incluso yo diría a tornearse de forma diferente, como si algunos de los músculos se desarrollasen y moldeasen para adecuarse a aquella postura" ["began growing stronger as a result of repeating that movement, and even I would say they became toned in a different way, as if some of the muscles developed and moulded themselves to adjust to that posture"] (165). Not only does her body change, but her movements and way of experiencing the world evolve, as well. She quits her job to spend all her time with her daughter. She begins to mirror her movements, using her wings less, moving only in ways in which her daughter can also move. Walking, crawling, and sitting on the floor with her child, the protagonist affirms that her daughter "me descubrió un mundo nuevo, un mundo a ras de tierra" ["revealed a new world to me, a world at ground level"] (165). This type of physical connection comes to represent a non-verbal communication, as the protagonist learns that "la madre que sostiene a su hijo en los brazos se comunica con él tan intensamente o más que la que lo arropa entre sus alas" ["the mother who holds her child in her arms communicates with him as much as, or more intensely than, the mother who tucks him between her wings"] (165). Mother and daughter redefine the meaning of an intimate relationship, creating a union based on emotions and the desire to be connected to another human being on a profound physical level that surpasses limited definitions of the mother/daughter experience. They have achieved a re-examination of the physical and sensual, as called for by Ann Ferguson in her description of affective energy, which "has a double-sided aim: the desire to be incorporated/ united with other social subjects and in doing so to achieve bodily pleasure (e.g. not merely orgasm: simple touching, as in hugging, satisfies this desire)" (11). The mother/daughter relationship in "La niña sin alas" provides physical pleasure that is not necessarily sexual but still powerful and emotionally fulfilling.

While motherhood research tends to focus on the way in which the child's identity is formed through her relationship to her mother, in Díaz-Mas's text, the mother's identity is reformulated through her relationship to her daughter.[7] In "Stabat Mater," Kristeva discusses motherhood's identity-forming potential for both mother and child, arguing that the two are simultaneously unified and separated, meaning that both must learn to live with the concept of difference that comes from within. Even though mother and child have two separate identities, "the mother proves that the other is within. A representation of the mother as a subject-in-process, as an open subjectivity which contains alterity, sets up a model of autonomy that still allows for connection, identity, ethics, and love" (Oliver, "Julia Kristeva's Feminist" 105). Kristeva's herethics calls for an understanding and acceptance of different ways in which the mother/child relationship may play out, allowing both participants to confront the "otherness, the stranger within" themselves, an exercise that "makes the ethical agent open to and accepting of others" (109). Through an awareness of what separates or differentiates mother from child, both individuals can accept and appreciate difference within others.

The protagonist acknowledges her physical differences from her daughter, but by assimilating to her child's way of moving in the world, the mother's identity begins to change, as she is focused on the child who has become "el centro de mi vida" ["the centre of my life"] (163). The protagonist isolates herself from patriarchal society, renouncing all ties to her old life to establish a female-centred connection with her child. As she begins to look at the world from her infant's grounded view, the protagonist discovers the pleasure of seeing from below rather than from above. "Me gustaba ver las cosas desde allí abajo, como ella las veía, sin la posibilidad de alzar el vuelo y colocarse en lo alto del armario o mirar la habitación desde una esquina del techo" ["I liked to see things from below, like she saw them, without the possibility of rising up into flight and placing myself on top of the dresser or looking at the room from a corner of the ceiling"] (166). The protagonist rejects patriarchal, ableist society and her marriage to focus on motherhood, a role that she had never intended to play. Adrienne Rich acknowledges how a mother's identity can alter after giving birth, proving that the experience of child birthing and rearing is also formative for the mother. Rich notes that most of the literature and research about individuation and identity formation after giving birth focuses on the child's process, with the parent's identity often assumed as an unchangeable truth. She was surprised, then, to realize that as a mother, she herself was "still in a state of uncreation" (cit. Rubin Suleiman 116), an individual with the potential to change in reaction to the new relationship and role in which she now found herself.

In "La niña sin alas," the mother's willingness to submit to a "state of uncreation" and choose this ancient form of motherhood – that relies on arms and legs rather than wings for nurturing children – could serve as a critique of her previous isolation, a hunger for human connection in a world that appears to place little value on such relationships. Superimposed on the leitmotiv of the handicapped child in the story is the recognition that these winged humans have lost some of their humanity in the process. What has been sacrificed in this future world where wings and flight are taken for granted, the story insists, is the human ability to connect through touch. In a world where "normal" mothers and children no longer embrace and instead rub wings, the protagonist's rediscovery of her arms and the pleasure of touch highlights the importance of the sensation of touch in the mother/child bond. In the first part of the story, the narrator laments the loss of the connection to the earth that has occurred as humans became airborne; the protagonist's physical relationship with her daughter presents itself as a possible path back to connection.

Self-Sacrificing and Castrating?: Ambivalent Mother Figure

The ambiguous representation of the mother/daughter relationship revealed in the ending of "La niña sin alas" is unsurprising for an author who employs "minefields of contradiction and ambivalence" in her work (Gould Levine, "The Female Body" 189), particularly concerning her female characters' relationship with patriarchy. An analysis of her 2001 novel *El rapto del Santo Grial* [*The Kidnapping of the Holy Grail*] asserts that Díaz-Mas's "portrayal of woman continually skirts the boundaries between subversion and convention" (189). Perhaps Díaz-Mas's ambiguity when it comes to her women characters is linked to the fact that she repudiates the labels of "feminist" and "woman writer," admitting to a "relación allí de amor-odio hacia esa crítica feminista" ["love–hate relationship towards feminist criticism"] (Ferrán 339) and believing that these categorizations make her work vulnerable to harsher criticism or classification as an "inferior" type of literature (Zomeño 428). While these two labels are often complementary, they are not identical. The term "feminist" implies that an author is dedicated to topics and themes that promote women's rights and equality. "Woman writer" is an overarching classification including all female authors who write about topics related to women, regardless of whether their perspectives are feminist in nature. Women who write may reject the term "feminist" because they do not want to be viewed as polemic or difficult; they might also dislike the term "woman writer" because of the notion that critics will interpret such work as less serious.[8] While much of her narrative incorporates a feminist viewpoint, Díaz-Mas's unwillingness to self-identify as feminist, asserting that "lo de las etiquetas me pone un poco nerviosa en la literatura porque me parece que te quitan libertad" ["labels in literature make me a little nervous because it seems to me that they take away freedoms"] (192), could be interpreted as detrimental to the advancement of her maternal figure in "La niña sin alas." Díaz-Mas's story can be read as a rejection of patriarchy in the attempt to build an alternate relationship outside of society's limitations or the designs of a controlling, castrating mother who destroys her daughter's freedom.

When the protagonist realizes that her daughter's wings are growing, she makes the shocking decision to bite them off, thus condemning her daughter to inhabit a handicapped body for the rest of her life. The mother's fright at seeing the child grow wings can be interpreted as a desire to keep the child in a state of innocence, but there is no denying the association between wings and freedom, or wings and flight. The fact that her child grows wings appears to indicate that the wings were already present and hers was a case of delayed development. While the mother's efforts to stifle or slow down the growth of the little wings may at first be read as a sign of the protagonist's utter dependence on her daughter for emotional nurturing, the act of biting her daughter's wings when they can no longer be kept from growing is indeed monstrous. In her words, "Levanté a mi hija en brazos, le desnudé el torso y mordí con toda la fuerza que me daban la rabia y la desesperación. Me llenó la boca un sabor asqueroso a polvo y ácaros" ["I lifted my daughter in my arms, I undressed her torso and I bit with all the force that rage and desperation gave me. A disgusting taste of dust and mites filled my mouth"] (167). This action seems doubly monstrous, first because she is eliminating her daughter's opportunity to be considered a fully functional member of society, but also because of the rather savage way in which she mutilates her daughter's body. It is difficult not to see here the transformation of the mother from one who protects a disabled child from a world that rejects her to a mother who will blunt the daughter's growth by stifling her development. In her willingness to mutilate her own daughter to keep the child entirely to herself, she becomes both the tyrannical mother under the guise of abnegation and self-sacrifice, and the castrating mother vilified by the Freudian mode of the family romance. The story ends with the mother assuring readers that order has been restored in their relationship. Her daughter:

> Ha vuelto a ser la niña que era y yo sigo entregada a ella. A quienes me dicen que me estoy enterrando en vida, que debería volver a trabajar, que he perdido a mi marido, que no puedo atarme a la niña de esta forma, les contesto que estoy contenta con lo que hago y que la obligación de una madre es sacrificarse por su hija. (168)

> [Has returned to being the girl she was, and I continue to be dedicated to her. To those who tell me that I am burying myself alive, that I should return to work, that I have lost my husband, that I can't tie myself to the girl in this way, I answer them that I am happy with what I am doing, and that the obligation of a mother is to sacrifice herself for her daughter.] (168)

The mother claims this act to be a sacrifice, as her daughter will now depend on her forever, but it is also a selfish gesture that curtails her daughter's freedom. By exerting her own will on her daughter's body and limiting her independence, the mother keeps her child subjugated in the status of female other.

In many ways, the protagonist embodies the Francoist and Catholic ideal of motherly suffering and self-sacrifice of her former selfhood. The extreme isolation the protagonist imposes on herself and her daughter, combined with the protagonist's willing abnegation of her former identity, aligns with many patriarchal or conservative accounts that proffer the rhetoric of motherhood as woman's highest aspiration and function in life, proposing motherhood as a defining identity marker that cannot be separated from womanhood. To some extent, the protagonist can be construed as a woman totally absorbed by the self-sacrifice of motherhood. Fascist, patriarchal agendas aside, various scholarly and anecdotal evidence corroborates the connection between motherhood and suffering. Kristeva argues that the child itself is the representation of maternal pain that never disappears: "One does not give birth in pain, one gives birth to pain: the child represents it and henceforth it settles in, it is continuous ... a mother is always branded by pain, she yields to it" (*The Portable Kristeva* 315). Díaz-Mas's protagonist accepts this maternal pain and suffering when she consciously decides to continue her pregnancy with the disabled fetus. The emotional connection that she feels with the fetus outweighs the potential burden that a disabled child will present in her life. She is willing to make such a sacrifice in exchange for the opportunity to forge a deep connection with her daughter. Biting off her daughter's wings, however, is more self-serving than self-sacrificing. The protagonist epitomizes the complexities of the parental role; mothers (and fathers) cannot be neatly divided into categories of good or bad parents. Parenthood is a series of actions and reactions, driven by a variety of motivations, rather than a static identity.

"La niña sin alas" offers readers an ambivalent example of a performance of motherhood, at times nurturing and joyful for mother and daughter and in other moments painfully restricting. The protagonist's performance of motherhood demonstrates that individual parental figures can enact their roles along a diverse spectrum of possibilities, and parents' actions and motivations may change drastically along that spectrum given the specific moments and situations in which they are performing their role. Díaz-Mas provided her interpretation of the ending in an interview, remarking that "el amor maternal puede ser abnegado y generoso en un principio, pero puede convertirse en obsesivo, absorbente y castrador si no se sabe dar libertad a los hijos" ["maternal love can be selfless and generous at the beginning, but it can become obsessive, demanding, and castrating if one does not know how to give freedom to their children"] (Jerónimo and Díaz-Mas 190). As an examination of the mother as monstrous other has shown, patriarchy commonly marks the female body in ways that relegate women to a powerless status:

> Of all the battlefields immortalized in the history of humankind for providing fertile terrain of the clash between ideologies and nations, the

> female body occupies a distinctive site ... its explorers and conquerors have inscribed and reinscribed on its complex geography the marks and signs of patriarchal dominance. (Gould Levine, "The Female Body" 181)

The protagonist's actions could be interpreted as the behaviour of a mother who is, in Paloma Díaz-Mas's words, "hiperprotectora" ["hyperprotective"] and "castradora" ["castrating"] (Jerónimo and Díaz-Mas 189), curtailing her daughter's opportunities for independence due to a wish to remain forever linked as mother and daughter in an unhealthy, co-dependent situation, not allowing her daughter to have any agency whatsoever. Her actions can be read as an exaggeration of maternal love, the negative consequences of this emotion carried to the extreme.

While this reading is the most obvious and cannot be dismissed, the mother's action in the story's conclusion can be framed in another light – as a violent yet subversive act against patriarchy. Mother and daughter are marginalized subjects on many levels; they are both women, the protagonist is considered a minority during her pregnancy as an older woman, and the daughter is physically disabled according to societal norms. Both characters are monstrous subjects in a heteronormative society. The concept of the mother as monstrous can be read from two perspectives, one patriarchal and the other subversive: "Those images which define woman as monstrous in relation to her reproductive functions work to reinforce the phallocentric notion that female sexuality is abject. On the other hand, the notion of the monstrous-feminine challenges the view that femininity, by definition, constitutes passivity" (Sempruch 66). By severing her daughter's wings from her body, the mother demonstrates agency. Monstrous as the act might be, she exhibits power in her decision to alter her daughter's body in a way that will keep her from belonging to (or perhaps becoming trapped within) heteronormative society. Kristeva writes about motherhood's perverse power of self-denial, wherein mothers feel pressured to make themselves "anonymous in order to transmit social norms ... which *one must* pass on to the child, whose education is a link to generations past" ("Stabat Mater" 149). By training their children to conform socially, mothers enjoy a modicum of social prestige and power. Kristeva further elaborates that this act of "social bonding ... can be frightening if one stops to think that it may destroy everything that is specific and irreducible in the other, the child: this form of maternal love can become a straitjacket, stifling any deviant individuality" ("Stabat Mater" 151–2). In "La niña sin alas," the mother does not participate in this social conditioning. She assures that she and her daughter will maintain their originality, their otherness. However, while she may have acted out of a genuine desire to protect her daughter, the mother's action frees her daughter from one straitjacket just to fit her for another.

The wings themselves are another site of ambiguity that beg a careful interpretation. In the protagonist's society, wings are a symbol of conformity, a sign of a body existing within social norms. By allowing her daughter's wings to grow, the protagonist would have permitted her daughter to be subsumed back into male-dominated society, which the protagonist assumes would have destroyed the powerful physical and emotional bond between mother and daughter. The wings could be viewed as a symbolic phallus, penetrating the baby's tender skin in order to bring her back into the patriarchal order as a "normal" female. When the wings finally break through the baby's skin, the description is reminiscent of a rape: "Durante la noche [las alas] habían brotado, rasgando la piel, y la sabanita de abajo estaba ligeramente manchada de sangre. Se me vino el mundo abajo" ["During the night (the wings) had broken through, scratching the skin, and the little sheet below was lightly stained with blood. My whole world came crashing down"] (167). By understanding the wings as a phallic symbol designed to return the daughter to a subjugated space, the mother's monstrous act becomes a violent rejection of patriarchy in their lives, a way of keeping them both out of a hierarchy where they are dominated "others." "La niña sin alas" questions the pressure toward social conformity experienced by women and mothers, providing a messy yet powerful example of a mother and child who elude patriarchal limitations. Alternately, the appearance of the wings could represent the daughter's symbolic first menstruation. In this interpretation, the sheet is "manchada de sangre" ["stained with blood"] (167) from a symbolic first period. In this case, the mother is not protecting her daughter from the dangers of patriarchal society, but instead is attempting to keep her daughter from growing up, as menstruation is recognized as a pivotal moment in many girls' development into women, signalling their upcoming independence. In either interpretation, the mother is trying to keep the daughter to herself, either by isolating her from patriarchal society or by preventing her daughter from growing up and leaving her.

The daughter is too young to know the damage she has suffered through the loss of her wings, but as the protagonist's affections turn violent, readers are asked to witness the dark side of maternal devotion. When, at the end of the story, the mother affirms that her daughter has "vuelto a ser la niña que era y yo sigo entregada a ella" ["returned to being the girl she was, and I continue to be devoted to her"] (168), readers must ask themselves if the price for indefinitely extending the mother/daughter bond is not the daughter's bondage. Ignorant of what the woman has done to keep her child from developing wings and thus gaining gradual independence, the protagonist's friends rebuke her for having sacrificed everything – job, husband, friends – for her daughter. Blindly, the protagonist continues to think of herself as a model of abnegation, repeating the cliché that mothers must sacrifice themselves for their children. It is unclear whether Díaz-Mas intends this last line to be ironic or merely accusatory, but the reader is likely to be disturbed, if not repulsed, by the mother's crime. The real sacrificial victim here is clearly the daughter. She will now be grounded and mutilated for life. She will also, therefore, remain entirely dependent on a mother whose love has become parasitic rather than symbiotic.

While a plethora of theory and research on motherhood explains how mothers are often constructed as monstrous others, Díaz-Mas's short story approaches motherhood from an ambivalent perspective, both in the evolution of the protagonist's feelings toward motherhood and in her performance of the role. Through her representation of the physical mother/daughter relationship, "La niña sin alas" explores the boundaries of motherhood and how this role can affect an individual's identity. Questioning depictions of the castrating and self-sacrificing mother, Díaz-Mas's protagonist embodies both stereotypes while simultaneously creating a fulfilling bond with her daughter through her rejection of patriarchal, ableist assumptions of what their (pregnant and disabled) bodies should look like, as well as how those bodies may interact with each other. The mother figure's eventual obsessive attitude toward her daughter, after asserting that her world revolves around her child, leads to her desperate and violent decision to sever the infant's wings. "La niña sin alas" offers a reflection on the multiple meanings and performances of motherhood, a role that is never static, demonstrating that enactments of motherhood will vary not just from woman to woman, but also for individual mothers, as they perform the role in diverse ways during different moments in time.

Chapter Three

The Shifting Face of Fatherhood

Rafa allows his wife Marina's lover Daniel to live with them because Daniel has impregnated Marina with the children that Rafa's impotence would never allow him to father. Leo cross-dresses as his dead wife to make his four-year-old daughter feel her mother's presence again. These scenarios might seem bizarre and unlikely to be tolerated or embraced by many men, but they are the plots of the movies *La buena estrella* [*The Good Star*] (1997, directed by Ricardo Franco) and *Todo lo que tú quieras* [*Anything You Want*] (2010, directed by Achero Mañas), wherein two men perform paternal roles in unconventional ways. Both father figures perform their parenthoods in ways that alternately align them with or distance them from the norms of hegemonic masculinity. In addition to re-envisioning fatherhoods, Rafa, Daniel, and Leo exhibit diverse ways of performing masculinity, each of which interacts with the concept of crisis often associated with hegemonic masculinity in distinct ways, presenting characters whose models of masculinity cannot live up to the ever-changing demands of hegemonic masculinity (as no one individual ever can), nor those of compulsory hetero-parenting (a term I have coined and will describe shortly). Characters' inability to meet the impossible hegemonic standards for masculinity and fatherhood reveal hegemonic masculinity to be an empty concept, whose fragility comes from the lack of a true definition or identity behind the term to uphold it. The qualities in Rafa and Leo that help them connect meaningfully with their children are also those that isolate them from dominant definitions of manhood and fatherhood, demonstrating the need to understand fatherhood (and motherhood) as a spectrum of performances that allows for non-normative parental love and experiences. In this chapter, I explore the performative nature of masculinities and fatherhoods, examine masculinities within a contemporary Spanish context, and discuss the connection between masculinities and the concept of crisis, linking Spanish masculinities to the concept of hegemonic masculinity as analysed through the lens of masculinity scholars Michael Kimmel, R.W. Connell, and Fintan Walsh. I then demonstrate the ways in which characters in these films are at times aligned with hegemonic masculinity, explore their desire to form families, analyse how body performances such as cross-dressing influence their identities and relationships with their children, show how various types of impotence distance them from hegemonic masculinity while allowing them to become closer to their children, and finally explore the relationship between hegemonic masculinity and violence in the lives of these characters. This analysis leads me to argue that the alternative masculinities and paternities in these films reveal a fluidity of paternal performance that facilitates a closer relationship between father figures and their children.

La buena estrella recounts the story of an unmarried butcher – Rafael, or Rafa for short (played by Antonio Resines) – who cannot fulfil his desire to have a family because he is impotent. One night, he happens across Daniel (Jordi Mollá), a typical tough guy and criminal who is beating his prostitute girlfriend Marina (Maribel Verdú), nicknamed "La Tuerta" ["The One-Eyed Woman"] because she is blind in one eye. Rafa threatens Daniel with his butcher knife and takes Marina to the hospital, where he learns that she is pregnant with Daniel's child. Rafa brings her to his house to recover. They become romantically attached, living as husband and wife and eventually raising Marina's daughter Estrella together, although Marina warns that Daniel will eventually return for her. Three years later, released from another sojourn in jail, a bloodied and beaten Daniel shows up on the couple's doorstep. Rafa lets him in, and his stay is prolonged indefinitely. Although Daniel is not interested in the daughter he has fathered, he wants to resume sexual activities with Marina, who is torn between her love for the two men. Rafa tests her by leaving her alone with Daniel for the weekend, only to return later that same day, entering the house to the sound of them having sex. Rafa chooses to forgive their dalliance, and they form a non-normative family until Daniel leaves again in pursuit of another ill-advised criminal scheme. Marina abandons Rafa and Estrella to follow Daniel, returning home pregnant to a still-forgiving Rafa after Daniel has been incarcerated once again. Daniel reappears in their home, released from jail as he is on his deathbed after contracting HIV/AIDS in prison. Daniel begs Rafa to euthanize him with a shotgun, a request that Marina carries out after Rafa refuses to do so. Marina dies soon after Daniel, leaving Rafa to care for their two daughters.

Todo lo que tú quieras details a different kind of fatherhood experience. Leo (Juan Diego Botto) is a perpetually busy lawyer who leaves most of the childcare for his four-year-old daughter Dafne (Lucía Fernández) to his stay-at-home wife Alicia (Ana Risueño). After his wife's unexpected death, Leo is completely unprepared to take on the responsibilities of caring for his daughter. Dafne constantly asks to see her mother, eventually requesting that Leo put on Alicia's lipstick and become her mother. After much hesitation, Leo complies with her request, believing that he is helping Dafne process Alicia's death. His transformation evolves into complete cross-dressing when he is at home, and later, at any time that Leo is with Dafne. Leo's public cross-dressing provokes a backlash of negativity from the community and the school counsellor, who threatens to call social services. When Leo is hospitalized after being beaten by a group of young men for dressing in women's clothing, Dafne is placed under the care of Alicia's parents, a rich, conservative couple. Since they refuse to return Dafne to Leo, he goes to retrieve her from school. That evening, Dafne asks if she can see her father, so Leo takes off the makeup, wig, and women's clothing to transform himself back into her father. Dafne says that if she wishes to see her mother, she will just close her eyes and think about her intently, and the film ends with this tidy resolution to Leo's experience with cross-dressing.

Although these films premiered more than a decade apart, I have chosen to analyse *La buena estrella* and *Todo lo que tú quieras* together due to their many thematic connections and their classification as examples of *cine social* [social issue cinema], which "seeks to address current social and political issues by presenting the spectatorship with an account of reality that will be recognizable as 'authentic' or 'truthful'" (Begin, "When Victim" 261). *Cine social* emerged in Spain in the 1990s, thanks to a group of filmmakers who wanted spectators to engage with a film's message and feel compelled to work toward social change (262). Many Spanish directors who made their cinematic debut in the 1990s came of age after Spain's transition to democracy, often choosing to produce films set in present-day Spain (Heredero 33). Among them is Ricardo Franco, director of *La buena estrella*, who has been described as a "pilar ... del cine de conciencia en la España en la transición" ["pillar ... of social awareness cinema in Spain during the transition"] (Mabrey). Achero Mañas, director of *Todo lo que tú quieras*, is another contemporary director whose work addresses various social issues in artistic ways; perhaps his most celebrated film *El bola* [*Pellet*] (2000) addresses the issue of child abuse. While social issue cinema makes a statement about current social problems, it has been criticized for its "rather explicit ... portrayal of social reality, the perception being that [social issue films] forgo artistic achievement for thesis statements which leave little wiggle room for critical interpretation" (Begin, "When Victim" 263). This criticism cannot be applied to the films under analysis in this chapter, both of which address social issues while maintaining artistic merit. These films address the shifting definitions of, and roles associated with, masculinities and fatherhoods in contemporary Spain through a focus on emotional vulnerability as a way for fathers to connect with their children, as protagonists enact fatherhood roles that alternately comply with and fall outside of the dictates of traditional hegemonic definitions of Spanish fatherhood. In *La buena estrella* and *Todo lo que tú quieras*, father figures explore the line between hegemonic and alternative performances of fatherhood, whose alignment with hegemonic masculinity varies given characters' situational performance of these roles.

Parenthood as Performance and Compulsory Hetero-Parenting

Hegemonic masculinity represents only one, often unsatisfactory, way of performing gender. In *Masculinities*, R.W. Connell defines hegemony as "the cultural dynamic by which a group claims and sustains a leading position in social life" (77). Connell notes that hegemony is fluid and changeable by nature, meaning that whatever iteration of masculinity is favoured at any one point will never remain the hegemonic model over time or in different societies or social contexts. A succinct explanation of hegemonic masculinity from Michael Kimmel describes the concept as "the image of masculinity of those men who hold power" ("Masculinity as Homophobia" 125), a definition that allows for the changing nature of characteristics or groups that are considered powerful at any given moment. Due to the constantly changing nature of which type of masculinity is valued most, and although hegemonic masculinity holds real consequences for men in many societies, it is a fragile concept not based on any "true" or authentic definition of masculinity, as such a thing does not exist, meaning that hegemonic masculinity is a fragile concept in constant need of defending. In *Gender Trouble*, Judith Butler demonstrates the instability of gender and the need to constantly uphold it through actions. Butler argues that gender should not "be construed as a stable identity or locus of agency from which various acts follow; rather, gender is an identity tenuously constituted in time, instituted in an exterior space through a *stylized repetition of acts*" (*Gender Trouble* 191; italics in original). Gender must be understood not as something that one is born with, but rather something that is constantly being formed, meaning that there always exists the possibility of reforming it in a different way. Due to the constant need to reaffirm one's gender and the inconstancy of any given model of hegemonic masculinity, men can easily be subject to "the panicked performativity of heterosexuality, as self-subjugating performatives towards mastery, insofar as the rigorous disciplining of desire, and the display of aggressive male prowess, ensure the subject's certain stability" (Walsh 10). This "panicked" enactment of heterosexuality affects the ways in which men are able to envision their performances of paternity.

Due to their changeable nature, concepts like hegemonic masculinity and gender are difficult to define. Hegemonic masculinity, the social and cultural prioritization of one version of masculinity over others, is relational, affected by class, race, and many other factors. Different versions of hegemonic masculinity, whose definitions vary situationally, may exist within one society at the same time. For example, hegemonic masculinity is performed differently by men in various social settings, such as the film industry, professional sports, the business world, and the prison system. Hegemonic masculinity is also difficult to define because gender (hegemonic or otherwise) is fluid, "constructed in interaction" (Connell, *Masculinities* 35). Some of the defining characteristics of hegemonic masculinity, which will be examined in relation to the male protagonists of these films, include compulsory heterosexuality (defined by Adrienne Rich in her seminal article "Compulsory Heterosexuality and Lesbian Existence" as the idea that everyone is assumed to be or "should" be heterosexual), sexual vigour and prowess, violence and toughness, and homophobia (which is often connected to violent attacks of men who are gay or who appear too feminine) (Walsh 61). Gender roles, like the ones just mentioned in relation to hegemonic masculinity, cannot provide concrete truths about gender, but they are informative to the extent that they describe the ways in which people engage in or perform gender, as well as "the effects of these practices in bodily experience, personality and culture" (Connell, *Masculinities* 71). Gender roles and their relationship to the concept or definition of gender will also change over time and in different situations.

Since gender is a socially established and patrolled performance, it is logical to conclude that parenthood (always gendered) is a part of that performance. Unfortunately, this performance often falls under the category of compulsory hetero-parenting, a term I have coined to describe the connection between hegemonic definitions of gender and parental enactments.[1] Drawing inspiration from Adrienne Rich's article "Compulsory Heterosexuality and Lesbian Existence," I define compulsory hetero-parenting as the deference to hegemonic, heterosexual models of parenthood as the ultimate, normative, and socially sanctioned type of parenthood. Compulsory hetero-parenting exalts the nuclear family – composed of a heterosexual mother and father, as well as their biological children – while stigmatizing and devaluing parenthood practices that deviate from these established constructions of the family. Compulsory hetero-parenting enforces strict gender roles that delimitate traditional responsibilities for fathers and mothers, encouraging fathers to remain (at least emotionally) distant from their children, while shaming mothers who attempt to define themselves beyond their maternal roles. Compulsory hetero-parenting describes the tendency in many societies to limit parental performance to hegemonic, heteronormative definitions of motherhood or fatherhood roles, whatever those roles are in a given society. Compulsory hetero-parenting is the antithesis of the spectrum of parenthood enactments and experiences I describe throughout this book in examples of non-normative Spanish families found in literature and film. The effects of compulsory hetero-parenting can be seen in the difference between the meaning of the verbs "mothering" and "fathering." Mothering a child refers to the repeated act of caring for a child's physical and emotional needs. Fathering, on the other hand, is generally understood as the one-time act of providing sperm for the conception of a fetus. The concept of fathering a child has nothing to do with the everyday practicalities of raising that child. Compulsory hetero-parenting, then, is a confining narrative of parenthood that isolates individual parents from one another, relegating them to ill-fitting roles shaped by gender stereotypes. Protagonists in *La buena estrella* and *Todo lo que tú quieras* do not adhere to compulsory hetero-parenting, and their relationships with their children are emotionally richer because of this decision.

Spanish Masculinity and Fatherhood in Crisis

While hegemonic masculinity plays a role in many Western cultures, before analyzing its impact on protagonists in *La buena estrella* and *Todo lo que tú quieras*, it is necessary to establish an understanding of masculinities and fatherhoods particular to contemporary Spain. As Ryan and Corbalán assert in *The Dynamics of Masculinity in Contemporary Spanish Culture*, any description of Spanish masculinities of the twentieth and twenty-first centuries must begin by acknowledging the multiple enactments of masculinities that have contributed to "the destabilization of normative masculinity" in Spain, in order to more accurately represent "the chameleonic nature of masculinity in Spain" (1).[2] The Spanish Civil War, near the beginning of the twentieth century, was a key moment for defining contemporary Spanish masculinities, as two dominant images of masculinity emerged: a Republican version and a fascist, National Catholic definition of masculinity. In her chapter "The Battle to Define Spanish Manhood," Nerea Aresti unpacks these constructions of Spanish masculinity, noting overlap between Republican and National Catholic definitions (both groups valued self-control), as well as marked differences. The fascist, National Catholic image of Spanish masculinity that became the hegemonic definition after the Spanish Civil War was strengthened throughout Franco's dictatorship and prized patriotism, self-control, austerity, monogamy, and virility (Aresti 149–54). In *Casting Masculinity in Spanish Film*, Mary T. Hartson argues that this model of masculinity, which also promoted fatherhood as an essential duty of men who should be "self-sacrificing and devoted to the State" (31), began to change in the 1960s when Spanish film and society began to promote more consumeristic values that encouraged the prioritization of individualism and personal advancement (9). The next great cultural shift in Spanish understanding of masculinities occurred after the Spanish Transition to democracy, wherein women's increasing role in the workforce necessitated a rethinking of masculinity for men who were no longer the only or primary breadwinners in the family. Spanish realities for masculinities and fatherhoods continued to evolve in reaction to the expanding definitions and roles of womanhood and motherhood. Spain's economic crisis, beginning in 2008, led to an even greater sense of instability in the definitions of Spanish masculinities.[3]

    Despite a multiplicity of enactments of masculinities, the traditional, hegemonic definition of the man as economic provider continues to influence constructions of fatherhood in Spain. With more women in the workforce, and with rising levels of unemployment caused by Spain's economic crisis, Spanish men's ability to provide economically for the family has become less of an achievable defining characteristic, yet economic expectations for Spanish men are still present in society. Spanish men must rethink their role within the family, potentially needing to assume more of the responsibilities for the home and childcare as they share the labour of working outside of the home with their partners. In 2019, Juan Antonio Rodríguez del Pino published a sociological study of masculinity in Spain, wherein he interviewed several Spanish activists and experts associated with groups seeking social equality between men and women. This study reveals that many Spanish men in heterosexual relationships are struggling to establish and maintain more egalitarian familial relationships. The study cites a "reluctance to change" (14) among participants, even for those who realize the "enriching" (17) nature of a deeper involvement in the home and childcare. Based on his interviews with Spanish men, Rodríguez del Pino asserts that, in "spite of the new possibilities offered by the kaleidoscope of masculinities, it is difficult to pinpoint exactly what an 'egalitarian man' is" (19). Even those Spanish men who wish to participate in more egalitarian families may feel unsure how to begin making those changes in their relationships. Not all Spanish men wish to establish more equitable childcare practices, of course, feeling that, along with caring for the home, raising children is part of "a female space," wherein men see themselves in the role of "helpers" (Borràs Català et al. 410) rather than equal partners. Spanish fathers who wish to enact their parental roles differently must step outside of the limiting hegemonic definition of Spanish masculinity, sorting through which aspects of the hegemonic definition (if any) they find useful in constructing a personal parental identity.

Although alternative versions of masculinity abound in Spain, hegemonic definitions of masculinity remain prevalent in Spanish society, contributing to a crisis of masculinity in Spain, as no individual person can fully and consistently live up to the expectations and demands of hegemonic masculinity. All those who attempt to do so will fail at some point, because hegemonic masculinity demands a continuously perfect performance. Some critics say that this Spanish crisis of masculinity began after Franco's death. Hartman writes of a "masculine hysteria" (76) caused by shifting hegemonic models at the end of the dictatorship, asserting that Spanish film in the 1970s produced "a profusion of new male models marked by failure, deviance, and 'perversion'" (76). In addition to the end of a dictatorship that had promoted the dominant model of masculinity, the value of men's labour shifted as Spain transitioned "from an agricultural to a globalized service economy [which] can be read as a form of masculine traumatization" (Ryan and Corbalán 7). Contemporary Spanish men receive the message from hegemonic society that their worth is tied to their economic potential. In many Western cultures, participating in paid labour is one of the ways in which men understand their identities, and when they are unable to work due to injury, unemployment, or retirement, this may cause an identity crisis (Borràs Català et al. 408–9).[4] After Spain's economic crisis of 2008, since which time Spanish men have no guarantee of their ability to fulfil the hegemonic role of economic provider, many Spanish men experience "insecurity … and a loss of confidence regarding their current and future roles in society" (Ryan and Corbalán 6), leading at times to depression and gender violence against their partners and children. Provoked by the impossibility of living up to hegemonic standards, Spanish men's relationship with crisis affects their role within the family. In *Cine (ins)urgente*, Isolina Ballesteros writes about "la crisis patriarcal" ["the patriarchal crisis"] (277), wherein the family must confront hegemonic models of masculinity and paternity that attempt to construct antiquated models of the family unit for family members who are adapting to new challenges or situations that the traditional model of the family does not have the capacity to address. Contemporary Spanish families include members who are grappling with generational differences while building new structures of parenthood and family that often involve chosen, non-biological families, monoparental families, and transnational families caused by immigration. Contemporary Spanish men must redefine themselves, both in terms of gender and fatherhood expectations, often creating new models and definitions as they parent, since more often than not, they have not "had fathers who demonstrated parental childrearing" (Trotman 29). Instead, these fathers help construct new family configurations through their lived experiences.

While the concept of masculinity in crisis was developed in the United States to describe phenomena related to masculinity within that context, it can and has been aptly applied to a Spanish-specific setting. As described in this section, Spanish masculinities have faced many challenges or moments of redefinition through contemporary history. Perhaps, then, it is more logical to state that crisis is simply a characteristic of masculinities. Spanish masculinities, tied to Spanish fatherhoods, are continually in a state of flux or transition, evolving in reaction to societal and cultural changes. Just as hegemonic standards of masculinity change over time, so do definitions of other enactments of masculinity, which influence definitions of fatherhood and impact the construction of family units. In his "Introduction to the Special Issue on Fatherhood," Robert L. Griswold asserts that fatherhood is changeable; rather than a stable definition, the role is "culturally constructed over time," an identity with "multiple, changing meanings" (251). Masculinity is an ever-changing category whose inherent instability will always bring with it a sense of chaos or crisis. In order to understand enactments of Spanish fatherhoods, which are influenced by constructions of Spanish masculinities, it is crucial to understand how and why these identities interact with the concept of crisis.

The Demands of Hegemonic Masculinity

The types of masculinities and paternities exhibited in these films both challenge and at times affirm the construction of hegemonic masculinity, described by R.W. Connell as societal acceptance of gender roles that support masculine supremacy over women (*Masculinities* 77).

Hegemonic masculinity is a relational concept, wherein one type of masculinity can be valued over others only through comparison to and coexistence with other, "less valued" enactments of masculinity. The concept of hegemonic masculinity supports the argument of a spectrum of masculinities (and therefore, fatherhoods), proving that various types of masculinities exist, although hegemonic masculinity ranks enactments of masculinity against one another, which the spectrum of parental performances and familial configurations does not. Connell asserts that, in order to maintain their dominant social position, members of a favoured hegemonic group in any society at a given time must attempt to subordinate or reject groups of men who do not achieve the standards of hegemonic masculinity. Connell asserts that we "must also recognize the *relations* between the different kinds of masculinity: relations of alliance, dominance and subordination. These relationships are constructed through practices that exclude and include, that intimidate, exploit, and so on" (*Masculinities* 37). In *La buena estrella* and *Todo lo que tú quieras*, characters' relationships to hegemonic masculinity shift, given their circumstances and performances of gender.

In each film, male characters display at least some of the characteristics of Spanish hegemonic masculinity. In *La buena estrella*, Daniel portrays the hardness and aggression of a "true" man. He admits that most of his thirty years have been spent either on the street, in jail, or in a correctional facility. The first glimpse of Daniel in the film shows him beating Marina, his pregnant girlfriend whom he forces into prostitution. Loud where Rafa is quiet, Daniel is not only violent but also oozes a barely contained sexuality, impregnating Marina twice. Marina is afraid to be left alone with him, concerned that she will not be able to contain her sexual desires for Daniel. While she loves Rafa, won over by his gentle nature and kindness, these qualities do not have the same sexual magnetism that she experiences with Daniel. The night that Daniel first appears on the couple's doorstep, wounded from a fight, Marina strips him down in the bathroom to clean his wounds. The camera angle takes in his body as he stands in an open, assertive stance, completely naked. His penis, the symbol of his masculine virility, is exposed for Marina and Rafa to see, reminding everyone of the contrast between the two men's bodies. Daniel also has a fitter physique than Rafa, who has a chubbier, softer appearance. Daniel has a full head of hair while Rafa is balding.

Although Daniel displays some characteristics of hegemonic masculinity, he is far from an accepted member of the "in" group, marginalized by his social class and lack of economic stability, factors that lead him to spend time in jail, an experience that further marginalizes him.

The Shifting Face of Fatherhood

Figure 3.1 Marina caring for Daniel in the bathroom

Daniel uses violent, heterosexual posturing to ensure his survival on the streets, accessing aspects of hegemonic masculinity associated with physical strength, even though such an extreme portrayal of violence would exclude Daniel from many other social spheres. Violence has purportedly served Daniel well during his incarceration, as he assures his lawyer as she retrieves him from jail that, "Aún soy virgen. Nadie me ha dado por culo" ["I am still a virgin. No one has given it to me in the ass"] (29:40). His words suggest both strength and violence, as he has been able to fend off those who would rape him, perhaps even implying that he was a sexual aggressor while incarcerated. Coupled with his denials of homosexual activity, Daniel alludes to possessing an excessive libido by sexually propositioning his lawyer. She does not appear to take his sexual suggestions seriously, ignoring his attempts with a smile that seems to indicate that she is accustomed to frequent, half-hearted advances from Daniel. His efforts appear compelled by hegemonic norms of masculinity in a bid to maintain the persona he has created for himself, proposing sex to his lawyer more as a formality or requirement for establishing his heterosexuality rather than an authentic attempt to sleep with her.

Very different from Daniel, Rafa's performance of masculinity and fatherhood aligns with other aspects of hegemonic masculinity. He is not loudly aggressive or hypersexual (in fact, he is sexually impotent), but Rafa represents many of the characteristics of hegemonic masculinity and fatherhood that were valued during the dictatorship and much of the twentieth century in Spain, particularly stoicism, patience, and self-sacrifice. He is "a monogamous, self-controlled man, hardworking and austere, an archetype associated with the ideas of progress, modernity, and civilization" (Aresti 149). Where Daniel is passionate and volatile, Rafa is patient and thoughtful, never quick to overreact. When he finds Daniel and Marina having sex in his bed, he feels anger but does not lash out in violence. Rafa embodies the idea of "[s]acrifice for the sake of the collective" (Hartson 28), putting the needs of the family before his own. While Daniel and Marina's betrayal wounds him, he always reacts in ways directed to protect the unity and well-being of his family. Rafa does not display some of the flashier characteristics of hegemonic masculinity, but he represents economic and emotional stability as a responsible partner and parent.

At the beginning of *Todo lo que tú quieras*, Leo is the perfect representation of hegemonic masculinity. Many aspects of his life function within a masculine, homosocial realm. As a lawyer, he spends most of his time in the office with homophobic male colleagues. At home, even when he is physically present, Leo is answering emails or working on a case. Leo loves his wife and daughter, but he did have an affair in the past with Marta, a woman with whom he still maintains occasional contact. Viewers might question Leo's motives for having an affair with Marta, since he does not want an established relationship with her, even after his wife Alicia's death. Nonetheless, Leo's co-workers know about the affair, which serves to bolster his image as a member of hegemonic masculinity, as Michael Kimmel describes masculinity as a "homosocial enactment," where "[w]omen become a kind of currency that men use to improve their ranking on the masculine social scale" ("Masculinity as Homophobia" 129). At the beginning of the film, Leo is presented as the kind of man who has access to the "markers of manhood – wealth, power, status, sexy women" (Kimmel, "Masculinity as Homophobia" 129), all factors that elevate him in the esteem of other men.

Leo also uses homophobia to establish himself firmly within the boundaries of hegemonic masculinity and call out those who do not comply with its standards. Álex, a friend of Marta's who is also a drag queen, becomes Leo's client for a legal matter. Although he is not dressed in drag in Leo's office, for the entirety of their meeting, Leo exhibits signs of being extremely uncomfortable around Álex. Leo obviously does not want his associates to see him with Álex, as his own sexuality may come under question through association. Marta later convinces Leo to go to one of Álex's drag shows with her. When Leo attempts to leave early, Álex detains him, only to have Leo push him to the ground and call him a "maricón de mierda" ["shitty faggot"]

(35:42), completing the image of Leo as a member of hegemonic masculinity who rejects any representation of masculinity that defies accepted patriarchal standards, an image that is so forcefully established early in the film in order to allow for a more drastic transformation in Leo later on. Leo is trying to get home to his daughter Dafne, who has suffered a minor cut on her finger when the babysitter wasn't looking. Even though Leo does exhibit inexcusable homophobic behaviours, his rapid departure from the drag show is not because he is repulsed or offended by the content of the show, as Álex and the audience members must assume. Leo is acting out of concern for his daughter, which foreshadows how his personality will change, but he resorts to a homophobic slur when Álex will not let him pass. In a moment of panic and anger, Leo utilizes the tools of hegemonic masculinity to aid him in reaching his goals.

As Leo, Daniel, and Rafa learn, hegemonic masculinity is a constantly shifting dynamic that varies not only by culture, but also among specific groups or organizations of men based on what they consider powerful at the moment. The instability of this power dynamic and the struggle to constantly achieve an enactment of masculinity whose criteria can change at any time can lead to what various masculinity studies scholars – including Michael Kimmel, R.W. Connell, and Fintan Walsh – have deemed the crisis of masculinity. This crisis is caused by feelings of powerlessness that one does not live up to the standards of hegemonic masculinity, which compels men to strive even harder to prove their masculinity, making them "repeatedly ... recuperate and reassert its terms" (Walsh 10). It could even be argued that crisis is "a condition of masculinity itself. Masculine gender identity is never stable; its terms are continually being redefined and re-negotiated, the gender performance continually being re-staged" (Walsh 9). Leo, Rafa, and Daniel all exhibit characteristics that fall outside of the realm of hegemonic masculinity, troubling on some level to themselves, as well as to the society in which they live. As a lawyer in family and marriage court, Leo sees various examples of masculinity in crisis where divorcing fathers feel powerless as they lose their children and money. One of Leo's clients complains, "No sé qué vamos a hacer los padres, de verdad ... No nos dejan ver a nuestros hijos, nos quitan la mayor parte de lo que ganamos" ["I don't know what we fathers are going to do, truthfully ... They don't let us see our children, they take the greater part of what we earn from us"] (1:09:31–9). Leo's client exemplifies the essence of what Michael Kimmel describes as masculinity in crisis, the changing role of masculinity in a world where the men in power must constantly struggle to stay on top, threatened by other groups of men, as well as by women who want more. As Kimmel asserts, men attempting to maintain their dominant status in society may "feel themselves beleaguered and besieged, working harder and harder for fewer and fewer personal and social rewards ... What's a man to do?" (*Manhood in America* 299). In court, as Leo listens to the arguments put forth by mothers and fathers in divorce cases, two different narratives of family life emerge. The fathers list the ways in which they have economically supported their children, while mothers criticize the caregiving shortcomings of their partners, as well as their lack of awareness of their children's and wives' daily realities. The fathers' bewilderment at their wives' discontent highlights the failings of hegemonic masculinity. They have been performing their paternity in socially accepted ways, shocked to find that hegemonic masculinity's hollow promises have left their families unfulfilled and ultimately victimized the fathers as well. Due to hegemonic masculinity's promise of power, these men have strived to live up to a set of expectations that they can never fully embody, instead becoming emotionally exploited by a system that traps men.

A Longing for Family

While being the patriarch of a family is certainly a characteristic of Spanish hegemonic masculinity, characters in both films express a longing for family that is driven not by power but rather by a deep-seated need for emotional connection. In *La buena estrella*, although Daniel is uninterested in a fatherhood role, both he and Marina have deep-seated desires to be part of a family. Both were abandoned by their parents as children and have never experienced a stable home life. Daniel was wrapped in a plastic sack and thrown into a dumpster as a baby, never to be adopted. Marina was given up by her father, who came back for her one summer, only to return her to the orphanage after a few months. As adults, Marina and Daniel at times both exhibit extremely childlike behaviours and are happy to have Rafa care for them. When Rafa brings Marina home after rescuing her from Daniel's beating, he leaves her alone while he goes to work, testing her with an open wallet overflowing with money on the coffee table. Marina takes some of the money to buy groceries for the two of them. She admits to spending a little of it on herself, showing Rafa the Kinder Egg she purchased, a childish candy selection. Another childlike element of her nature is revealed through a crayon drawing from her youth that she still carries with her; it depicts a father, mother, and daughter standing next to a cheery house. She explains to Rafa that child psychologists told her that she "era burra porque tenía graves carencias afectivas ... quiere decir que a mí de pequeña nadie me ha querido mucho. Por eso yo voy a querer tanto a mi niño" ["was stupid because I had serious emotional deficiencies … this means that when I was little, no one loved me very much. That's why I am going to love my child so much"] (22:02–24). Although Daniel tries to make her abort Estrella, Marina desperately wants to have the child and love her as she longed to be loved during her childhood. Marina asks Rafa if he has ever felt abandoned; he affirms that he was abandoned when his mother died. Marina tells him confidently that he has never felt abandoned (like she did), and she vows to never cause those feelings for Estrella. She does leave Estrella, though, to follow Daniel, and again later, when she dies of what Rafa describes as "la misma tristeza a la que yo me abandonaría si no fuese porque alguien tendría que ocuparse de nuestros niños" ["the same sadness to which I would abandon myself if it weren't that someone needed to take care of our children"] (1:35:30–6). Marina craves the security of a stable home life that Rafa offers to her, but her lived experiences have not prepared her to establish roots or to form emotional attachments.

When Marina leaves Rafa and their daughters to follow Daniel, she makes a choice that would surely be judged harshly by heteronormative society, which "encourages us to see 'staying with' or 'leaving' a child to be an all-or-nothing matter" (Park, *Mothering Queerly* 122). However, just as the father figures in these films perform paternity in non-normative ways, Marina enacts an alternate expression of motherhood. Shelley Park suggests that for a mother, leaving can be an act of resistance against having one's entire identity defined as the self-sacrificing mother figure, searching for a definition of the role that allows more agency for the woman who is also a mother (*Mothering Queerly* 184). Motherhood does not encompass Marina's entire life or identity. Because Rafa cares for their daughters so well, Marina can step back from mothering, conceptualizing her role within the family differently than that of a traditional mother figure. Her children are well cared for in her absence, and when she returns, she is able to mother them in a way that both she and her daughters find fulfilling.

Daniel also seems to be looking for the family that he never had, although his behaviour indicates the desire to assume a childlike role instead of a parental one. On the first night he spends in Rafa's house, Rafa moves the sleeping Estrella into the master bedroom so that Daniel can sleep in her bed. Symbolically, Daniel occupies a child's space within their home and family. Marina bathes him and tends to his wounds, while Rafa brings him a glass of water, essentially tucking him in and turning off the lights. He accommodates himself cosily in Marina and Rafa's house, and they tell everyone that he is Marina's brother. Later he accompanies Rafa to work at the butcher shop, where Rafa interacts with him like he might with a teenage son, scolding him for using the informal you ("tú") with customers. Daniel accepts this criticism cheerfully, apparently happy to be spending time with Rafa and eagerly following Rafa's orders. On his deathbed, Daniel expresses gratitude for being welcomed into the family. Without a home to go to, he would have been left in jail to die. Daniel comments, "Ventaja de tener familia. Si no es por vosotros, me hubieran dejado morirme en el trullo como un perro" ["Advantage of having a family. If it weren't for you all, they would have left me to die in the slammer like a dog"] (1:27:16–23). In the end, this group of adults does indeed form a non-normative familial unit. The movie ends with Rafa and his daughters at the cemetery. Daniel and Marina are both buried alongside Rafa's parents, showing that just as he has accepted Marina's daughters as his own, he has also come to consider Marina and Daniel as members of his family.

While compulsory hetero-parenting discourages fathers from being closely involved with their children, Rafa experiences a great longing for fatherhood and family life. He seems resigned to his inability to engage in sexual activity, but not to the possibility of never becoming a father. Although he has a good job and a house big enough for children, the house seems to taunt him, a constant reminder of the heteronormative family life from which he has been excluded. Even before Marina moves in with Rafa, the house is staged as if a family lived there, with pictures of Rafa with his sister and her children in every room. The rooms are tidy and presentable; there are even flowers on the living room bookshelf and a cartoon Babar poster in what will later become Estrella's room. Marina tells Rafa that if she had a house like his, she would fill it with children; however, she admits that she could never have such a nice house. In this moment, they realize that, together, they can fulfil their desires – a house for Marina and children for Rafa. When Rafa tells his sister of his plan to form a family with Marina and her child, she asks if he will adopt the baby. Rafa replies, "Yo no voy a adoptarlo. Lo voy a reconocer" ["I'm not going to adopt her. I'm going to legally recognize her"] (24:30–3). He goes on to explain the pain of not being able to have children, saying that he suffers when he sees "a todo el mundo con su familia, su mujer y sus hijos y tú sabes que eso, no podrás tenerlo nunca" ["the whole world with their family, their wife, and their children, and you know that you can never have that"] (24:16–19). While Rafa describes his relationship with Marina as "una locura" ["madness"] (25:26), recognizing its non-normative nature, his sister corrects him by saying that it is actually "un milagro" ["a miracle"] (26:02). She admits that until Marina's appearance, she had often pictured him growing old alone in his big house, a symbol of permanently unfulfilled normativity.

In the eyes of all three protagonists, Rafa becomes the legitimate and unquestionable father of Marina's daughter. Rafa gives her the name Estrella, his mother's name, as a way of preserving his family's lineage and history. Marina asks him if he would abandon Estrella in the case of her absence. Rafa responds that Estrella is his daughter, too. Marina wants Rafa to swear to her that he will always look after Estrella, but Rafa responds, "No tengo que jurar nada. Somos una familia y para eso estamos. Para cuidarnos los unos a los otros" ["I don't need to swear anything. We are a family, and that's what we're for. To care for each other"] (1:15:15–23). Marina does eventually abandon the family, living with Daniel for a brief time before returning to the house, impregnated once more by Daniel. Upon her return, she tells Rafa, "Vamos a tener otro hijo, sabes" ["We're going to have another child, you know"] (1:19:28). Rafa accepts and recognizes the second child as his own. The family created by Rafa, Marina, and Daniel is unique because, while Rafa remains monogamous, Marina's polyamory allows Rafa to have children. Although Daniel is the biological father of Marina's daughters, Rafa is emotionally connected to them. Both Daniel and Marina see Rafa as Estrella's father, most likely because he can provide something for her that neither of her biological parents can: economic stability. In Marina's eyes, this makes him an excellent paternal candidate, in addition to his caring nature and desire to take on caregiver duties for the children. Although society might characterize Rafa as foolish for economically supporting children who are not biologically his, Rafa's economic resources are a source of masculine power for him. At one point, he offers Daniel money to leave Marina for good, which Daniel accepts. Although Daniel is physically and sexually more virile, Rafa is the more stable man, asserting his masculinity through his economic power, steady and ever-present love for the children, and reliability. Members of Rafa's non-normative family are happier when Rafa does not feel the need to prove his masculinity and family members can interact in more peaceful and authentic ways.

Although Daniel is the biological father of Marina's children, she does not believe that he has any paternal rights to them, as he will not be the one to raise and support them. Daniel neither wants nor considers himself to be a candidate for paternal rights. Rafa is afraid that Daniel might reclaim Estrella, but Daniel very clearly tells him, "No te equivoques. Que la niña es tuya" ["Don't get it mistaken. The girl is yours"] (43:12–14). During Daniel's final incarceration, Rafa visits to tell him of the second daughter's birth, saying, "Hemos tenido otra niña"

["We've had another girl"] (1:20:11). He is referring, of course, to the second daughter that was conceived between Daniel and Marina. This is an interesting scene for many reasons, as it seems almost comical that Rafa tells Daniel of the birth of a child that he himself helped to create. Rafa's word choice is curious. By using the subject pronoun of *nosotros, we* have had another daughter, does Rafa wish to include Daniel in the parental group responsible for raising the baby? Perhaps so, or he could be referring only to himself and Marina with the use of "we." Either way, his ambiguous word choice creates space for various potential parental configurations in the children's lives. Daniel wholeheartedly congratulates Rafa on the birth of his child, as Daniel himself has never felt the desire or pressure to become a father. Although fatherhood is one of the ways in which Spanish men may access part of hegemonic masculinity, it is not an aspect of Daniel's identity. By refusing to value a biological connection with a child over an emotional connection, Daniel and Rafa break away from compulsory hetero-parenting.

In *Todo lo que tú quieras*, Dafne is the one who demonstrates an intense longing for family after her mother Alicia's death, and the family that Dafne hopes to recreate is a traditional one centred around the importance of the stereotypical mother figure, most likely because in her limited experience, her mother was always the parent who cared for her emotional needs. Before asking Leo to cross-dress, Dafne expresses an insistent desire to see her mother, or if that is not possible, to establish an alternate mother figure, as she suggests that Marta become her "madre postiza" ["fake mother"] (30:32). Marta and Leo had a sexual relationship in the past, during Leo's marriage to Alicia. When Leo admits (before Alicia's death) to his co-worker and confidant that he will be meeting with Marta because she is introducing him to a new client, the friend urges him not to see her, saying that Marta has always been "jodiéndote la vida" ["fucking up your life"] (11:04), calling her crazy and describing her as a villain. This is a misogynistically one-sided interpretation of the relationship between Marta and Leo, as he chose to cheat on his wife. Although Marta cares for Leo and appears to want an established romantic partnership after Alicia's death, none of her actions suggest a needy or diabolical personality. After Alicia's death, when Leo and Dafne begin to spend time with Marta, Dafne clearly gravitates towards her because she is a woman. In a café where the three of them have met, Dafne kisses Marta on the cheek without being prompted, a stark contrast to earlier when she would not give Leo a kiss as he dropped her off at school, even though he expressly asked her for one. Leo and Marta go on a date, after which Marta plans to spend the night. When Dafne cannot sleep in the middle of the night, she calls for Marta instead of her father, upset to learn that Marta has left. Dafne's experiences up to this point have clearly taught her that women take on emotional roles, leading her to assume that it would be easier to get a new "fake" mother rather than ask for emotional support from her father. Leo considers having a relationship with Marta for Dafne's sake but decides against it because it would not make him happy. After their date, Leo and Marta have sex, an example of Leo's emotional impotence: he continues to call her Alicia during intercourse, even though Marta tells him that she is not Alicia. Both Leo and Dafne are tentatively searching for a substitute mother/wife figure to replace Alicia.

Body and Identity Performance

In both films, body performance becomes an important way for characters to explore non-normative familial creation, particularly in relation to hegemonic masculinity. *La buena estrella* is divided into sections – "La Tuerta" ["The One-Eyed Woman"], "El guapo de cara" ["The man with the handsome face"], and "El manso" ["The docile one"] – that correspond to Marina, Daniel, and Rafa accordingly while focusing on their physical attributes or personality. Marina's body is an important social signifier. In the beginning of the movie, she is a prostitute with one blind eye. Daniel views her as an object, a source of income created by renting out her body. He tells her, "Yo hago contigo lo que me da la gana ... Eres una puta" ["I will do with you what I feel like ... You are a whore"] (3:46–9). He also never calls Marina by her name, instead referring to her as "la Tuerta" ["the One-Eyed Woman"]. With this nickname, Daniel relegates her identity to a physical characteristic, one that recalls her subjugated social status, as she was blinded in the orphanage when another girl stuck a fork in her eye. When Rafa takes Marina to live with him, he buys her a contact that makes her eye seem normal. When Daniel first sees her from afar after being released from jail, Marina appears to be a completely different person. Dressed in a demure skirt, sweater, and flats, she is pushing a baby stroller. Marina is now performing the role of traditional housewife, as advertised by the image that Rafa has created for her body to project.

Although she can perform either role, Marina will never fully be one or the other. Her desires are split between wanting a life with both Rafa and Daniel, along with everything that those very distinct lives imply. She therefore floats in between these roles, able to perform as either but representing a perplexing and perhaps threatening (to hegemonic society) ambiguity. At an impasse between the virgin/whore dichotomy,

Marina complicates the notion that "through social institutions and discourses, bodies are given social meaning" (Connell, *The Men* 58). She is indeed defined by social institutions such as marriage and prostitution; however, she can choose which body performance to enact in any given moment. Patriarchal society does not wish to associate motherhood with prostitution:

> The modern discourse on prostitution was part of a broader discursive production of female sexuality which separated the female body into the reproductive body and the un(re)productive body: normal female sexuality was defined in terms of woman's reproductive functions; deviant female sexuality was defined in terms of prostitution. Reproductive sexuality, which denied woman active sexual desire and pleasure, was the respectable norm; prostitution was its inversion. (Bell, *Reading, Writing & Rewriting* 41)

Marina/La Tuerta refuses to stay fixed within either category. She is simultaneously mother and sex object, respectable housewife and prostitute. Switching between the two roles is as easy as removing a contact lens.

Daniel is also defined by his body performance. The film's subtitle that corresponds to Daniel is "el guapo de cara" ["the man with the handsome face"], which suggests his sexual potency and ability to attract and impregnate women. Daniel exudes heterosexuality, making advances toward any woman he encounters while fervently rebuffing markers of homosexuality. He defines himself not only through his attractive face, but also through the vitality of his sexual appendages. During a conversation with Rafa, Daniel asks him various questions about his sexual organs, feeling perplexed, horrified, and intrigued by Rafa's impotence. He asks Rafa whether he actually has a penis and testicles, and whether he can get hard enough to have sex with Marina. For Daniel, masculinity and identity are defined through the body, specifically the genitals and the way in which one performs with them, because these are some of the only markers of hegemonic masculinity that Daniel can access. In the next breath, Daniel asserts, "Yo sin cojones, tío, preferiría estar muerto" ["Without balls, man, I would prefer to be dead"] (1:07:46–50), showing his preoccupation with hegemonic masculinity and sexual potency. When illness begins to physically deteriorate his body, Daniel is ready to die, understanding his life as a man to be already over after losing his physical and sexual strength. While Daniel seems obsessed with the trappings of compulsory heteroparenting, the ability to biologically father a child, these aspects become very superficial for him and the children he fathers. What hegemonic society suggests makes a father – his ability to procreate – is actually the furthest away from defining true paternity in *La buena estrella*.

Rafa's body performance does not necessarily highlight his membership within hegemonic masculinity, as the film's denomination of him as "el manso" ["the docile one"] suggests. While "manso" translates to "meek" or "docile," it is also a word frequently employed to describe less aggressive bulls. The image of Rafa as a tame bull is an interesting contrast to the way he performs his masculinity as a butcher. His butcher's coat and knife evoke images of violence, blood, and gore; in the rest of his life, Rafa is not drawn to violence, although he can access or threaten violence when necessary. When he confronts Daniel for beating Marina at the beginning of the movie, Rafa's darting eyes betray his nervousness and distaste for confrontation, but he challenges Daniel because he feels protected by the signifiers of masculinity that he carries with him. A brief flash of his long butcher's knife causes Daniel to abandon the scene without a fight. While Rafa is averse to violence, he is also quietly confident in his ability to defend himself and Marina in this moment. The type of masculinity that Rafa embodies is quieter than Daniel's but just as powerful. Rafa follows a code of honour, protects those weaker than him or in need, and exhibits patience and reliability. After Daniel has moved into the house, Rafa finds that one of his knives is missing, only to learn that Daniel took it. Daniel later returns it to him, revealing that he had taken it in order to purchase a leather carrying case for the knife. Thanking Daniel for the gift, Rafa adds (while looking at Marina), "pero no toques mis cosas" ["but don't touch my things"] (1:02:07–8), an admonition with a double meaning. Just as Daniel tampered with his knife, he has also slept with his wife, a threat to Rafa's masculinity that Rafa responds to with a quiet assurance of reprisal for future transgressions on Daniel's part.

For Leo in *Todo lo que tú quieras*, his cross-dressing is an example of body performance that leads him to fall short of hegemonic masculinity (and compulsory hetero-parenting, as its ideals align with those of hegemonic masculinity). Cross-dressing is an act with complex motivations that can be done by homosexual or heterosexual individuals. Some heterosexual men cross-dress due to the sexual pleasure that wearing women's clothing affords them or the desire to express a more feminine side of their personalities (Reynolds and Caron 71). There are various interpretations of the meaning behind cross-dressing. Cross-dressing has been described by various critics as a societal tactic to subordinate and belittle women while reaffirming male power. Described as "one of the last preserves of a virulent misogyny, the minstrel show of sexist culture" (Showalter 122), cross-dressing's somewhat ridiculous juxtaposition of male and female characteristics, the "deep voice, the wig that is removed, the deployment which is not 'quite right'" (Hawkes 266) can lead to a comical portrayal of women that reduces them to an amalgam of their physical parts. Cross-dressing can also become yet another way for men to make themselves feel more powerful at women's expense. In Elaine Showalter's analysis of the US film *Tootsie*, she argues that by assuming the female body, cross-dressers imply their ability to be better women than biological women; they are "phallic" women who "with practice will become a better woman than a biological female if he chooses to do so" (123).[5] Showalter argues that, in this case, cross-dressing is not done to celebrate feminine characteristics but rather "as a way of promoting the notion of masculine power while masking it" (123), implying that certain men who cross-dress believe they can teach women how to perform femininity. Others view cross-dressing as an attempt to honour women and acknowledge their worth through imitation. Cross-dressing can be a positive, liberatory experience, representing a blurring of gender lines that defies patriarchal society's need for dichotomous gender divisions. Charlotte Suthrell writes about men who cross-dress, stating that they "have been censored for ... dressing as the inferior sex and for transgressing the binary rule, for blurring the boundaries" (23). Cross-dressing can be an empowering act for gay or trans people, as well as any individual who does not feel comfortable within the rigid confines of heteronormativity. Judith Butler describes it as yet another form of gender performance, something that all humans engage in, arguing that by "*imitating gender, drag implicitly reveals the imitative structure of gender itself – as well as its contingency*" (*Gender Trouble* 187; italics in original). *Todo lo que tú quieras* opens with several images of nondescript men, unsmiling and in grey or black suits, followed by images of the same men dressed in drag, colourful outfits, often smiling. From the beginning, then, viewers are aware that they will be confronted with representations of masculinity that are not hegemonic. Whatever an individual's reasons for cross-dressing might be, the performance itself allows for the practice of fluidity.

After Leo explains to Dafne that certain men dress up as women, she becomes fixated on the idea of Leo transforming into her mother. At bedtime, she asks him, "¿Por qué no te pintas los labios y me haces de mamá?" ["Why don't you put on lipstick and do Mom for me?"] (42:39–42). After some resistance, Leo puts on Alicia's lipstick and reads Dafne a bedtime story. Dafne focuses on his lips for the entire story, transforming Leo into her mother by concentrating on this isolated body part that has been appropriated as female by the application of lipstick.

Figure 3.2 Leo reading a bedtime story to Dafne while wearing Alicia's lipstick

Leo later buys a wig that resembles Alicia's hair, excitedly bringing it home to show to Dafne while putting on a fashion show in one of Alicia's dresses. While the montage of Leo trying on Alicia's clothes for Dafne is presented to the soundtrack of lighthearted music, there is an element of the macabre in the fact that Leo dresses as and imitates his dead wife. Dafne enjoys the upbeat fashion show, a performance that Leo uses in an attempt to achieve emotional connection with his daughter, but Dafne admonishes Leo because she can see the hair on his legs. Even four-year-old Dafne realizes that gender is performative; she polices her father's performance of motherhood to make sure that he is as accurate as possible. Dafne exhibits a high level of agency and self-awareness for a four-year-old, seeking out the image of her mother as it is inscribed on her father's body because she already understands gender constructions and needs a maternal figure on which to model her own identity. Later in the movie, however, Leo does become "mamá" ["Mom"] for Dafne, and she struggles to separate the two identities.

Through cross-dressing, Leo assimilates his physical appearance to that of Dafne's mother and attempts to fill the gap that Alicia's absence leaves in both of their lives. Although he claims that the cross-dressing is just a game, asserting that both he and Dafne can differentiate between fantasy and reality, Leo's attitude is clearly changing, his identity becoming blurred. At first, he does not want to dress as Alicia, protesting to Dafne, "Escúchame una cosa, flaca. Papá también tiene el derecho de existir, ¿no?" ["Listen to me, skinny one. Dad also has a right to exist, right?"] (56:01–6), to which she responds, "Yo prefiero que me hagas de mamá" ["I prefer that you do Mom for me"] (56:07–8). While the Leo who had a wife at home hardly spent time with his daughter and would much less cross-dress for her, the widowed Leo cross-dresses in public because it is what Dafne wants. Although Leo's cross-dressing does not alter the type of activities the two do together – such as negotiating how many vegetables Dafne must eat before dessert, reading stories, and dropping Dafne off at school – Dafne seems much happier when Leo dresses as Alicia. Leo even begins to go into the women's restroom with Dafne instead of taking her to the men's room, evidence of a psychological change within him in relation to his parental connection to Dafne. When a client asks Leo about Dafne's mother, he responds that he is Dafne's mother. Not only has Leo's relationship with Dafne changed to make him a more involved parent, but his ideas about gender roles have shifted to become more inclusive. Later in the film, when his colleague asks how his case for the "maricón" ["faggot"] (1:06:44) is progressing, Leo replies, "Álex. Se llama Álex" ["Álex. His name is Álex"] (1:06:45). His response comes naturally and is non-confrontational. However, Leo now refuses to participate in the shaming of a man who falls outside the confines of hegemonic masculinity.

Leo's cross-dressing elicits societal backlash from various groups. Dafne's school psychologist cautions Leo to stop cross-dressing because it confuses Dafne, threatening to report him to social services if the behaviour does not stop. Leo pushes back against the counsellor's advice, asking why he would know better than Dafne's father what is best for her in her grieving state. Leo exhibits a confidence in his enactment of parenthood here that he would not have had before becoming Dafne's primary caregiver. Now, he trusts his own judgment when it comes to Dafne's well-being, even if that requires something unconventional or uncomfortable from him as a father. Leo does indeed face many consequences for his decision to cross-dress. He is almost refused service at a motel while dressed in Alicia's clothes. The most serious repercussion is the beating he receives from a group of young men. While Leo is recuperating in the hospital, Dafne is taken to Alicia's parents, who will not let Dafne call Leo "mamá" ["Mom"] (1:20:27) on the phone nor will they give her back to him. While in the marginalized state of a cross-dresser, Leo's maternal experience reveals some of the struggles that women, homosexual and transgender individuals, and others who do not fit into the privileged category of hegemonic masculinity face daily, particularly the ever-present threat of violence. Having benefited from hegemonic masculinity for so long, Leo finds it difficult to negotiate his existence without the societal privileges to which he is accustomed. Achero Mañas addresses this topic in an interview about the film, saying:

> La liberación de la mujer ha sido una falacia. Ha sido ficticia, un *bluff*. Y por eso están luchando tanto, ¿no? Lo que pasa es que la mujer, una vez que ha salido, ha reivindicado sus derechos para estar equiparada y no estar desfavorecida. Pero en el caso del hombre protagonista de la película no ha sido voluntario: [...] ha sido una especie de trauma. (Queipo)

> [Women's liberation has been a lie. It has been fiction, a *bluff*. And that's why they are fighting so hard, right? What happens is that the woman, once she has come out, has reclaimed her rights to be on the same level and not at a disadvantage. But in the case of the male protagonist of the film, it has not been voluntary: (...) it has been a type of trauma.] (Queipo)

Although Leo's willingness to cross-dress for his daughter presents a positive message of bending the gendered rules of parenthood, it must be noted that the film's conclusion returns to a reliance on traditional gender stereotypes. After Leo has retrieved Dafne from the school where her grandparents were sending her, father and daughter begin the drive home. They stop at a roadside restaurant and eat in their car, instead of risking a confrontation by trying to dine inside while Leo is dressed in women's clothing. They watch through the restaurant's window as a family consisting of a father, a mother, and one child eats their meal. The scene is sombre, as both Leo and Dafne watch the family with longing or nostalgia, a moment of closure and grief for Dafne's lost mother. They spend the night in a motel, arriving when it is already late and dark. Dafne becomes frightened and says that she wants to see her father again. She removes the makeup from Leo's face, signalling her readiness for Leo to resume presenting himself as her father. At this moment, they come to the agreement that Dafne will just close her eyes and imagine her mother's presence whenever she misses her. Leo's willingness to cross-dress to help Dafne achieve this closure clearly brought the two of them closer together emotionally. As Dafne observes the "pupas" ["booboos"] (1:32:30) on Leo's face from his beating, she gently kisses them to make them better, demonstrating the increased emotional attachment between them. Just as Ragan writes about *La buena estrella*, Leo (and Rafa) create "'comunidades afectivas' que sustituyen la familia tradicional. También coinciden en que la masculinidad es dónde se ubica el mayor obstáculo a la felicidad de las mujeres y a la de los hombres mismos" ["'affective communities' that substitute the traditional family. They also coincide in that masculinity is where the biggest obstacle to happiness for women and for the men themselves is found"] (Ragan 125). This example of fluid parental performance is contrasted with the heteronormative message of the film's ending. In her moment of fear, Dafne wants a father – not a mother – to care for her, because strength and protection fall under the responsibilities of the traditional father figure. Leo's engagement with a non-normative performance of parenthood has allowed him to enjoy a closer, more meaningful relationship with his daughter. His choices are not without consequences, however. The movie ends with the endearing scene between the two, although the sound of sirens fills the background, suggesting that perhaps the police are coming for Leo, who has taken Dafne from school without permission. This is a reminder that those who deviate from performances of hegemonic masculinity face societal backlash.

The Positive Potential of Impotence

By the end of both films, Rafa, Daniel, and Leo are clearly invested in participating in some version of family, but they have different ways of establishing their place with the family. Whether they act in accordance with hegemonic masculinity or stand in opposition to it, their performances of gender and paternity expose the fallibility of the concept. One important component of hegemonic masculinity is sexual virility, which defines impotence as an indicator of masculine crisis. Sexual impotence is of such concern because it is emblematic of a more widespread impotence: "Although the term has been used for centuries to specifically refer to partial or complete loss of erectile ability, the first definition dictionaries give for 'impotence' never mentions sex but refers to a general loss of vigor, strength, or power" (Tiefer 165). Rafa, Daniel, and Leo – like all men – experience some type of impotence that leaves them powerless. Their specific experiences with different types of impotence, which I will discuss in this section, isolates them from the ideals of hegemonic masculinity, a concept that has been socially constructed as "a kind of triumph over impotence" (Walsh 65). Since impotence can lead to a crisis of masculinity, men look for other ways to compensate their shortcomings.

Rafa is the most obviously impotent of the three protagonists, as he cannot father children, nor can he maintain an erection long enough to have intercourse. When Rafa first brings Marina to his house, she immediately asks him if he wants to have sex with her, assuming that this is the motivation behind his kindness. Although he refuses her offer, the two begin to kiss, leading Marina to direct Rafa into manually stimulating her to orgasm. Rafa repeatedly shuts down Marina's attempts to initiate intercourse, not wanting to confront his impotence. When she finally convinces him to try, Rafa claims afterwards that he enjoyed himself. However, when Marina asks if he had an orgasm, Rafa responds, "No sé, pero no importa" ["I don't know, but it doesn't matter"] (21:07–10). He leaves the bedroom to go to his butcher shop, fleeing from his impotence to a site of masculine enactment.

Rafa performs "abjection as endurance [which] becomes a useful strategy to counteract male impotence. For the masculine to survive, its (repressed) constitutive abjection must be strategically collapsed into the glamour of the wounded hero" (Walsh 80). He stoically endures his impotence and his sexual lack. When Marina cheats on him with Daniel in his house (as he sits and listens downstairs instead of marching to the bedroom to confront and stop them), Rafa does not become violent or seek revenge on either of them. Instead, he passively endures their infidelity in silence, ignoring his part of the blame for the situation – as he was the one who left the two alone in order to test them, despite Marina's pleading that he should not leave her in such a situation. Although sexually impotent, Rafa demonstrates throughout the film that having a family with Marina is more important to him than having a sexual relationship with her. Compulsory heteronormativity holds sexual virility in great importance, but Rafa establishes a familial unit with Marina and the children without meeting this requirement.

Although he does not experience sexual impotence, Daniel's entire life is an example of masculinity in crisis. He attempts to live up to the hegemonic standards of masculinity that he believes will allow him to survive a life on the streets as a marginalized individual: through violence and toughness. His lack of emotional connection, which can be viewed as a form of self-preservation, is not an intentionally acquired characteristic, but rather a result of being abandoned as a child and never learning how to connect with others. Writing about Spanish films in the later part of the Transition, Mary T. Hartson describes the impact of hegemonic masculinity for "many male characters who do not learn to forge new bonds with others [and] become isolated and insecure. They seem stuck on a dead end street and often turn to violence or self-absorbed individualism as coping mechanisms" (163). Although *La buena estrella* premiered decades later, Daniel's relationship with hegemonic masculinity mirrors earlier patterns of masculinity that Hartson describes. His hyper-aggression is an attempt to protect himself, but instead, this lifestyle leads to several incarcerations and a solitude that is only broken by Marina's love and later Rafa's reluctant support. Trapped within a jail cell toward the end of his life, Daniel's impotence is evident both in his lack of freedom and his rapidly failing physical health. The jail scene between Daniel and Rafa shows a role reversal. Rafa appears to be the powerful, free man who is announcing his paternity, while Daniel coughs weakly, trapped behind the glass and seemingly holding back tears. Daniel even says, "Ahora soy menos hombre que tú" ["Now I am less of a man than you"] (1:23:10–11), referring to the debilitating illness that has left him physically powerless. Daniel then affirms that other men do not have "la mitad de cojones" ["half the balls"] (1:21:20) that Rafa does. Despite Rafa's physical impotence, Daniel finally acknowledges Rafa's manliness, a realization that there is more than one way to enact manhood. Daniel realizes that the ways in which he tried to perform his masculinity were dangerous and ultimately unproductive, landing him in jail, while Rafa's quieter, less showy masculinity has better served him. The two men seem unified in a homosocial way in this scene. The camera alternates between shots of each man's face next to the reflection of the other's face in the glass. At the end of their visit, both men touch their hands to the glass in a prolonged embrace, a vulnerable show of emotion that unites the two men as members of a non-normative family. Here, Daniel and Rafa exhibit an alternative performance of masculinity that breaks with the standards of hegemonic masculinity to show connection through emotional vulnerability, a reflection of the alternate family they have created with Marina and the children.

Daniel asks Rafa to take good care of "nuestras mujeres" ["our women"] (1:22:43), indicating that he thinks of them all as part of his family. It has been suggested that the characters of Daniel and Rafa enact a "demystification of traditional patriarchy through the juxtaposition of two competing models. The dissection of patriarchy is then carried out through the contrast between the 'biological' father, Daniel, and the adoptive father, Rafael" (Begin, "Picking a Fight" 131). Both men display aspects of patriarchal behaviour and compliance to hegemonic masculinity, but neither can fully live up to its demands. Moreover, the components of their personalities that diverge from patriarchal constructions of manhood and fatherhood are those elements that truly make them human and better candidates for fatherhood. Although Daniel and Rafa have formed a non-normative family with Marina and the children, it is important to point out that these characters are simply performing their roles within the family without consciously having constructed the family in an alternative way. Their enactments of family and parenthood are natural, not studied.

In *Todo lo que tú quieras*, Leo experiences emotional impotence when it comes to connecting with his daughter. While his wife was alive, Leo did not – and was not expected to – engage in childcare activities. After Alicia's death, Leo is unsure of how to connect with Dafne without Alicia's presence to facilitate their interactions. This film addresses Spanish men's changing role within society and the family. While mothers are becoming more involved in the labour force, leaving them with less time to dedicate to the home, men must renegotiate their social and familial roles, which can provoke panic in men who have not been accustomed to taking on these responsibilities. Of course, as the multiple examples of non-normative families in this book have demonstrated, there are myriad ways of performing fatherhood. Even though, as discussed earlier in this chapter, sociological studies have shown that many Spanish men are uncomfortable with changing expectations that require their greater presence and emotional vulnerability with their children, other Spanish men have already been involved in and comfortable with more intense childcare roles. Leo's struggle to find a way to connect with Dafne embodies one type of Spanish paternity, explained by the film's director Achero Mañas in the following way: "Se trata de una metáfora de lo que está sucediendo: al varón no le queda más remedio que cambiar porque si no, se queda fuera de juego" ["It addresses a metaphor of what is happening: man doesn't have any other solution but to change because if not, he will fall by the wayside"] (Carrón). While Leo struggles to adapt and take on more caregiving and emotional responsibility for Dafne, a brief scene with Leo and his father reveals a different option for enacting paternity. When Leo admits to his father that he feels unable to care for Dafne, his father replies, "No vas a tener tiempo de pensarlo. ¿Y sabes por qué? Porque los hijos afortunadamente son más importantes que uno mismo. Dejarás de pensar en ti porque su felicidad te va a importar más que tu sufrimiento" ["You're not going to have time to think about it. And you know why? Because fortunately, children are more important than oneself. You will stop thinking about yourself because their happiness is going to matter more to you than your suffering"] (20:39–50). This is an emotionally vulnerable moment between Leo and his father, where Leo's father exhibits a mindset of traditional (especially Catholic) masculinity in which the father figure enacts abnegated self-denial, focused on the best interests of the child. Both masculinities (Leo and his father's) have at one point been hegemonic models of masculinity in Spain, even though their approaches toward relationships with one's children are very different.

Leo is not the only father in the film who suffers from emotional impotence. Álex, the drag queen whom Leo insults but later convinces to teach him how to cross-dress, has been permanently rejected by his son Hugo because of his homosexuality. Álex is deeply troubled by his lack of relationship with his son. At the drag show and scene of Leo and Álex's confrontation, Álex tells Leo that he reminds him of someone (his son, although he does not specify this in the moment). As Leo attempts to leave the room, Álex throws himself to the ground and grabs Leo's leg, shouting, "No me abandones así entre todo este mugre" ["Don't abandon me here among all this filth"] (35:27–9). While this is meant to be a humorous moment for the audience's benefit, Álex is simultaneously acting out the pain of being abandoned by his son. Álex is not trying to live up to the standards of hegemonic masculinity, having long ago acknowledged his non-normativity. Acknowledgment is not acceptance, however; Álex clearly suffers from internalized homophobia. In his drag show, he dresses as Dracula.[6] While this choice provides him with many humorous opportunities, Dracula is a marginalized, monstrous figure. Perhaps Álex chose Dracula as a way of mirroring or expressing his feelings about his own sexuality and social role. When Leo explains why he wants to cross-dress, Álex says that his own homosexuality and cross-dressing "no ha sido por una causa noble como la tuya" ["has not been for a noble cause like yours"] (59:47–9). Álex contrasts Leo's cross-dressing for his daughter with his own cross-dressing, which is part of his expression of his homosexuality, about which he carries guilt, as it has created a separation between himself and his son. When Leo is surprised to learn that Álex has a son, he retorts, "Los heterosexuales no tenéis un monopolio en la paternidad. Nosotros también cometemos fallos" ["You heterosexuals don't have a monopoly on paternity. We also commit errors"] (1:21:59–22:06). Álex is deeply troubled by his inability to reconnect with his son, and this aspect of his story demonstrates that emotional connection with one's children can be a struggle for all types of fathers.

The chinks in the men's armour of patriarchal power – their moments of failure to live up to heteronormative standards – are undoubtedly the aspects of their identity that hold the most positive significance for their children. Daniel does not feel compelled by any patriarchal impulses of ownership to claim paternity of the daughters whom he has fathered. Instead, Rafa fulfils this role, both men acknowledging that Rafa is more suited for it and more willing to take it on. Rafa does not allow his enactment of paternity to be hindered by feelings of inadequacy stemming from the fact that he did not biologically father the girls. Each man disregards the heteronormative script set out for them, technically failing to live up to hegemonic masculinity. Through their failure, they gain the ability to assume roles within their non-normative family that are satisfying for both themselves and their daughters. Similarly, Leo ignores the dictates of hegemonic masculinity, choosing to cross-dress to be closer to his daughter. His failure is powerful, as it allows him to create a strong bond with Dafne. Álex is the only character whose impotence does not provide him with an alternate way of connecting with his son. In the impotence of the other three men, there is power to reclaim and recreate the family outside of the boundaries of patriarchy.

Hegemonic Masculinity and Violence

In addition to their relationship with various types of impotence and the ways in which they perform bodily enactments of masculinity, protagonists in both films also negotiate their relationship with hegemonic masculinity through their relationship with violence. Violence is an important tool in the process of upholding hegemonic masculinity, used to subjugate individuals who are not part of the dominant group, as well as to maintain order within the confines of hegemony. However, violence is an indication of the crisis of masculinity, because a system that already had complete domination over its members would not need to employ such tactics to maintain order (Connell, *Masculinities* 84). Especially in *La buena estrella*, the suggestion of violence is almost always present. It must be noted that violence is not a factor in the relationships formed between these men and their children, perhaps because all the children are daughters, and masculine homosocial violence is often used to teach young men their place within a hegemonic system.

Although Rafa is described as the "manso" ["docile one"] of the film, because he does not constantly perform an aggressive version of masculinity, he has the strength and potential for violence within him. Rafa understands the system of violence, and although he prefers not to engage in it, he shows Daniel that he can manipulate this system when needed. When the two go hunting together, Rafa does not allow Daniel to touch his shotgun, stating that he fears him. In this scene, Rafa switches his knife for a shotgun, replacing one phallic symbol of masculinity and potency with another, all the while denying Daniel access to a marker of masculinity. At one point, Rafa aims the gun at Daniel, saying, "Estaba pensando lo fácil que sería pegarte un tiro y enterrarte por aquí" ["I was thinking how easy it would be to shoot you and bury you here"] (1:11:25–7). Although he does not murder Daniel, it is not for lack of desire. Rafa admits that he is not a good liar, and he would have to live his life in fear, always wondering if the murder would be discovered. Rafa takes a non-violent, passive approach throughout much of his life, although he does threaten Daniel, playing with the idea of violence. He allows Daniel to live with them, despite his fears that Daniel will take his wife and daughters away from him. The moments when Rafa does attempt to perform a version of hypermasculinity always seem to go poorly for him. After Marina and Daniel have sex in his bed, Rafa begins to initiate violent sex with Marina, who accuses him of performing sexually in a way that he imagines to be an imitation of Daniel. Marina does not appreciate this, as she admires Rafa's gentle qualities.

Throughout his time living on the streets, Daniel has adopted a hyper-violent performance of masculinity as a way to protect himself from the violence that has frequently been enacted upon him. Daniel is beaten after his first stay in jail, and the sexual violence of rape is implied due to the fact that he contracts HIV/AIDS while in prison for the second time. Prison is one of the primary sites where violence is used on (mostly) men in order to "teach" behaviour modification. Those who wish to be part of the "in" group of hegemonic masculinity "must submit themselves to the gender's specific violent laws if they are to be accommodated within the male order ... those subjects who fail to realize gender cohesion must willingly subject themselves to violence at their own or others' hands in order to be assimilated by the group" (Walsh 60). When Daniel arrives at Rafa's doorstep, he is covered in blood and bruises; wounds also have the capability to masculinize an individual because they show a person's level of endurance (Walsh 92). Once Marina has cleaned his wounds and put him in bed, however, Daniel does not seem so tough. Rafa checks on him in the middle of the night because he is whimpering in his sleep. As Rafa touches his forehead to see if he has a fever, the two men have another emotional moment where Rafa demonstrates his caring abilities. Daniel has been converted into the sick child, not a powerful man capable of inflicting and receiving extreme violence. Daniel's character embodies what Mary T. Harston describes as thematic masculinities in contemporary Spanish film:

> traumatized or unmoored and melancholic masculinities that may express themselves through reactionary or violent means; hypersexual, self-indulgent, and/or self-absorbed masculinities; and clearly modern masculinities which attempt to find new grounding, often basing themselves in friendship or alternative family relationships. (163)

When Daniel realizes the promise of hegemonic masculinity found through violence is an empty one, he turns to alternate ways of performing masculinity that allow him to connect emotionally with his non-normative family.

Leo is another victim of masculine violence. As he waits in his car while Dafne attends a friend's birthday party, a brick is thrown at his car. When he gets out of the car, dressed as a woman, a group of four young men beat him to the point of hospitalization for no other reason than his gender-bending appearance. Members of hegemonic masculinity fear being excluded from the group; one way to fit in is to reject and punish any type of feminine behaviour (Connell, *The Men* 217). Leo's cross-dressing is a reminder to other men that all masculinity is subject to question and even change. As a cross-dresser, Leo experiences a way of living unconcerned with – and therefore threatening to – hegemonic masculinity.

As Leo, Daniel, and Rafa demonstrate, compulsory hetero-parenting and hegemonic masculinity are standards that no father can completely and consistently live up to, nor should they necessarily even want to, as, in the case of these protagonists, hegemonic masculinity offers a limited, flawed way of connecting with one's progeny. From the first, extremely graphic scene in *La buena estrella*, hegemonic masculinity is being questioned. In this scene, cows and bulls in a butcher shop are being sliced apart, their bloody, fragile undersides exposed. The image of the bull, so closely associated with Spanish masculinity, reveals the potential weakness or fragility of hegemonic masculinity and, by association, performances of fatherhood that are tied to the concept. As both films show, Rafa, Daniel, and Leo's performances of masculinity at times allow them to align themselves with hegemonic definitions of masculinity and fatherhood. However, the moments in which they are willing to ignore or fail at hegemonic masculinity are those times in which they are free to enact their masculinities and fatherhoods in uninhibited and meaningful ways. In these moments, they place their children's needs before their own, performing their parenthood as they see fit, not as society dictates they should.

Through their portrayal of masculinities, at times aligning with the demands of hegemonic masculinity and at other times greatly deviating from them, *La buena estrella* and *Todo lo que tú quieras* are films that create space for a larger dialogue about how masculinities influence a variety of performances of fatherhoods. Rafa, Daniel, and Leo show the difficulties of living up to the standards of hegemonic masculinity and compulsory hetero-parenting, as well as how the experience of this crisis is enacted through sexuality, cross-dressing and other body performances, and violence. The moments in which these men are most truly connected with their children and their own identities as fathers and individuals occur when they eschew hegemonic constraints to perform their parenthood in a way that feels genuine to them at the time. This continuum, while not a perfect elaboration of a new social construction of parenthood, provides a framework for beginning to reimagine meaningful and authentic ways in which men (and women) can enact their own personalized interpretations of parenthood.

Chapter Four

Lesbian Maternal Community Formation

In *Tras la pared* [*Behind the Wall*] (2010), the second novel in Mila Martínez's trilogy, the interwoven themes of motherhood and female community are central to both plot lines, which converge by the end of the novel. The first plot centres on the worries and excitements experienced by Carla and Mel, a lesbian couple embracing a surprise pregnancy. Meanwhile, Sara and Patricia serve as volunteers in Mozambique while Sara struggles to attune her religious beliefs with her sexual desire for Patricia. Through its diverse configurations of women-centred familial structures, *Tras la pared* establishes an empowered lesbian community of motherhood that extends far beyond biological connections. Although contemporary Spanish narratives of motherhood are expanding to include multiple representations, *Tras la pared* stands out in Spanish literature and film as a positive vision of lesbian motherhood, as the topic is not often discussed or portrayed in an affirmative way. In this chapter, I demonstrate that mother figures in *Tras la pared* reject the concept that there can be only one type of acceptable motherhood by expanding the definition through the legitimization of non-biological motherhood and the celebration of pregnant women's sexuality away from the male gaze. Although some instances of magical realism reveal vestiges of internalized homophobia in the novel's characters, the women in *Tras la pared* come together to form a non-normative motherhood community, wherein women alternate fluidly between the roles of mother (caregiver) and child (care recipient).

Tras la pared is a novel that rejects patriarchal constructions of the family through the creation of a maternal community of women, composed mainly of lesbians, where all members share caregiving responsibilities for one another. Martínez weaves various plot lines and characters through each novel in the trilogy, which begins with *No voy a disculparme* [*I'm Not Going to Apologize*] (2009) and finishes with *Autorretrato con mar al fondo* [*Self-portrait with the Sea in the Background*] (2011).[1] Mel and Carla, a lesbian couple on the brink of motherhood, are the primary focus of this analysis, although Sara and Patricia's storyline is also relevant to an understanding of the construction of a motherhood community in the novel. Mel is in her forties, while Carla is the bisexual, twenty-something daughter of Álex, a heterosexual woman who is Mel's best friend. The novel begins with Carla's realization that she is pregnant after a recent one-night encounter with a male lover that occurred before Mel and Carla officially became a couple. Carla quickly moves from surprise, panic, and shock when the "artilugio maldito con las dos rayas de color rosa, acusadoras" ["damn contraption with the two accusatory, pink-coloured lines"] (24) reveals she is pregnant, to excitement and certainty about the prospect of motherhood. Mel, initially devastated because she never wanted children, becomes accustomed to the idea of motherhood as Carla's pregnancy progresses, even finding that Carla's changing body arouses a powerful sexual desire within her. In a fantastic twist, the fetus begins to speak to Mel from within the womb. Carla cannot hear the fetus's words, believing that the stress of the pregnancy is causing Mel to become mentally unbalanced. Despite Carla's disbelief, the telepathic connection between Mel and the fetus transforms her feelings on motherhood and foments her excitement for the baby's arrival. Once she can hear the fetus, Mel is unable to have sexual relations with Carla during the pregnancy because she is disturbed by the knowledge that the fetus is constantly watching them. Carla's frustration with Mel's strange behaviour, coupled with Mel's inability to perform sexually, creates a tension in their relationship that is not resolved until the baby's birth.

Tras la pared's second storyline centres on the romantic entanglement between Sara and Patricia. Sara has been raised by nuns in a convent since she was a baby. Her dying mother, Pilar, entrusted Sara to the care of Asunción, the mother superior and Pilar's sister. Sara suspects her true relationship to Asunción is biological, although the mother superior never reveals this connection to her niece. Asunción wishes for Sara to become mother superior one day, while Sara is secretly pursuing opportunities to travel to Africa to volunteer as a nurse, desirous of a more action-filled life. Their convent shares a wall with the library where Patricia, businesswoman and serial seducer, spends her free time. Through the wall, Patricia hears of Sara's plans and becomes enamoured – almost obsessed – with Sara from listening to her voice. Patricia arranges to follow Sara by volunteering her time in Mozambique, and the two women grow close. Given her religious upbringing, Sara fights her sexual desire for Patricia while Patricia attempts to seduce her. Their relationship is complicated by the fact that Sara's touch physically burns Patricia. When Sara learns how Patricia spied on her and arranged for them to meet, she flees the country. Their storyline ends with no resolution, to be continued in *Autorretrato con mar al fondo*.

Motherhood beyond Biology

Almost all characters in *Tras la pared* describe motherhood as a fulfilling journey upon which they are eager to embark. Carla's pregnancy is unplanned, but she immediately knows that she wants to keep the baby, even though she and Mel had never discussed the possibility of children. Carla tells Mel, "[Q]uiero que sepas que es algo que siempre he querido hacer, aunque no deseaba que fuese de esta forma. Quiero tener este bebé, Mel, puede que sea mi última oportunidad de tener un hijo" ["I want you to know that it is something that I've always wanted to do, even though I didn't want it to happen like this. I want to have this baby, Mel, it could be my last opportunity to have a child"] (33). The couple had never previously discussed raising children, yet Carla asserts that she has always felt the desire to do so. For her, the only aspect of pregnancy that evokes negative emotions is the fear that Mel will reject the baby and abandon her. Mel struggles with her lack of desire to be a mother, the only character in the novel who expresses any concerns or lack of interest in mothering. When Carla informs her mother of Mel's original lukewarm reaction to the news, Álex reminds her daughter that pregnancy causes different reactions for every woman, saying, "Tienes que entender que si para ti esto supone algo tremendo en tu vida, para ella es un cataclismo que desmorona su estabilidad" ["You have to understand that, if for you this means something tremendous in your life, for her it is a cataclysm that destroys her sense of stability"] (46). Mel decides to stay with her partner and commit herself to raising Carla's biological child as a second maternal figure, coming to see the pregnancy as a positive event in their lives. Although she is unsure of what her maternal role will be in their new family, she is willing to embark on this journey with Carla, and she will establish a unique and meaningful relationship with their child. Through Mel's initial hesitancy to embrace motherhood and Álex's understanding attitude about her reaction, *Tras la pared* demonstrates that the role is not a biological imperative nor a universally inherent desire.

Neither Sara nor Patricia are mothers, but Sara's experience of being raised in the convent by a bevy of maternal figures highlights the reality that motherhood can be configured in many ways. Not her biological mother, Asunción finds that mothering Sara gives her life meaning, a strong statement for a woman who had already dedicated her life to God. After Pilar leaves Sara at the convent, Asunción's life "comenzaba a tener sentido … Adoraba a aquella niña, que se convirtió en la luz de sus pasos, su tesoro, su posesión" ["began to make sense … She adored that girl, whom she made the light of her life, her treasure, her possession"] (65). Asunción's understanding of motherhood is a very traditional one; she sees Sara as a treasured belonging, someone under her authority, to be directed as she sees fit. Asunción attempts to control Sara's future by keeping her in the convent and choosing a career path for her. The way in which she mothers Sara does not allow for many emotions; instead, Asunción establishes "con su sobrina una relación de protección autoritaria. Asunción se aseguró de que a la niña no le faltara nada, excepto la expresión de su cariño" ["with her niece a relationship of authoritative protection. Asunción assured herself that the girl would be lacking for nothing, except the expression of her affection"] (65). Sara loves and appreciates her aunt, but she benefits from the mothering of other nuns in the convent as well, especially that of Sister Teresa, who "se había encargado de compensar con creces la ausencia de manifestaciones de ternura de la madre superiora hacia su pupila, inundando a Sara de mimos y cariño" ["had taken it upon herself to more than compensate the Mother Superior's lack of manifestations of tenderness toward her pupil, overwhelming Sara with cuddles and affection"] (65). Sara is raised by a community of mothers in the convent whose complementary strengths work together to meet her needs.

Tras la pared offers a unique portrayal of motherhood not centred exclusively on biological motherhood. Sara's childhood shows that she clearly benefited from the emotional support of a multitude of mothers. In fact, one might argue that Sara was better placed with this group of non-biological mothers than she would have been with her biological mother, Pilar. *Tras la pared* does not describe Pilar's life in any detail. She ran away from home at a young age, acting out against strict, religious parents. When she leaves Sara with Asunción, she reveals that doctors have given her just months to live, asserting, "La vida no me ha tratado bien" ["Life has not treated me well"] (62). Pilar is not presented as a stable person. The many questions surrounding her life and her apparent lack of connections to a community imply that Sara has a better life because she was raised by Asunción and the stability of the convent. Mel is another mother who is not biologically related to her child; however, the close-knit relationship she has with Carla's fetus leaves no room to question Mel's motherhood. Mel has the agency to consider whether she wishes to be a mother when Carla becomes pregnant, making a conscious decision to take on this role. With exceptions like Asunción and Mel, non-biological mothering rarely comes as a surprise. Even in Asunción's case, she still made the choice to accept Sara instead of sending her to an orphanage. For Mel, the news of Carla's pregnancy is shocking, but she is not forced to commit to the pregnancy. Mel could have decided to walk away from her relationship with Carla and the motherhood role.

Even though Mel is not the baby's biological mother, she is physically connected to the infant in various ways. Shelley M. Park writes about the temptation "to define adoptive maternal bodies in terms of the bodily experiences that they lack," in an attempt to portray adoptive or non-biological mothers as "inferior to (less real than)" biological mothers (*Mothering Queerly* 61). Non-biological mothers may be physically better suited to the demanding tasks of motherhood immediately following birth, as they are not coping with post-partum emotions or managing the physical recovery required after childbirth. Park asserts that non-biological mothers "are less physically exhausted and-or traumatized from childbirth than biological mothers of infants and thus have more energy; we do not suffer the tenderness of breasts laden with milk" (73). Mel is better situated to care for the infant's needs while Carla's body heals. Essentialist descriptions of motherhood tend to focus on nursing as a bond that only biological mothers can form with their children, disregarding situations where biological mothers struggle to produce milk or simply choose not to breastfeed. Such choices or situations do not delegitimize an individual's motherhood in any way, nor should nursing be considered the only way for mothers to connect with their infants. Park elaborates on Margaret Homans's (2002) argument that "all forms of parenthood include intense bodily experiences" (*Mothering Queerly* 61), emphasizing that activities such as feeding a baby with a bottle, changing its diapers, and providing flesh-to-flesh contact are a few of the multiple ways in which infants and their parents establish a bond through physical touch.

Maternal Sexuality and the Mysterious Womb

While some descriptions of motherhood in *Tras la pared* – particularly Asunción's understanding of motherhood – are traditional, Carla and Mel are non-normative mother figures who reconfigure the role outside of the limitations of society. With her high libido, Carla rebuffs the myth of the pure, desexualized, and vulnerable pregnant body. In both social and medical spheres, pregnant women have often been relegated to a childlike role – weak and desexualized. The "implicit male bias in medicine's conception of health" has created an understanding of pregnancy as a problem that must be taken care of, perhaps a disease "with 'symptoms' that require 'treatment'" (Young 57). In patriarchal societies, women's ability to bear children is one of the "functions [that] render women vulnerable, in need of protection or special treatment, as variously prescribed by patriarchy" (Grosz 14). Therefore, the heteronormative stereotype of the pregnant woman is that of a fragile person in need of protection, "often not looked upon as sexually active or desirable" (Young 53), an image that does not reflect the portrayal of the pregnant body in *Tras la pared* or the relationship between Carla and Mel.[2]

Perceptions of the pregnant body (worldwide and in Spain, in particular) vary greatly, ranging from infantilization to sexualization of pregnant individuals. As I discuss in chapter 2, medical professionals and other members of Spanish society often infantilize pregnant individuals, in many cases leading to obstetric violence where pregnant individuals are made to feel dehumanized as the medical community denies them agency and access to information about their pregnant bodies (Mena-Tudela et al. 2). One such example is that of the late Carme Chacón, who was highly scrutinized as Spain's first woman to not only serve as Defense Minister, but to do so while pregnant (Socolovsky). The traditional, hegemonic characterization of pregnancy and motherhood in Spain produces a rhetoric that associates pregnant individuals and mothers with "[p]urity, chastity, and lack of sexuality," constructing motherhood as an asexual state of being (Nash, "Un/contested Identities" 40). While infantilization of pregnant individuals can be a way to control them, another common reaction is to sexualize pregnant individuals, rarely in a way that allows the pregnant individual to express agency. The plethora of pregnancy pornography that I mention in chapter 2 affirms that many people find pregnancy arousing. In her article "Motherhood, Sexuality, and Pregnant Embodiment," Kelly Oliver reviews several US films from the last few decades that feature pregnancy, arguing that the pregnant women in these films are portrayed as sexual objects for the male gaze, where pregnant "bodies and their desires are imagined for others, for men, for the viewing audience, and not for themselves" (765). As a whole, these films do not explore the sexual desires of pregnant individuals, nor how pregnancy affects their relationship to sexuality. Within the Spanish context, Magdalena Romera's article about sexy maternity examines the representation of pregnancy and motherhood in seven women's magazines (five Spanish and two international), finding that in many cases, maternity is now constructed as sexy (referring to the MILF trend), but requires "reparación" ["repairs"] of the maternal body after pregnancy and birth "dañan" ["damage"] women's bodies (979). In Romera's findings, Spanish magazines send the message that motherhood can be sexy, as long as the mother's body retains no physical signs of the experience of pregnancy. Perceptions of the pregnant body, therefore, vary greatly within Spanish society; whether the pregnant individual is infantilized or sexualized, heteronormative society strives to control the narrative about pregnancy.

Far from infantilized and innocent, pregnancy heightens sexual desire for both Carla and Mel in *Tras la pared*. Carla's changing body arouses Mel, even though she is conscious of the fetus's awareness of their sexual activities. A description of Carla's body during a sexual encounter with Mel emphasizes her breasts, her rounded stomach, and the "door" that guards the pleasures of paradise, as well as the entrance to the fetus's dwelling:

> Sus pechos, hinchados por el embarazo, se erguían desafiantes ante la boca de Mel y ésta no pudo evitar que su lengua, ávida, humedeciera los labios, relamiéndose ante el placer esperado. Bajo el contorno redondeado de su cintura, el delicado vello negro se ofrecía como la puerta que guardaba, celosa, los goces del paraíso. (182)

> [Her breasts, swollen from pregnancy, rose defiantly in front of Mel's mouth, and Mel could not keep her eager tongue from wetting her lips, licking themselves in anticipation of pleasure. Below the rounded contours of her waist, the delicate black hair offered itself as the door that jealously guarded the pleasures of paradise.] (182)

Mel's erotic focus on the parts of the female body altered by pregnancy reinforces the connection between maternity and sexuality. Although Mel will struggle to have sexual relations with Carla throughout her pregnancy, this is not due to a lessened sexual desire for Carla's pregnant body, as she finds her wife "enormemente sexy" ["enormously sexy"] (69). The clear sexual desire between Carla and Mel during the pregnancy – both Carla's desire as a pregnant woman and Mel's desire for her partner's pregnant body – repudiates patriarchal constructions of the pregnant body that would seek to deny any maternal sexuality not focused on pleasing the heteronormative male gaze. While the pregnant body may be sexualized, it is usually simultaneously marked as an othered body lacking in sexual agency. In her analysis of US films featuring pregnancy from the last few decades, Oliver asserts that the male gaze focuses its scopophilic desire on the sexualized pregnant body, combining lust with distaste or fear of the pregnant body "as both gross and a sex object" ("Motherhood, Sexuality" 766). Enclosed in their women-centred community, Mel and Carla are free to enjoy the sexuality of Carla's maternal body in a space devoid of any voyeuristic masculine influences.

Although Carla's maternal sexuality is a refreshing contrast to desexualized depictions of pregnant individuals, it contributes to the construction of Carla as a monstrous (m)other, described by her friends as a "bruja" ["witch"] (123) due to her magical powers. Before Carla and Mel become a couple (in *No voy a disculparme*), Carla buys a magical bottle of perfume that allows her to engage in a spectral type of sexual relationship with Mel. Whenever Carla has sex or masturbates, she first applies the perfume and imagines that she is with Mel. During these encounters, Mel also has a sexual experience – seemingly with an invisible person – where she loses control of her body, her clothes come off as if someone is removing them from her body, and she orgasms. This aspect of Carla and Mel's sexual relationship is disturbingly akin to rape with its violent overtones and lack of consent between partners. For Mel, these sexual experiences are both pleasurable and frightening because she is not fully aware of what is happening and has no idea what force is leading Mel to have "un orgasmo brutal nacido del más absoluto terror" ["a brutal orgasm born from the most absolute terror"] (*No voy* 52). Her terror comes from having a real sexual experience with a seemingly invisible figure that Mel cannot name or say no to. In a trilogy that otherwise subverts patriarchy, this detail stands out as problematic. Although Carla believes the magic comes from the perfume, Mel is convinced that Carla herself is magical, a theory supported by the telepathic communication between Mel and Carla's fetus. The figure of the witch can be a positive one, especially in women-centric communities, and there are benefits to Carla's magic. Mel does receive sexual pleasure from Carla's orgasm-inducing perfume, and she enjoys the closeness and feeling of parental legitimacy brought on by her telepathic communication with the fetus. However, the primary characterization of Carla as a witch in Martínez's trilogy is in keeping with patriarchal society's image of the dangerous and marginalized female figure. Mel's friends assert that Carla and the fetus she carries are both witches, meaning that Mel will have to "sufrirlas a las dos" ["suffer them both"] (123). Mel's magical sexual experiences cause her great terror, and even the communication with the fetus distresses her by causing a rift between Mel and Carla.

The dual nature of Carla's magic reflects societal constructions of the pregnant body, which often portray a split image. Kelly Oliver describes how the "seemingly contradictory cultural valuation of pregnancy and motherhood as good and proper for women and the abjection and debasement of the maternal body have gone hand-in-hand" ("Motherhood, Sexuality" 765). Pregnant individuals may experience the "pregnant body as being ugly and alien" (Young 53), considered by society to be both "a 'dark continent' and a 'holy vessel'" (Gould Levine, "The Female Body" 181). The womb itself is a site of mystery and at times suspicion, linked to life and death. Representing both a fearful invocation of death – unsurprisingly compared to a tomb in Freud's *The Interpretation of Dreams* – and a space of growth and creation, the womb becomes a symbol for the double-edged role of maternity. While mothers are driven to protect and nurture their children, this behaviour can become stifling and controlling. From this perspective, "[s]ometimes the womb is described not as incubator but as prison ... the fetus as 'bricked in, as it were, behind ... an impenetrable wall of flesh, muscle, bone and blood'" (Bordo 85). Martínez plays with the significance of the womb in the multifaceted title of the novel, *Tras la pared*. The wall described in the novel's title defines the boundaries of Carla's womb, which can be construed as a separation between the fetus and her mothers. The fetus is enclosed, but not imprisoned, within the womb, as she can communicate with Mel from within the womb. Mel states, "Tras aquella pared de piel crecía un ser excepcional" ["Behind that wall of skin, an exceptional being was growing"] (90), something she knows because the wall has not completely separated them. The fetus often tells Mel that she is happy, providing no indication that her stay in the womb is frightful or reminiscent of death. The wall of the womb, then, is not an absolute barrier but rather provides opportunities for communication and connection.

The fetus shares Carla's monstrous magical powers, perhaps exceeding her mother's capabilities, as she can express emotions and desires for both herself and Carla. The first time that Mel hears the fetus's voice, she says that Carla wants a yogurt, articulating Carla's desire before she can formulate the thought on her own. When Mel brings Carla the yogurt, she is surprised but happy, saying, "No te lo he llegado a pedir, pero me encanta que te adelantes a mis deseos" ["I hadn't gotten around to asking you yet, but I love that you anticipate my desires"] (60). The fetus differentiates between her own needs and Carla's. She tells Mel when she is happy, announces "Tengo sueño" ["I'm sleepy"] (71) when she is tired, and informs Mel when Carla wants to be hugged or needs to rest.

In addition to the wall of the womb, *Tras la pared*'s title refers to the wall between the library and the convent that separates Patricia and Sara. This wall, while also a barrier, provides a one-way communication;

Patricia can hear Sara, although Sara does not know Patricia is there. The convent is a symbolic womb for Sara, a limited space that has protected her while she grew and matured. While the womb of the convent has sheltered Sara, she can no more remain in the convent for her entire life than Carla's fetus could remain in her womb indefinitely. Sara has outgrown the convent and wishes to strike out on her own. An important difference between the symbolic and the real womb in *Tras la pared* is that Sara does not know that Patricia is listening to her. Patricia's obsessive behaviour becomes a problem in their relationship, causing Sara to have less agency in certain situations than Carla's fetus, who can always communicate her desires to Mel.

The image of the convent as womb is reinforced when Patricia asks Pepa, her doctor friend, to borrow her stethoscope so that she might better hear Sara's conversations on the other side of the wall. Patricia "[l]e había pedido un favor a Pepa, su ginecóloga y amiga desde hacía algunos años, y llevaba bien oculto en el bolso un estupendo fonendoscopio. Pepa no había querido hacer preguntas: únicamente se había limitado a sonreírle con picardía cuando se lo prestó. 'Úsalo bien' – le dijo con expresión reprobadora" ["had asked a favour of Pepa, her gynaecologist and friend since some years ago, and well hidden in her bag, she carried a stupendous stethoscope. Pepa had not wanted to ask questions: she had limited herself only to smile at Patricia mischievously when she lent it to her. 'Use it well' – she told her with a disapproving expression"] (25). Pepa's response to Patricia's request to borrow the stethoscope is curious. From her disapproving look and refusal to ask questions, Pepa seems to believe that Patricia wants the stethoscope for some type of mischievous purpose, such as sexual roleplaying. By comparing Sara's confinement in the convent to the time a fetus spends in the womb, *Tras la pared* once again links maternity, pregnancy, and sexuality, showing the womb's potential to shelter and stifle.

The communication between Mel and the fetus, while two-way, is also problematic, as it negatively affects Mel and Carla's relationship. Carla does not believe that Mel is communicating with the fetus. Instead, she imagines that her unplanned pregnancy is provoking a nervous reaction in Carla, growing angry with her and coercing her to see a male psychiatrist for her "problema" ["problem"] (151). The psychiatrist, "sombrío y oscuro" ["sombre and gloomy"] (151) with his "mirada inquisidora" ["inquiring look"] (151) and "voz grave e impersonal" ["serious and impersonal voice"] (151), dismissively prescribes Mel anti-anxiety medication after spending a mere hour with her. Mel does not take the medication, as she knows the fetus's voice is a magical occurrence, not the side-effect of anxiety. The encounter with the psychiatrist – one of the few male characters in the novel – demonstrates patriarchal society's desire to control and subdue the unfamiliar or unknown and the extent to which, in this case, Carla is willing to participate in patriarchal society. While *Tras la pared* ultimately constructs a woman-centred community of mothers that positively isolates itself from heteronormative dictates, the characters do, at times, adhere to the patriarchal norms that have surrounded them throughout their lives. Pregnancy is an experience often influenced by some type of masculine control, either by husbands in heterosexual relationships or by the traditionally male-dominated medical field. A pregnant individual's sexuality may also be controlled by men; her male partner "may decline to share in her sexuality, and her physician may advise her to restrict her sexual activity" (Young 53). While Carla does not face these challenges, she places her partner's mental health care in the hands of a man, believing his diagnosis over Mel's explanation of her behaviour. In this moment, Carla exhibits internalized misogyny, wishing for Mel to comport herself in a more normative way to such an extent that she prioritizes a male doctor's opinion over her wife's viewpoint. Carla effectively marginalizes Mel in a way that is reminiscent of how the medical field often deals with pregnant individuals, as the "tendency of medical conceptualization to treat pregnancy as disease can produce alienation for the pregnant woman" (Young 57). Carla later comes to believe Mel, but not before subjecting her to evaluation by the patriarchal institution. Mel forgives her partner's misogynistic doubts, relieved to be close to Carla again and harbouring no resentment about the time it took Carla to believe her.

Perhaps Carla reacts so strongly to Mel's assertion that she can communicate with the fetus because such a relationship would be taboo, signifying that the fetus not only maintains a physical and mental connection with her mothers, but also retains an awareness of their sexual activities. Maternity and sexuality intersect in the connection between the fetus and her mothers, establishing a relationship that includes taboo forms of physical contact and is threatening to patriarchal society because it falls beyond heteronormative confines. The fetus is conscious of Carla's physical, emotional, and sexual needs, while she has a telepathic connection with Mel. This awareness is shocking, primarily due to the belief that children should not have any awareness of their parents' sexual lives. Iris Marion Young's canonical work on pregnancy and sexuality states that one of the ways in which patriarchy subjugates women is through a denial of maternal and pregnant sexual desire. According to Young, patriarchy is founded on the "border between motherhood and sexuality … Freedom for women involves dissolving this separation" (85, 88). *Tras la pared* clearly shows maternal sexuality, as pregnancy only increases Carla and Mel's desire for one another. Carla's "subida hormonal ... provocaba encuentros amorosos cada vez más frecuentes y satisfactorios. Carla buscaba a Mel, la provocaba, la volvía loca, llevándola a explorar nuevos y excitantes terrenos" ["hormonal increase ... provoked even more frequent and satisfactory romantic encounters. Carla looked for Mel, she provoked her, she drove her crazy, leading her to explore new and exciting terrains"] (69–70). Their sexual life is stymied, not by lack of desire, but by Mel's awareness of the fetus's subjectivity and what might be described as her voyeuristic presence. Whenever they attempt to have sex during Carla's pregnancy, the fetus speaks to Mel, making comments such as, "Me habéis despertado. Estoy cansada" ["You two woke me up. I'm tired"] (83). This upsets Mel, impeding her ability to perform sexually. Mel is reluctant to reveal her communication with the fetus to Carla, fearing that Carla will react in a sceptical way, which she does. Carla doesn't believe Mel's explanation, instead worrying that Mel does not find her pregnant body attractive, or that Mel is panicking over the idea of motherhood. After many sexless weeks, the fetus speaks to Mel about Carla's sexual needs, telling her, "Te necesita" ["She needs you"] (96), in an attempt to unify her mothers.

While the concept of children's sexuality – or the simple idea that children understand what sexuality is – can be uncomfortable, in this case, the fetus is trying to help her mothers maintain a strong relationship. Although seen as a taboo, the fetus understands that a sexual relationship between her parents is necessary for the health of the family, and she encourages her mothers to prioritize and normalize the sexual aspects of their relationship. This is a subversion of traditional familial roles, wherein the child looks after the parents' needs and physical and sexual boundaries have become more fluid to allow for the creation of greater connections between the three.

Magical Realism and Homosexuality

The fetus's telepathic powers and the characterization of Carla as a witch because of the magical sexual control she exerts over Mel are both examples of the unique reality that Martínez creates for her characters through the use of magical realism. In his analysis of magical realism, Márquez Rodríguez asserts that magical realism transforms reality into something magical by ignoring laws of nature and logic (40, 50). Martínez uses the telepathic communication between Mel and her non-biological child to legitimize their relationship and make space for lesbian, non-biological motherhood in a society that has not always been accepting of this role. Not only in Spanish lesbian and gay literature,[3] but in queer literature worldwide, the inclusion of magical elements or the use of magical realism often plays an important role in the genre (Crisp 340). While the use of magical elements is as diverse as the authors who employ them, it is often tied to characters' exploration or acceptance of their identities, examining "the meaning of going from 'invisible' to 'visible' identities" (Faucheux 569). In *Tras la pared*, Martínez lends visibility to another enactment of motherhood through her descriptions of a lesbian maternal community. Some queer literature relies "on magical realism to suspend reality, imagine away homophobia" (Crisp 336), and present a more cheerful vision of a discrimination-free world. *Tras la pared* creates a world where the primary conflict in the story of two lesbian women having a baby together is not their sexual orientation. No one in their social circle or society condemns them for their sexual orientation or motherhood choices. Instead, the conflict comes from Carla's lack of belief in her partner's magical connection to their fetus, a situation that strains Mel and Carla's relationship but simultaneously connects Mel to her daughter in a powerful and pleasurable way. The telepathic communication is an affirmation of the mother/child connection, allowing the novel to develop a fully actualized example of a non-normative family.

While the telepathic communication between Mel and the fetus fosters an empowering, non-normative mother/child relationship between them, the novel's elements of magical realism suggest a dual and contradictory interpretation – at times positive, and in other instances highlighting characters' internalized homophobia. Mel's connection to the fetus, while legitimizing her motherhood, threatens and weakens her relationship to Carla. Mel is unable to engage in sexual relations with Carla because she hears the fetus's voice and is aware of its presence. Throughout most of the novel, Carla does not believe that Mel can communicate with the fetus, blaming her sexual distance on anxiety about their upcoming motherhood. Carla accuses Mel of not wanting to share her feelings, or perhaps of being mentally unstable, saying, "Está claro que ahora no estás por la labor de decirme lo que te pasa. O peor, si realmente te crees lo que cuentas, deberías ir a un psiquiatra. Hasta que no lo soluciones no quiero que vuelvas a tocarme" ["It's clear that right now you're not up to the task of telling me what's going on with you. Or worse, if you really believe what you're telling me, you should see a psychiatrist. Until you figure this out, I don't want you to touch me again"] (99). This conflict keeps the two women from having sex, as Mel most often hears the fetus's voice when she is about to be intimate with

Carla. No coincidence, these instances of communication are based in internalized homophobia about lesbian sex on Mel's part. Mel's repeated rejections of Carla's sexual advances mirror the self-denials of someone struggling with their sexual orientation. Mel laments her "cobardía" ["cowardice"] (92) and the fact that she is hurting Carla by not being able to tell her why she cannot have sex with her. Despite the benefits of this telepathic connection, Mel abhors the physical distance imposed between herself and Carla because of her magical link to the fetus, calling the entire situation a "pesadilla" ["nightmare"] (141).

In Patricia and Sara's relationship, moments of magical realism are also connected to their sexuality and romantic connection. Whenever Sara touches Patricia, she leaves painful burns on her skin. On the one hand, this magic is heavy-handed symbolism for the burning nature of the sexual desire between them. On the other hand, the physical burning caused by their touch can be interpreted as internalized homophobia on Sara's part, as she has struggled to suppress her homosexual desire throughout her life, due to her conservative, religious upbringing. During her years in the convent, Sara has tried to excise any sexuality from her identity: "Estudiaba con ahínco, trabajaba hasta caer agotada y, sobre todo, rezaba y rezaba, día y noche, pidiendo que el instinto sexual desapareciera de su cuerpo. La vida de oración y de retiro espiritual, incluso su trabajo en el centro sanitario, no habían sido suficientes para callar sus anhelos" ["She studied with effort, she worked until she fell down exhausted, and above all, she prayed and prayed, day and night, asking that the sexual instinct would disappear from her body. The life of prayer and spiritual retreat, including her work in the health centre, had not been sufficient to quiet her longings"] (67). When this did not work to shut down her sexuality, Sara turned to missionary work in Mozambique as the answer, hoping she could erase this part of her identity through service to others.

Patricia, a veritable don Juan, tries everything in her power to seduce Sara and break down her defences. When Patricia is close to her, Sara "sintió de pronto que ardía. Toda ella se deshacía en ascuas en los labios de Patricia, viéndose arrastrada por un río de lava que ascendía desde sus entrañas y le prendía fuego" ["soon felt that she was burning. All of her was dissolving in embers on Patricia's lips, seeing herself pulled away by a river of lava that climbed from her insides and set her on fire"] (193). While this is a romantic and sexual interpretation of the magic between them, Sara acknowledges a dangerous component to her desire. Her feeling of dissolving in embers and being swept away by a river of lava indicate a fear of losing control and giving in to what she characterizes as a dangerous sexual desire, as she feels "perdida en su íntima lucha" ["lost in her personal battle"] (193). Sara describes her desire for Patricia as the "pecado más grande del mundo" ["greatest sin in the world"] (88). When Sara does touch Patricia, she leaves "una mancha rojiza con la forma de unos dedos" ["a reddish stain in the shape of fingers"] (103) on Patricia's skin. A negative burn rather than the flames of desire, Sara's touch causes Patricia pain, a physical manifestation of her internalized fears of loving another woman.

When Sara finally gives in to her desire for Patricia, their sexual encounter happens in nature. Sara sees Patricia masturbating and flees from the house they share. Patricia pursues her into the African landscape, symbolizing Sara's need to leave civilization and its norms behind before she feels free to have a sexual relationship with another woman. The entire encounter is described in conjunction with wild or savage descriptions of the setting around them. As they kiss, "[u]n grito animal sonó en lo alto de una rama. A lo lejos, el retumbar de los tambores cargó el ambiente de deseos antiguos. Las manos de Sara se enredaron en la melena de su amiga, atrayéndola con más fuerza hacia ella" ["[a]n animal yelled high on a branch. Far away, the echoing of the drums charged the atmosphere with ancient desires. Sara's hands tangled in her friend's long hair, forcefully drawing her close"] (162–3). Sara is afraid of her sexual desire for Patricia, fearing the repercussions of letting herself lose control. Sara identifies herself in this moment as a wild horse, running free through dangerous surroundings. Sara "[s]e vio a sí misma convertida en una yegua negra, salvaje, envuelta en llamas, mientras era cabalgada por una amazona exacerbada por el éxtasis, derritiéndose como oro fundido sobre su lomo" ["[s]aw herself converted into a black mare, savage, covered in flames, while she was ridden by an Amazon heated up by ecstasy, melting like gold molten onto her flank"] (193). Only by breaking away from society and her religious upbringing is Sara able to have this experience with Patricia. While some critics might explain away the magical burning as Sara's uncontrolled lesbian desire for Patricia, the negative aspects of the burning and Sara's many attempts to silence this part of her identity necessitate a more complex analysis that takes into account her internalized homophobia.

In *Tras la pared*, magical realism marks Carla, Mel, and Sara as powerful others, to some extent celebrating their difference. The magic that all three can access serves as "a powerful metaphor of the relationship between power and the body […] whereby the body becomes the visual signifier of a person's identity as other" (Faucheux 569). These protagonists are othered by their unique abilities, an experience that at times reflects the homophobic messages from society that they have internalized, while at other times provides them the basis for creating a better, more magical space for their relationships within their world.

Construction of a Motherhood Community

Despite their potential connections to internalized homophobia, the elements of magical realism in *Tras la pared* help to establish the novel's women-centred community, which is vital to the construction of motherhood embodied by Martínez's characters. The depiction of motherhood as a role that seeks unity, connection, and community is important, as so often, critics and scholars view childbirth and motherhood as a series of separations. In "Stabat Mater," Julia Kristeva elaborates on the ways in which childbirth elucidates the separations and connections between mother and child. Childbirth begins a process of rupturing that establishes the child as an "other" who must construct her identity as a separate entity. Kristeva questions exactly what ties mother and child together after they no longer share the same body, asserting:

> A mother is a continuous separation, a division of the very flesh. And consequently a division of language – and it has always been so. Then there is this other abyss that opens up between the body and what had been its inside: there is the abyss between the mother and the child. What connection is there between myself, or even more unassumingly between my body and this internal graft and fold, which, once the umbilical cord has been severed, is an inaccessible other? (Kristeva, *The Portable Kristeva* 324)

Kristeva expands on the idea that the most important aspect of mother/child relationships does not come from a biological link. In her personal experience of motherhood, Kristeva highlights the importance of emotions in creating a connection between mother and child, ranging from all-consuming anguish to a "demented jouissance" or "opaque joy" that binds mother and child (*The Portable Kristeva* 325, 320). Such a perspective on motherhood certainly widens the definition of the word, as a woman does not need to be a biological mother to have an emotional connection with a daughter, as evidenced in *Tras la pared*.

Within Mel and Carla's family formation, the use of telepathy serves as a validation of lesbian co-parenting and proves that biological requirements are not necessary for motherhood. Telepathy has been defined as "an occult force that troubles known categories by forging new and inventive associative relations" (Marder 50), such as a non-normative construction of family. Through telepathy, Mel enjoys a level of connection with the fetus that not even the biological mother has with her growing child, showing that Mel's emotional relationship to the fetus is just as valid as Carla's physical link to the fetus. Mel quickly comes to accept and value this magical relationship, confident in the fact that she "[h]abía oído claramente *la voz*. Lo que no comprendía era por qué Carla no la oía: al fin y al cabo era su hija y la llevaba dentro. Se suponía que durante el embarazo existía siempre una conexión especial entre la madre y el bebé" ["[h]ad clearly heard *the voice*. What she did not understand was why Carla couldn't hear it: after all, it was her daughter and she carried her inside her body. One would suppose that during pregnancy a special connection always existed between the mother and baby"] (84). As the non-biological mother, Mel had been worried about how to approach her maternal role, but the fact that only she can hear the fetus's voice creates a special bond between the two, reassuring her that there will be a unique place for her in the child's life. Through their telepathic connection, Mel learns months before the sonogram that the baby will be a girl, information to which Carla does not have access. This non-normative physical and mental relationship between Mel and the fetus brings them closer as a family. Telepathy can transform "its magic into a form of revelatory power that claims the capacity to produce new discourses of truth and knowledge" (Marder 50). Here, telepathy affirms the creation of a non-normative family.

Mel and Carla's relationship is strengthened as they come to see themselves as a legitimate family, each with a unique connection to the fetus that Carla carries. They form a family outside of the limitations of heteronormative society, in this way avoiding what Luce Irigaray views as the patriarchal family's main function as "the privileged locus of women's exploitation" (142). Another method of rejecting patriarchal constraints is found in *Tras la pared*'s construction of lesbian motherhood through the minimization of the male role in the process of childbearing and rearing. When Carla realizes that she is pregnant, she feels that she and Mel have created the baby; although she was physically having sex with Jean-Marc (an ex-lover), she was thinking of Mel, who was also having a sexual experience, due to Carla's magical perfume. When Carla tells Mel of her pregnancy, she says, "Lo que quiero decirte es que realmente este hijo lo hice contigo. Él sólo fue el vehículo, pero tú estuviste allí todo el tiempo" ["What I want to tell you is that really, I made this child with you. He was only the vehicle, but you were there the whole time"] (32). This connection between Carla and Mel is a way of legitimizing their lesbian motherhood together, creating an emotional and sexual connection that Carla never had with Jean-Marc, despite their physical union.

In *Tras la pared*, Martínez reverses the patriarchal attempt to control the female body through a similarly problematic appropriation of the male body. Carla uses Jean-Marc's masculine body only for its reproductive purposes, an action she finds empowering but that nonetheless objectifies Jean-Marc. Carla never tells Jean-Marc that he has impregnated her, seeing his role in the process as completed. Her mindset is reminiscent of the "theory of the maternal imagination," an idea prevalent in Europe from the sixteenth to the early eighteenth century that asserted a pregnant woman's desires and passions "were capable of *directly* inscribing themselves upon the body of the fetus" (Kukla 15). Although this type of inscription was viewed as negative, thought to produce "deformities and monstrosities that retained the semantic content of the original impression" (Kukla 15), Carla takes a negative assumption about pregnancy and twists it into an empowering personal conviction, as her sexual thoughts about Mel during intercourse with Jean-Marc allow her to believe that she has created a child with her lesbian partner. Carla uses her magical powers to legitimize Mel's maternity in her mind, yet another way of creating a non-normative family.

Interchangeability of Motherhood Roles

Beginning with Carla's pregnancy, she and Mel create an exclusively woman-centred community of mother and daughter figures – linked either symbolically or biologically – who support one another; at times, these women rotate between mother and daughter roles interchangeably. The type of community created in Martínez's novel is reminiscent of Adrienne Rich's lesbian continuum, a community of women who have bonded together in defiance of phallocentric, patriarchal society, similar to Kristeva's herethics or Ferguson's definition of the erotic.[4] In Rich's words:

> I mean the term *lesbian continuum* to include a range – through each woman's life and throughout history – of woman-identified experience, not simply the fact that woman has had or consciously desired genital sexual experience with another woman. If we expand it to embrace any more forms of primary intensity between and among women, including the sharing of a rich inner life, the bonding against male tyranny, the giving and receiving of practical and political support ... we begin to grasp breadths of female history and psychology. (252)

Tras la pared contains additional mother/daughter relationships beyond the one constructed between Mel, Carla, and the fetus. Carla has a strong connection to her mother, Álex, a heterosexual woman and ally who forms part of the motherhood community.[5] Álex celebrates the special bond she has with Carla, recalling the first time she held her daughter and how she realized "ese sapito arrugado que fue parte de su cuerpo, algo cambió en su interior. Ya nada en su vida sería igual. Un hilo de conexión las uniría para siempre" ["that little wrinkled toad was part of her body, something inside her changed. Nothing in her life would ever be the same. A thread of connection would unite them forever"] (*No voy* 44). Mel and Carla continue the circle of female community by naming their daughter Alejandra in honour of Álex. In fact, the fetus tells Mel of her desire to be named Alejandra, showing the intergenerational extension of the community of women. *Tras la pared* is replete with examples of positive, women-centred community building. As Carla and Mel experience the journey of pregnancy, they have several supportive women friends who encourage them along the way. Eva and María are two of Mel's closest friends, who support her even when Carla thinks Mel is lying about hearing the fetus's voice. Their names, symbolic of two of Christianity's iconic mother figures, further cement the bond between motherhood and community formation.

The interchangeability of the symbolic mother/daughter roles between women is an integral element of the motherhood community. During Carla's pregnancy, the fetus cares for Carla by expressing Carla's needs to Mel, in the same way that a mother might anticipate a child's needs. The fetus understands Carla's emotional requirements, as well as physical needs, like hunger and exhaustion. The fetus warns Mel when the time for her birth has arrived by saying "Voy a salir" ["I'm coming"] (195) before Carla is aware that childbirth has begun. The symbolic mother/daughter relationship between Mel and Carla is another representation of the fluid nature of maternal roles. Kristeva asserts that "the relation to the mother is always, in some way, reproduced between women," a statement reflected in the relationship between these women (Gallop, *The Daughter's Seduction* 116). Fifteen years older than Carla, Mel could potentially be her mother. The fact that Mel is good friends with Álex and has watched Carla grow up adds a familial (and perhaps incestual) element to their story. In *No voy a disculparme*, when Carla first returns to Spain after a long stay in Paris, Mel recalls Carla as a child, saying, "La recordaba como una niña inteligente, encantadora y algo tímida, a la que había querido como a una hermana pequeña necesitada de protección" ["I remembered her as an intelligent child, charming and somewhat timid, whom I had loved like a little sister in need of protection"] (23). While Mel describes a familial bond between the two women, she also sees Carla as a desirable sexual partner. She ignores the confines of patriarchal society in her unwillingness to divorce the familial from the sexual. In the same way, Carla seems to view Mel as an acceptable substitute for the parental figures in her life. As she thinks back to when she left Spain as a young teen, her biggest challenge was leaving Mel behind: "El hecho de irse de España supuso para ella, en aquellos momentos, algo mucho más terrible que la muerte de su padre. Dejar de ver a la amiga de su madre fue lo que realmente dejó su vida sin sentido" ["The reality of leaving Spain meant for her, in those moments, something much more terrible than the death of her father. Leaving her mother's friend was what really left her life without meaning"] (*No voy* 21). This statement shows the depth of the connection between the two women. On another level, Carla's desire for Mel could be interpreted as a sexual desire for her own mother. Although Álex and Mel were never sexually intimate, Carla imagines that they might have been, telling Álex, "¿Sabes? Hubo un momento en que pensé que habíais sido amantes" ["You know what? There was a moment when I thought that you two had been lovers"] (*No voy* 32). *Tras la pared* blurs the boundaries of mother/daughter relationships and identities to challenge heteronormative limits.

Martínez's novels create a community of women-centred narratives, a goal of many lesbian-identified texts, as suggested by Rodríguez Pérez: "In general, lesbian critical reading proposes the blurring of boundaries between self and other, subject and object, lover and beloved, as the lesbian moment in any text" (97). Although Sara and Patricia are lovers, they care for each other in ways that are at times reminiscent of a mother/daughter relationship. During their time in Mozambique, Patricia becomes very ill with dengue fever. Sara devotes herself to caring for Patricia, much like a mother might. In *Tras la pared*, female and maternal energy and love are at no time directed toward the phallus, which allows women to create strong communities focused only on each other, where they can alternately fulfil the role of mother or daughter for one another as needed.

A unique aspect of motherhood revealed in *Tras la pared* is the importance of the relationship between two (or more) mothers, a connection that must be nurtured and cared for so that all relationships in the family can thrive. Park makes insightful points about the importance of the mother/mother relationship when it comes to the family and the motherhood role. Park insists that a "queer account of mothering needs to explore the third arm of the mother-mother-child triangle, namely the affective relationship between the mothers themselves" (*Mothering Queerly* 11). Park considers the Oedipal question, asserting that a family with two mothers does not allow the child to identify with just one parent: first the mother and then after rejecting her, the father. Rather, "such families (minimally) triangulate the mother-child relationship, thus propelling us away from a romanticized version of mother-child love as a dyadic relationship of mutual recognition" (*Mothering Queerly* 10). Park considers how family constructions could be theorized or lived differently if the bond between mother and child was not the all-encompassing focus of the family, but if instead the erotic or romantic relationship between mothers was more highly prioritized (*Mothering Queerly* 12). In *Tras la pared*, the family unit constructed by Mel, Carla, and Alejandra creates space to value and foster Mel and Carla's relationship, in addition to their relationship with their child. The mothers and daughter acknowledge maternal sexuality as a good and necessary element of a healthy family. Mel and Carla are better at the motherhood role because their relationship with Alejandra, and the motherhood community they are part of, gives them the space to focus on their relationship and not be subsumed by the maternal aspects of their identities.

Tras la pared concludes with the birth of Alejandra, delivered by Sara, who has returned from Mozambique, while her relationship status with Patricia remains unclear. The novel does not offer a neat resolution of the conflict between these two women, although the third novel in the trilogy will continue to follow Patricia and Sara's lives. Sara's presence at Alejandra's birth connects the two story lines and emphasizes the importance of women-centred relationships. Alejandra begins her life with a strong community of women and mother figures that is established at her birth. Despite the internalized homophobia hinted at by the examples of magical realism in the novel, the overall vision of motherhood in *Tras la pared* is multiple, expansive, and inclusive. Characters in the novel create an empowered definition of motherhood wherein maternal sexuality is not overlooked or denied, pregnant individuals are not infantilized or sexualized for the benefit of the male gaze, and women move fluidly between mother and daughter roles. The development of an all-inclusive narrative of Spanish motherhoods that examines both hetero- and homosexual motherhoods faces various challenges, but at the very least, Martínez's trilogy provides an example of mothering differently, inviting conversation and comparison with many other types of mothering. Through a normalization of non-biological motherhood, maternal sexuality, and fluidity of maternal roles in a motherhood community, *Tras la pared* suggests a version of motherhood that offers agency to mothers and daughters, who are able to both care for and be cared for by one another.

Chapter Five

Beyond the Biological Family

Biological reproduction, although not necessary for familial formation and certainly not the only way that Spanish families acquired children, was lauded as part of the idealized vision of the traditional Spanish nuclear family under Franco's regime. The National Catholic rhetoric that equated biological parenthood with personal fulfilment of destiny and good citizenship pervades the contemporary Spanish collective consciousness. This is evident through the pronatalist messaging (which advocates for and encourages higher birthrates) that can easily be found in contemporary Spanish society and culture. Although – or perhaps because – Spain currently has one of the lowest birthrates in the world (Zecchi 147), many contemporary Spanish films contain pronatalist messages about motherhood. While decreasing natality rates are caused by both partners, in the article "All about Mothers," Barbara Zecchi analyses several contemporary Spanish films that present "the birth of a child as the only meaningful event in a woman's life" (158). Such a focus on the supposedly inherent naturalness and correctness of the biological familial unit leaves little space for dialogue about alternative familial structures, which have always existed in Spanish society, literature, and film. Luisa Castro's short story "El amor inútil" ["Useless Love"] (1997) and Esther Tusquets's *Varada tras el último naufragio* [*Stranded after the Last Shipwreck*] (1980) reveal two examples of non-biological parenthood, wherein the parental figures do not adopt the children but form affective relationships with them and take on the responsibilities of caring for them. In their enactments of parenthood, these parental figures blur boundaries between traditional gender roles and obscure the limits between the roles of parent, friend, and lover. While Tusquets's novel may seem like an odd selection for inclusion in this book due to its earlier publication date in comparison with the other novels and films I analyse, I chose Tusquets's work because it is part of the Spanish canon, in addition to the many thematic connections between *Varada* and "El amor inútil." Readers may not be surprised that a more unconventional text (like *¿Por qué me comprasteis un walkie talkie si era hijo único?*) presents alternative versions of Spanish family formation, but I wish to emphasize that the non-normative nature of contemporary Spanish families can be found in a diverse range of texts and films, including canonical ones. The spectrum of non-normative familial formation is not an alternative topic, but rather one that is also found within mainstream Spanish literature, film, and society.

"El amor inútil" and *Varada* challenge assumptions about biological parenthood through an examination of alternative, non-biological parent/child relationships. This chapter will demonstrate how these texts repudiate biologically driven, pronatalist definitions of the family. I will assert that the children in these texts have unhealthy ties with their biological family members and show how these children form non-normative relationships with their non-biological parental figures (who experiment with the traditional gender roles associated with childcare) that are supportive at times and unhealthy or incestuous at other times. Finally, I will describe the parental figures' attempts to create alternate versions of themselves in their children as doppelgängers, establishing a cyclical parent/child relationship that ultimately exposes the limitations of the parent/child relationship. I use the concept of the doppelgänger, generally understood as a physical double, to analyse emotional similitude between parental figures and children, as part of an examination of how even non-biological parents seek to replicate their identity within their children.[1] While assessing parental affinity toward moulding their children into personal doppelgängers, Castro's and Tusquets's non-biological parental characters expose the confines of traditional motherhood and fatherhood, critiquing the pressure for parents to stay within these rigid roles. The parent/child relationships in these texts end in dissolution of the family; however, they present two examples of non-normative family formation that have nothing to do with biological reproduction.

In Luisa Castro's "El amor inútil," the protagonist Alberto experiments with his performance of parenthood. The short story focuses on Alberto's relationship with his good friends Fidel and Nora and their newborn daughter Fidelia, providing readers with an example of the recurring theme of "las relaciones padre-hija, hombre maduro-mujer joven" ["father-daughter, older man-young woman relationships"] (Encinar 154) found in Castro's work. As Fidelia's godfather, Alberto begins to take over Fidelia's daily care, exhibiting a strong inclination toward nurturing. Alberto takes Fidelia for walks in the park every week, not correcting strangers who assume that she is his biological child. Because of their infrequent excursions with Fidelia, Fidel and Nora are seen as imposters in the eyes of onlookers in the park who presume Alberto's parental legitimacy. The narrator affirms this when the "verdaderos padres sustituyeron en el paseo de Fidelia al padre supuesto y algún curioso tuvo que morderse la lengua para no indagar más de lo que aconseja la discreción entre desconocidos" ["true parents substituted the supposed parent on Fidelia's walk and curious people had to bite their tongues so as not to inquire more than discretion permits among strangers"] (142). When Fidelia turns three months old, Alberto realizes that he is in love with her and wants to eventually marry her. He shares his feelings with Fidel and Nora, afterwards choosing to move away. Alberto does not see her again until he invites Fidelia and her boyfriend to celebrate her eighteenth birthday at the hotel he manages in Palma de Mallorca with his wife (who is only mentioned briefly). They only spend a weekend together, but Fidelia immediately feels a strong connection to her godfather upon reconnecting after so many years. The short story neither describes their sexual encounter nor explains how they avoid Alberto's wife and Fidelia's boyfriend in order to be together, but two weeks after returning from her visit, Fidelia is pregnant. Her boyfriend is never mentioned again, and no one suspects or suggests that he could be the father. The narrator confirms that the baby is Alberto's, even though Fidelia does not reveal this information to her parents, who assume Alberto is the father but do not attempt to confront him. The story ends as, from afar, Alberto watches Fidelia with their son in the park, never attempting to communicate with her again.

Alberto's parenthood offers an interesting counterpoint to that of Eva, a maternal figure in Esther Tusquets's *Varada tras el último naufragio*.[2] The novel's main plot revolves around Elia, a middle-aged woman undergoing a trial separation from her husband Jorge after learning that he no longer loves her.[3] Elia travels without Jorge to the summer house the couple shares with her best friend Eva and Eva's husband Pablo. While it is one of the novel's subplots, Eva's relationship with Clara, an often overwrought orphaned teenager, is the aspect of the novel I will focus on in this chapter, as it provides an engaging example of non-biological parenthood.[4] Eva meets Clara after an unidentified character takes the girl to Eva's office so that she can seek legal counsel to escape from her current living situation with a presumably abusive aunt and uncle. Eva takes Clara on as a summer project, unofficially adopting her and relocating her to the summer house. Eva – accustomed to mothering all types of needy individuals – finds that she is unable to focus her edifying energies on Clara, nor can she appreciate or accept Clara's overwhelming adoration toward her. Instead, Eva is sidetracked by suspicions that Pablo is cheating on her. When Clara tells Eva that she witnessed Pablo in the couple's bed having sex with a teenage girl, Clara unwittingly provokes the unravelling of her mother/daughter relationship with Eva. Full of jealousy and rage and unable to disassociate Clara from the upsetting news that she has delivered, Eva expels her from the house permanently, deciding to forgive Pablo and move on with her marriage. *Varada* and "El amor inútil" end with familial disbanding and the separation of non-biological parents and children.

Non-Biological Parenthood as a Challenge to Reprosexuality

Parental figures in both texts are not biologically connected to the children for whom they perform parenthood, revealing another potential familial configuration along the spectrum of Spanish familial formation. Best described as non-biological parental figures, there is no official adoption in either narrative, even though both parental figures assume responsibility for the children's physical and emotional needs. While it appears that Castro and Tusquets's parental characters genuinely attempt to care for their "adopted" children, parental figures in both narratives espouse a certain level of naivety regarding these relationships. To care for a child without adopting her disregards social norms and laws about childcare. Failure to recognize the social fragility – or even illegitimacy – of such a connection may be related to the ultimate failure of these relationships.

In Spain, non-biological parenthood occurs in a variety of configurations, but research on non-biological parenthood focuses on adoption. Starting with the Constitution of 1978 and throughout the Transition in the 1980s, Spanish law modified codes relating to adoption policies and established children as a legal group with particular needs and requiring specific protections. Spanish law also protects parental rights, which cannot be revoked as a "punishment to the parent" but only "for the benefit and interest of the child" (Segado et al. 160). Due to the importance that Spanish society places on blood-based familial connections (an attitude that is slowly shifting towards individualism, according to sociologist Inés Alberdi in her sociological study titled *La nueva familia española*), the numbers of inter-country adoptions in Spain are low and have progressively decreased. Inter-country adoptions and foster care placements that do occur in Spain are primarily kinship placements (70 per cent of foster care placements in Spain), a higher rate than other European countries (Segado et al. 166). After becoming a legal option in Spain in the mid-1990s, the country experienced a 273 per cent increase in international adoptions between 1998 and 2004 (Selman 578). The Spanish social work system, legal structure, and society overwhelmingly view heterosexual couples who cannot biologically have their own children as the "default candidates for adoption while all other configurations are treated as problems by the system" (Poveda et al. 37). Single-parent adoptions can be challenging in Spain, as psychologists' and social workers' training documents, research reports, and interviews often indicate a negative stigma (at times unconscious) against single parents, even though post-adoption assessments give no indication that single-parent adoptions are detrimental to the child or worse than dual-parent adoptions in any way. Single-parent adopters in Spain are often paired with more "complicated" children, such as older or special-needs children (Poveda et al. 35–7, 46). Queer individuals or couples who wish to adopt in Spain also face many obstacles, despite the fact that Spain was the third country in Europe to legalize gay marriage in 2005, the same year that the Spanish government legalized gay adoption (Messina and D'Amore 64). Little research has been conducted on queer adoptive parents in Spain, but existing studies show that they experience internal struggles, such as self-doubt when comparing the family they will construct to heteronormative societal standards, as well as external challenges, including potential discrimination from birth families (Messina and D'Amore 69, 73). The most recent research in Spain suggests a decrease in international adoptions, due in part to Spain's economic crisis, long wait times, restrictions from other countries against queer adoption, and an increase in international surrogacy (a trend hard to track because surrogacy is illegal in Spain) (Álvarez "In Spain, International"). While the way in which non-biological parenthood occurs has changed and will most likely continue to do so, Spain has a long history of non-biological parenthood.[5]

While lived familial experiences often tell a different tale, Spanish media and society contain many examples of pronatalist messages, including increased prominence of pregnant bodies in commercials and magazines, as well as talk shows and newspapers that promote having more children earlier in life (Zecchi 147–8). Some pronatalists and similar-minded groups seek to invalidate the legitimacy of adoptive parents by ascribing a negative otherness to the adoptive role, defining "motherhood as a natural, biological phenomenon including both a gestational and genetic connection to one's child. From this perspective, there is something queer about any adoptive maternal body – a body that poses as, yet is not a 'real' mother" (Park, "Adoptive Maternal Bodies" 202). In this way, parental bodies that cannot – or do not – biologically reproduce a child represent an anomaly, breaking with reproductive norms. Although the quote from Park focuses on maternal bodies, the implications of otherness extend to paternal bodies as well, and the heteronormative expectations linking masculinity to the ability to engender a child.

Any variation of parental identity that is not biological opposes "reprosexuality," a concept coined by Michael Warner to describe a set of values anchored within the confines of heterosexuality and a sense of fulfilment achieved through biological reproduction. According to Warner, reprosexuality complements "repro-narrativity," which espouses the belief that "our lives are somehow made more meaningful by being embedded in a narrative of generational succession" (7). Reprosexuality and repro-narrativity offer only one perspective on how individuals should perform parenthood. Every parental figure, biological or not, engages in a performance of parenthood that varies depending on the gender roles and social norms that have been ingrained upon her or his psyche as a member of any given society. Just as Simone de Beauvoir asserts that an individual is not born a woman but becomes one, Judith Butler describes gender as a fluid identity, maintained through repetition of actions. In Butler's words:

> gender is in no way a stable identity or locus of agency from which various acts proceede [sic]; rather, it is an identity tenuously constituted in time – an identity instituted through a *stylized repetition of acts*. Further, gender is instituted through the stylization of the body and, thence, must be understood as the mundane way in which bodily gestures, movements, and enactments of various kinds constitute the illusion of an abiding gendered self. ("Performative Acts" 519)

According to these arguments, gender is performed through actions; if individuals or groups change their actions, so will the meaning of gender. It therefore stands to reason that, because parental identity is intricately interwoven with sexual identity, individuals come to understand the parental role that society has foisted upon them as part of a larger performance of gender. Just as individuals may modify their performances of gender, so might they adapt their enactments of parenthood.

Whether or not they are aware of doing so, parental figures are constantly performing, because "family situations are comprised of roles (e.g. husband, wife, mother, father, child) that become performed, both for a familial audience, and a wider social audience (at which point the familial audience becomes complicit in creating a performance)" (Lauster 545). Adoptive or non-biological parents are likely to be more mindful of their performance, as "adoptive mothers know that their status as mothers depends on mastery of the social script for good mothering; the contingency of their status as mothers is largely invisible to biological mothers, who embody the norms regulating their status as mothers" (Park, "Adoptive Maternal Bodies" 211). Performances of parenthood must be repeated, much like performances of gender, which Butler affirms "is not a singular 'act' or event, but a ritualized production, a ritual reiterated under and through constraint, under and through the force of prohibition and taboo, with the threat of ostracism and even death controlling and compelling the shape of the production" (*Bodies* 95). While Castro and Tusquets's characters are continuously cognizant of how society expects them to perform gender, sexuality, and parenthood, as well as the stakes for performances that deviate from expected social norms, they are often estranged from these scripts. In Castro's and Tusquets's texts, parental figures break from normative enactments of parenthood in their attempts to reproduce themselves in a child figure. Their performances of parenthood exist as part of a diverse spectrum of potential enactments of parenthood, playing with the notion of stereotypically gendered parental roles, as Alberto embraces stereotypically maternal roles and Eva at times performs her parenthood with many of the characteristics attributed to a traditional father figure.

Unhealthy Biological Ties

Clara and Fidelia are fitting examples of children in non-normative relationships with parental figures because, although they readily and freely give themselves to their non-biological parents, they nonetheless have biological relatives who are involved in their lives. In "El amor inútil," Fidelia feels linked to Alberto by an intense familial bond stronger than her connection to her biological parents. While Fidelia's biological parents are passive and distant around their daughter, Alberto is obsessed with Fidelia, compelled to minister to her every need. He admits, "Sueño con cuidarla, con respetarla" ["I dream about taking care of her, respecting her"] (140). Their attachment is not severed by time and distance. When Fidelia sees her godfather after sixteen years of separation, she feels more strongly drawn to him than to Fidel and Nora. The narrator reiterates Fidelia's feelings of connection to Alberto, stating, "Escuchándole hablar de su infancia, de sus padres y de ella misma cuando era pequeña, aquel hombre al que no conocía de nada le resultaba más próximo que toda su familia, incluido también el joven que la acompañaba" ["Listening to him talk about her infancy, her parents, and herself when she was little, that man whom she didn't know at all became closer to her than her family, including the young man who accompanied her"] (143). For Fidelia, Alberto fulfils the roles of father, mother, and romantic interest.

Fidelia's and Clara's relationships with their non-biological parents present a challenge to reprosexuality through the negation of the need to construct one's identity based on biological ties. Many individuals feel the impulse to seek self-definition through links to biological parents. Adopted or orphaned children often pursue knowledge of their biological parents as well, even when they are happily incorporated members of an adoptive family (Sobol and Cardiff 477). In contrast, Clara and Fidelia's rejection of biological ties refutes the supremacy of emotional ties between biological parent and child, proving that other, non-normative, parent/child configurations can provide a bond of equal or greater meaning.

The biologically related characters in these texts exhibit a distant or even abusive attitude toward Fidelia and Clara. Regardless of genetic ties, these individuals are participating in only the most distant and unengaged performance of parenthood. A healthy, connected parental performance is a decision that each parent must continuously and consciously make, as "[e]ven biological parents must make an active choice to keep and rear the children they bear" (Homans 266). Fidel and Nora maintain distance between themselves and Fidelia, happy to concede parental tasks to Alberto. After admitting his romantic feelings about Fidelia to her parents, Alberto stops visiting the family's home, leaving Fidel and Nora disconcerted about their parental abilities. During this time, "Fidel y Nora intentaron construir una normalidad que les protegiera de sus pensamientos, pero todas las conversaciones acababan en desesperados malentendidos y advertencias crispadas sobre cómo bañar a Fidelia o de qué modo era mejor dormirla" ["Fidel and Nora tried to construct a normality that would protect them from their thoughts, but all their conversations ended up in desperate misunderstandings and tense warnings about how to bathe Fidelia or what was the best way to get her to sleep"] (140). Although society would concede parental authority to Fidel and Nora as biological parents, they are less prepared than Alberto to care for their daughter.

Despite the fact that Alberto has expressed romantic feelings toward a three-month-old – no doubt alarming news for most parents – Fidel and Nora ask Alberto to return to their house, ostensibly out of concern for Fidelia. Nora tells Alberto that they do not wish to deprive Fidelia of her godfather, expressing the "alivio" ["relief"] (140) she feels just hearing his voice again. Nora and Fidel justify their decision to not sever ties with Alberto by alleging that "en ningún caso podemos obligar a nuestra hija a vivir en una burbuja" ["in no way can we obligate our daughter to live in a bubble"] (141). Perplexed in their parental role, Fidel and Nora ignore the paedophilic nature of an adult man who harbours romantic feelings for an infant. Although he does not act on his feelings nor indicate a desire to do so until she is older, Alberto expresses his sexual or romantic desire for Fidelia while she is an infant, beginning many of his monologues to her with the phrase, "Cuando seas mayor ..." ["When you are older ..."] (141), the ellipses signifying the implied sexual and romantic ways in which their relationship will change. The repetition of this phrase shows his fixated desire toward Fidelia. Fidelia's parents encourage Alberto to reinstate his visits so they might have someone around to perform the responsibilities of parenthood. Not only are Nora and Fidel not alarmed by Alberto's confession, they seem to approve of a romantic or sexual relationship between Alberto and their daughter once she is older. When Alberto explains that he must move away so that Fidelia can eventually see him as a potential romantic partner and not just a father figure, Nora and Fidel agree with his plan, "convencidos como él de que sólo la familiaridad impedía a su hija el enamoramiento" ["convinced like him that only familiarity would impede their daughter from falling in love with him"] (142). Fidelia's biological parents seem to take comfort in the idea of Alberto marrying their daughter, allowing them to further negate any responsibility for her. Their enactment of parenthood demonstrates that some individuals have no innate ability or desire to parent, while others can learn how to fulfil the role regardless of biological ties.

In *Varada*, Clara is another child who feels an intense emotional connection with a non-biological parental figure rather than connecting with the adults to whom she is biologically related. She is an orphan, but she lives with her biological aunt and uncle, to whom she feels no filial or emotional connection. In fact, Clara describes her aunt as an "impostora" ["imposter"] (62) who is enacting an "innoble parodia de la maternidad y del afecto" ["ignoble parody of maternity and affection"] (64). Clara's account of her uncle is yet more negative, portraying him as a monstrous, predatory individual, envisioning him as the:

> hombre sapo, tan bajo y tan sucio y tan feo, viscoso el cuerpo lleno de escamas, que ha pretendido también jugar a ser su padre, que lo llame papá, y cómo podría ser su padre ese ser procedente de otros mundos que no se le parece en nada, en nada, por más que la siga como un perrillo fiel, y la mire con sus ojos pequeños, sanguinolentos, y la acaricie torpe con sus zarpas húmedas y duras. (64)

[toad man, so low and so dirty and so ugly, the viscous body full of scales, who has also pretended to play at being her father, whom she called dad, and how could that being originating from other worlds who wasn't like her at all, at all, be her father, no matter how much he followed her around like a faithful little dog, and he looked at her with his little eyes, bloody, and he caressed her clumsily with his damp, hard paws.] (64)

The lascivious gaze and caresses of her uncle, in addition to his animalization as "el hombre sapo" ["the toad man"], point toward the probability of sexual abuse, although it is never explicitly stated. Clara's perception of her family life must be interpreted with a certain amount of caution, as this "chiquilla medio loca" ["half crazy little girl"] (71) provides an unreliable narration of her own life, wavering between reality and the fantasy worlds she creates, perhaps at times unable to distinguish between the two. As Eva takes Clara from her aunt and uncle's home, Clara's aunt warns Eva that, "no conseguirá usted nada, se está equivocando usted de medio a medio, le repito que es una chica mentirosa, una mocosa llena de malicia que la ha embaucado a usted con sus embustes, porque quién sabe lo que le habrá contado de nosotros" ["you won't achieve anything, you are making a mistake from start to finish, I repeat that she is a lying girl, a brat full of malice who has swindled you with her lies, because who knows what she will have told you about us"] (62). Despite Clara's affinity for embellishing the truth, the family narrative that she presents must be based in truth, as it seems unlikely that she would be taken to Eva's office in search of relocation if she were not in a difficult living situation. Clara is desperate to recreate her identity by linking herself to Eva and forgetting her problematic home life.

The relationship Clara hopes to establish with Eva is not as easily achievable as she would like, due to Eva's distracted, at times impatient, performance of motherhood. The distant and cold mother juxtaposed with the absent father is a theme throughout Tusquets's work. Negative descriptions of mother/daughter relationships have autobiographical roots for Tusquets, as the writer admits to an unhappy childhood and an unsatisfactory relationship with her mother (Ichiishi 18).[6] According to Stacey Dolgin Casado, "Healing the emotional scars left by an unsatisfactory mother-daughter relationship" is one of the "primary tasks that the collective female psyche of Tusquets's protagonists must perform successfully in order to propel into motion the psychological development" (17). Various characters in *Varada* suffer through unhappy familial relationships in their childhood. Elia remembers her mother as "una madre prepotente, espléndida, invasora" ["an overbearing, splendid, invading mother"] (173), while her father has been replaced by a gaping absence in her memories, converting her childhood into a "niñez sin padre [y una] carencia básica de afecto" ["childhood without a father (and a) basic lack of affection"] (173). Likewise, Eva's parents did not occupy themselves with the care of their children, expecting Eva to look after herself and her siblings. Clara, the orphan who desires nothing more than the comfort of a mother's love, has never experienced parental solicitude.

In addition to the physical and emotional absence of parental figures in *Varada*, Elia and Eva's biological children hover at the novel's periphery, vague and shadowy beings with whom the narrator is unconcerned. Elia's son Daniel is away at summer camp, but even when he is physically present, Elia rarely thinks about him. As Eva states, "ni de su hijo parece que [Elia] se acuerde este verano, ni de su propio hijo se ha responsabilizado en realidad jamás" ["it seems that Elia doesn't even remember her son this summer, in reality, she hasn't ever taken responsibility for her own son"] (125). Eva and Pablo have children of their own who are summering with them, although the narration offers no description of these children, neglecting to specify how many exist, what their names or ages are, or any identifying characteristics about them. This numberless amalgam of children "sólo comparecen puntuales para recibir provisiones en forma de enormes bocadillos o para caer rendidos en la cama" ["only appear punctually to receive provisions in the form of enormous sandwiches or to fall exhausted into bed"] (88). The children are selfish, only emerging for food or interacting with their mother when it benefits them. Eva does not seem concerned for their well-being beyond satisfying their basic needs, focusing instead on Clara, the girl she has chosen to mother for the summer. At this moment, both Clara and Eva are more invested in their non-biological relationship than in cultivating connections with those biologically related to them.

Incestuous Gaze

Although Alberto and Eva provide a level of physical and emotional care for their non-biological children, the parent/child relationship in each narration is complicated by incestuous or sexual desires. In *Interrogating Incest*, Vikki Bell links incest to the sexualization of children that often occurs in Western cultures. Bell argues that women are often infantilized (citing baby doll nightgowns for adult women as one example) while girls are sexualized in ways designed to make them appear older (Bell references toddlers in bikinis). Incest, then, "is theoretically placed at the intersection of discourses on predatory masculine (hetero) sexuality," where children are characterized as both "sexually attractive and ... as possessions" (79). In such a patriarchal understanding of children where young girls are sexualized and patriarchs may view their daughters as property, Bell asserts that the leap to incest can be a short one when a father understands his female children to be imbued with a sexuality that falls under his purview as leader of the family. Feminist critics have discussed the heteronormative functions of father/daughter incest, suggesting that:

> given the power dynamics of male-dominated society and the understandings of sexuality which we live out, incestuous abuse is in a sense unsurprising. In feminist analysis, incest signals not the chaos it did (and does) for sociological functionalism, but an order, the familiar and familial order of patriarchy, in both its strict and its feminist sense. (Bell, *Interrogating Incest* 3)

In "El amor inútil," even though Alberto is not biologically related to Fidelia, he still thinks of himself as Fidelia's parent during her infancy, making any sexual relationship between them taboo and symbolically incestuous, in addition to the age difference that complicates power dynamics between the two. Alberto is a non-normative parental figure for Fidelia, as he is the one who assumes the primary caregiver role for the first two years of her life. Alberto's parenthood in relation to Fidelia does not need to be biological to be authentic, as I argue throughout this book that non-normative parent/child relationships are legitimate. The sexual relationship between Alberto and Fidelia breaks the emotional limits and sexual taboos between parent and child, meaning that it is incestuous. Alberto's firm belief in the legitimate parent/child connection between himself and Fidelia is confirmed when he sits in the park at the end of the story, watching Fidelia with their child, and the narrator describes him as an "abuelo" ["grandfather"] (137). This is a role he can have in this situation only through an incestuous connection with his daughter Fidelia, an encounter from which the baby – both Alberto's son and grandson – is born. Alberto sees himself as both Fidelia's father and lover. Perhaps his sexual relationship with Fidelia can be explained as his attempt to reclaim the daughter figure, to reverse the figurative castration he might suffer due to the fact that he did not biologically father her. According to Stefani Engelstein, incest can be interpreted as a father's attempt to "reinstitute his paternal claim to his daughter" (53). By committing symbolic incest with Fidelia and having a child with her, Alberto returns to the realm of patriarchal heteronormativity and hegemonic masculinity.

To some extent, the narration in "El amor inútil" reflects Alberto's delusional beliefs that baby Fidelia welcomes Alberto's romantic attention or even plays a seductive role in her relationship with Alberto, indirectly suggesting that she is complicit in the incestuous relationship and establishing her as a Lolita figure. The narrator states that, despite her age, Fidelia "contaba con su paseo dominical cada semana" ["counted on her Sunday walk each week"] (138), implying an agency and awareness beyond the capabilities of an infant. Alberto senses his life beginning to change when Fidelia is three months old and Alberto believes, as insinuated through the narration, that the infant develops a romantic interest in him: "Los ojos azules y grandes de Fidelia empezaron a mirarle y a reconocerle, la sonrisa de su carita redonda se llenaba de complicidades y guiños para él, sus bracitos se extendían para que Alberto la levantara de la cama, y con cada demanda él iba experimentando una felicidad desconocida" ["Fidelia's big, blue eyes began to look at him and recognize him, the smile of her round face filled with mutual understanding and winks for him, her little arms extended so that Alberto would lift her out of the bed, and with each demand, he was experiencing an unknown happiness"] (139). The narrator insinuates that, at three months of age, Alberto finds her gaze flirtatious, which awakens his sexual feelings toward her, indicating that he finds her to be the instigator – or at least complicit – in this evolution of their relationship. Fidelia's face full of "complicidades y guiños" ["mutual understanding and winks"] (139) is understood by Alberto as her consent, as the narrator describes how Alberto interprets the universally normal act of a baby lifting her arms to be held as Fidelia's romantic demands for Alberto's attention, a way for Alberto to rationalize her as a willing participant in his delusion.

The notion of gaze as an element of control – prevalent in "El amor inútil" – is one tool used by perpetrators of incest. In Laura Mulvey's seminal writing on the power of the male gaze, she describes scopophilia as the process of "taking other people as objects, subjecting them to a controlling and curious gaze" (450). Alberto feels justified in pursuing a romantic relationship with Fidelia, assuming or pretending a consensual nature to the connection based on his interpretation of the infant's gaze. "El amor inútil" concludes with gaze, as well, as Alberto watches his daughter/lover and son/symbolic grandson from afar while they play in the park. With his gaze, Alberto maintains both himself and Fidelia in the roles prescribed for them by heteronormative society. Although his son starts to wander toward him, Alberto makes no move to reach out to him, remaining immobile and passive as the stereotypical father figure.

Gaze is deeply invested with a powerful and often incestuous meaning in *Varada* as well. Both Pablo and Clara's uncle attempt to use their lascivious gaze against her, forcing her to constantly discern between appropriately affectionate parental gaze and incestuous sexual advances. An incestuous parent can use his gaze to control his victim, who is constantly "unsure whether his attentions were motivated by affection or sexual intent" (Bell, *Interrogating Incest* 64). Before living with Eva, Clara's uncle has incestuous desires toward her, which he quite possibly acts upon. Later, in Eva's house, Clara feels an intense aversion and wariness toward Pablo, who technically would be her adopted father, since he is Eva's husband. Although Clara is often portrayed as emotionally unbalanced or out of touch with reality, she has good reason to avoid Pablo, as he often stares at her in a sexual way and admits his lust for her in soliloquies. To Pablo, Clara is "esa muchacha tan extraña y tan hermosa, con un cuerpo estallante de mujer adulta, de mujer bandera, y esa mentalidad propia de una niñita de nueve años, que le rehúye a él" ["that girl, so strange and so beautiful, with the explosive body of an adult woman, of an irresistible woman, and that mentality belonging to a little girl of nine years old, who shies away from him"] (104). What he finds so appealing about Clara is her mixture of childlike and womanly traits. When he hears her crying in the night, "esos maullidos roncos de leona en celo" ["those hoarse meows of a lion in heat"] (105), Pablo wishes that he could be the one to go to her instead of Eva. His fantasy of this nighttime scene wherein the father comforts the child is violent and paedophilic. Instead of consoling her like Eva does, Pablo imagines using sex as an aggressive act of possession and control, fantasizing about how he would like to

> arrancarle a manotazos ese ridículo camisón de ursulina en que se ahoga, y montar sobre ella y cabalgarla, con energía y con cuidados infinitos, y hacerla gritar al fin de gozo y de dolor, de genuino gozo y de dolor real, no ya de ansiedades confusas y de vanos miedos, un gozo de mujer que ha descubierto en el varón la auténtica ternura, el definitivo apoyo que le permitirá dejar atrás sus sofocos sin causa, sus fantasías vanas, sus miedos infantiles, tan evidente es lo que anda buscando y necesitando. (105)

> [strip her of that ridiculous, goody-goody nightgown that she is drowning in, and mount her and ride her, with energy and with infinite care, and finally make her yell from pleasure and pain, from genuine pleasure and real pain, not from confused anxieties and vain fears, the pleasure of a woman who has discovered authentic tenderness in a man, the definitive support that would allow her to leave behind her feelings of suffocation

without cause, her vain fantasies, her infantile fears, it is so evident that is what she is looking for and needing.] (105)

The bedroom becomes a site of doubling, for it can either represent the scene of parental comfort after a child's nightmare or a space of sexual activity. For Pablo, Clara's frightened nocturnal whimpers remind him of a woman's orgasmic cries of pleasure. The act of going to Clara's bed in the middle of the night to comfort her as a parent could easily be substituted with a lover's advances, goaded on by the goal of conferring sexual pleasure (although for Pablo, it seems that such an act would be laced with violence).

While Pablo has incestuous thoughts about Clara, she is sexually attracted to her non-biological mother. In her interactions with Eva, the object of her incestuous desire, Clara also appropriates the power of gaze. Clara watches Eva vigilantly and relentlessly; when Eva is able to sneak out of the house, Clara is not calm until Eva returns and reports where she has been and what she has done. While Clara's gaze can be interpreted as an attempt to control Eva, she also values it as a way to be closer to Eva: "Clara entonces la acecha por la ventana, oculta tras las cortinas y visillos, no para averiguar qué es lo que la otra hace, en modo alguno para espiarla, sino sólo para verla aunque de lejos unos minutos más" ["Clara then stalks her by the window, hides behind the shutters and curtains, not to find out what the other one is doing, by no means to spy on her, but just to see her for a few minutes more, even if it's from far away"] (72). By watching Eva, Clara feels connected to her, as opposed to feeling controlled by the male gaze. While Clara strives to connect visually with Eva, she never considered such a potential relationship with her biological aunt. Clara describes her aunt as "la mujer serpiente ... la mujer de cera ... la mujer sin ojos – porque esa impostora que ha pretendido con increíble insolencia durante años ocupar el lugar de su madre tiene vacías y terribles las cuencas de los ojos, aunque nadie lo note, tiene la piel de cera" ["the serpent woman ... the wax woman ... the woman without eyes – because that imposter who has pretended with incredible insolence for years to occupy the place of her mother has empty and terrible eye sockets, even though no one notices, she has wax skin"] (62). Through the description of her aunt's empty eyes, the narration indicates that Clara does not see herself as linked or belonging to this biologically related stranger but prefers to form a non-normative familial relationship with Eva instead.

Eva is so distracted, however, that she barely notices the girl for whom she has vowed to care, much less Clara's sexual feelings toward her. Clara follows Eva around adoringly, eager to lap up any signs of affection that she might bestow upon her. Clara views her relationship with Eva as "una historia simplísima de amor y desamor" ["a very simple history of love and indifference"] (120), wishing that Eva would give her more than a goodnight kiss. Clara's bodily reactions to Eva belie her physical attraction to her. When Eva scolds Clara, her body responds in an extreme manner, as if reacting to a lover, as "le tiemblan las manos ... y siente que le arden más y más las mejillas, que le zumban los oídos, que se le cierra la garganta y le supone un grave esfuerzo respirar" ["her hands tremble ... and she feels that her cheeks burn more and more, that her ears buzz, that her throat closes and this creates for her a serious effort to breathe"] (142). Her feelings for Eva are so intense that Clara "piensa que si en algún momento Eva llega a besarla, va a tener ella inevitablemente que morir" ["thinks that, if in some moment, Eva kisses her, she inevitably is going to have to die"] (67). Clara is never afforded consummation of her incestuous desire for Eva, but their affective connection creates a non-normative, non-biological parent/child relationship that is an example of alternative familial construction, even though the relationship is temporary.

Non-Normative Parental Identities

Alberto and Eva enact alternative performances of parenthood that interact with and question the limits of what Spanish patriarchal society has generally understood as stereotypically maternal or paternal roles. Alberto adheres to stereotypically maternal behaviours and thoughts in his relationship with infant Fidelia, and Eva often exhibits stereotypically masculine, paternal reactions to Clara. Even when Alberto and Eva perform stereotypical roles, they are those associated with the opposite sex, which becomes another way for these characters to question the limits of gendered parental roles and explore non-normative enactments of parenthood, in line with one of the purported goals of queer theory, "a certain unsettling in relation to heteronormativity" (Freccero 17). Queer theory provides a useful understanding of these parental figures, as they challenge gender binaries that inform society's conceptions of motherhood and fatherhood. Queer theory "circumvents fixed identity and promotes indeterminacy by exploring the interstices of the constructions of gender, sex and the identity markers dependent on them ... challenging the queer theorist to re-think binary divisions and 'simplistic' classifications" (Davis 64). Alberto and Eva perform their parental roles in ways that question or break from the binary, positioning their performances of parenthood on a diverse spectrum of potential parental enactments.

In "El amor inútil," Alberto narrates his own doubled or skewed reflection about parenthood, set against the traditional example of Fidel and Nora. Symbolically fulfilling both stereotypically maternal and paternal roles, Alberto becomes a different yet familiar reflection of Fidelia's biological parents. He establishes the nature of his relationship with Fidelia when she is still a baby, too young to provide any input to the incestuous desire behind the narrative he generates, wherein Alberto plays the role of parent and lover to the woman whom he has imagined that Fidelia will grow up to be. When Alberto takes baby Fidelia for walks in the park, he mentally constructs their future life together. Alberto always "supo que cuando Fidelia fuera mayor no vivirían en aquel barrio. Aunque no podía haber otro más bonito en toda la ciudad, Alberto había renunciado a culminar su historia con Fidelia en el mismo lugar en que ésta había comenzado" ["knew that when Fidelia was older they wouldn't live in that neighbourhood. Although there couldn't have been a prettier one in the whole city, Alberto had refused to finalize his history with Fidelia in the same place where it had begun"] (138). Alberto plans to take Fidelia away from the place where various individuals observed his paternal role toward her as she grew up, making it easier to redefine their relationship in an unknown place.

In Alberto's fantasies of their life together, as in Castro's text itself, Fidelia has very little agency or even personality. For example, "El amor inútil" includes no description of her personality or physical characteristics, aside from Alberto's opinion of her upon seeing her after sixteen years of absence, when Alberto thinks that his "ahijada se había convertido en una mujer muy bella, de una belleza un tanto empañada por el vestuario excesivamente juvenil y por la compañía de aquel muchacho sin gracia" ["goddaughter had become a very beautiful woman, of a beauty a little tarnished by her excessively youthful clothing and by the company of that graceless youth"] (143). This description of Fidelia, minimal as it is, highlights many of the ways in which her character complies with patriarchal ideas of womanhood. She is pretty, young, and always has a man around to guide her. Alberto is satisfied by this image of Fidelia.

Alberto exhibits a non-normative parental identity, but in many cases he does so by performing his parenthood as a traditional (except for the incestuous aspects of his parenthood, of course) mother figure due to the emotional limitations of the heteronormative father role. As a father figure to Fidelia, Alberto would have remained trapped within the strict gender confines of hegemonic masculinity, not allowed to take on a primary role in caregiving for Fidelia, as Spanish women are more likely to be caregivers than men (Alberdi 326). Even in a study of Spanish families where both adults worked outside of the home and both agreed that responsibility for the house and children should be equally shared, only 25 per cent of respondents reported that caregiving responsibilities were equally divided, with the extra work generally falling on women (Bourland Ross, "Why We Are" 18). In a society that is theoretically amenable to men being more involved in the day-to-day parenting of children but whose reality does not live up to this idea, the concept of men engaging in caregiving

> announces a predisposition to reframe caregiving to something different ... generally something less ... when the caregivers are men. This is a tyranny of sorts. As members of a culture, are we so conditioned by our beliefs and assumptions about gender that it becomes difficult to envision men as caregivers? (Thompson 21)

Since the way in which Alberto interacts with Fidelia and assumes a caregiving role does not fit within the borders of hegemonic masculinity, he must find another way to define his performance of parenthood.

To do so, Alberto begins to understand his relationship with Fidelia within the context of mother/daughter roles. Even though Alberto's performance of parenthood as motherhood is non-normative, it often falls into heteronormative expectations of the traditional mother figure. The all-consuming, sacrificial love for Fidelia that Alberto experiences as her "mother" aligns itself with patriarchal rhetoric about motherly abnegation. The narrator states that "Alberto era uno de esos hombres que aman como las mujeres, con cierto desencanto implícito, con una resignación teñida de generosidad y de esperanza, con absoluta consciencia de lo que es querer: estar ahí para lo que se ofrezca" ["Alberto was one of those men who love like women do, with a certain implied disillusionment, with a resignation tinged with generosity and hope, with absolute awareness of what it is to love: to be there for whatever is offered"] (138). Alberto's initial impulses toward parenthood are driven by a need to love another human being, a desire so selfless that he even embraces the mundane aspects of such a relationship, eager to meet any of Fidelia's physical needs: "Como para las mujeres, el amor para Alberto tenía más que ver con la limpieza que con los sentimientos; se parecía más a abrigar bien a la pequeña que a colmar su cara de besos" ["Like for women, for Albert, love had more to do with cleaning than feelings; it looked more like bundling up the little girl's coat well than showering her face with kisses"] (141–2). Alberto understands maternal love to be all-suffering, practical, and action-based; therefore, he is happy to complete the thankless duties of a caregiver rather than simply bestowing affection on Fidelia.

Alberto's performance of parenthood, non-normative in that it transforms him into a stereotypical maternal figure, traps him through his intense love for Fidelia and through the expectations of the motherly role. Alberto is smitten by baby Fidelia, loving her, "como una mujer puede querer, sin esperanzas y sin desesperanzas, contento de tenerla en sus brazos y de cargar con aquel peso dulce, contento de poder disfrutar de su compañía y de su indiferencia" ["like a woman can love, without hope and without despair, content to have her in his arms and carry that sweet weight, content to be able to enjoy her company and her indifference"] (141). This description indicates that loving "like a woman" (or a mother) implies no guarantee of reciprocation, simply the need to put forth unconditional love while waiting and hoping that the object of one's affection's feelings will evolve from indifference to love over time. This is an extremely isolating type of love, leaving Alberto alone with his emotions as he remains focused on fulfilling every need of a child who cannot return his love as he desires.

When Alberto biologically becomes a father to Fidelia's son after Fidelia's weekend visit to the hotel Alberto manages, his performance of parenthood is drastically different than the way in which he enacted his parenthood of infant Fidelia. With his son, Alberto complies with the heteronormative image of the father as an authoritative figure who is unengaged in the practicalities of childcare. Through the emergence of this biological connection, Alberto loses the stereotypically feminine side of his nature and is no longer a traditional maternal figure. The parental change in Alberto is linked to his lack of sexual desire toward his son. While Alberto has paederastic feelings toward Fidelia, this is not the case with his son, due either to his gender, their biological connection, or both considerations. Although the story does not indicate whether Alberto consciously felt ashamed for not having had a biological child sooner in his life, something he apparently has not done with his wife either, "norms of reproductive masculinity perpetuate the idea that the ability to father biological children is essential to one's standing as a man. This ideal has led historically to ... the denigration of men who fail to live up to this ideal" (Daniels 164). Fathering a biological child with Fidelia allows Alberto to participate in the homosocial culture so prevalent within the heteronormative world, wherein "men define their masculinity, not as much in relation to women, but in relation to each other" (Kimmel, *Manhood in America* 7). Alberto has finally succumbed to pressures toward behavioural conformity, quickly reverting into an uninvolved, absent father.

In a way, Alberto now mirrors Fidel's behaviour by showing a lack of interest in Fidelia's life. Both men are passive and disinterested, as their reactions to Fidelia's pregnancy reveal. "Cuando nació el pequeño, Fidel también confirmó sus sospechas, pero nunca, ni antes ni después del nacimiento, hizo nada por hablar con su amigo, y Alberto, por su parte, tampoco volvió a llamar ni a escribir" ["When the little one was born, Fidel's suspicions were also confirmed, but never, not before or after the birth, did he attempt to talk with his friend, and Alberto, for his part, did not call or write again either"] (144). In an article for *El País* titled "Los hijos como propiedad" ["Children as Property"], Luisa Castro writes about the downfalls of hegemonic masculinity, addressing the problem of men's lack of involvement in their children's lives, touching upon the masculine perception of children as property, or "mercancía" ["merchandise"]. While Alberto maintained an emotionally vulnerable (yet problematic) connection with baby Fidelia, his perspective toward his son is emotionally reserved. He may feel in some way that his son is his property, or at the very least has allowed him to regain his masculine and paternal societal status, but Alberto loses the intimate aspects of a parent/child relationship that he found so fulfilling when Fidelia was a baby.

Alberto's foray into a maternal relationship with Fidelia reveals the restrictive nature of the traditional Spanish maternal role, but his enactment of his role as a stereotypical father figure for his son is limited as well. Alberto enjoyed caring for Fidelia in her infancy, but he distances himself from his son, and readers never know if Alberto wished to be more of a presence in his son's life or not. Fathers often act differently with sons and daughters, at times behaving in a more distant manner with sons (Morman and Floyd 395). Alberto has found – or been forced into – the escape hole from love that the narrator insists all men are looking for, explaining, "Los hombres nunca se enamoran como las mujeres. En el amor de los hombres siempre hay una fuga, un agujero por el que acaban desapareciendo" ["Men never fall in love like women. In men's love, there is always an escape, a hole through which they end up disappearing"] (137). While the narration in "El amor inútil" describes gender roles in very stereotypical ways, as evidenced in this quote's rigid delineation of the differences in the ways in which men and women love, the narrator's voice is often tied to Alberto's thoughts or beliefs rather than expressing a universal truth about Spanish society. The narration may present such essentialist assertions about gender and parental roles, but characters play with those roles in their lived experiences. The title of the text, "El amor inútil," emphasizes how Alberto never finds a way of expressing parental love that is fulfilling for him, Fidelia, or their son, because he can never escape the worthlessly rigid gender roles imposed on parents. Alberto fails miserably – both as a stereotypical mother and a stereotypical father – to truly connect with his children. His disappearance at the end of the story can be interpreted as the pursuit of freedom or the loss of familial connection.

While Alberto's understanding of paternity evolves with time, in *Varada*, Eva's non-normative parental identity stems from a personality that has always been defined by a combination of stereotypically masculine and feminine attributes.[7] Her husband Pablo finds that Eva defies categorization on many levels. She sleeps with him the first night they meet, astonishing Pablo by choosing to skip the perfunctory drink and small talk that often precedes the first sexual encounter. Eva's focus on developing the couple's physical relationship before concentrating on its emotional or verbal components could be interpreted as a step away from the stereotypical feminine role in romantic relationships. Pablo finds it "imposible alinearla entre los coros de las vírgenes o en los supuestos aquelarres de las prostitutas" ["impossible to categorize her within the choirs of virgins or in the supposed covens of prostitutes"] (41). Although Eva and Pablo are married, they maintain an open relationship, since they both have "tantas reservas sobre las relaciones de pareja, tantas dudas sobre la monogamia" ["so many reservations about romantic relationships, so many doubts about monogamy"] (166). Pablo also complains about Eva's emotional and physical independence, a character trait that he finds frustrating, admitting that it is "muy difícil convivir año tras año con una mujer que no nos pide nada, que nunca necesita nada, que no espera ... nada, terriblemente exigente y difícil tras esta aparente ausencia de demandas" ["very difficult to live year after year with a woman who doesn't ask anything of us, who never needs anything, who doesn't want ... anything, terribly demanding and difficult behind that apparent absence of demands"] (83). While Pablo allows himself to lean on Eva's strength, he simultaneously admires and resents her for not fitting into stereotypical roles of femininity.

Eva assumes the duties of mothering, which she often views as a burden. Despite her successful career as a lawyer, Eva finds herself taking on the entirety of the household responsibilities, even though she despises them:

> interpretando ella día tras día el papel de ama de casa heroica y mortificada, un papel que en modo alguno le va, que no encaja, agobiada por unas tareas que ha desempeñado siempre sin aparente esfuerzo, desabrida y hostil, haciéndolos sentirse a todos, hasta a Clara, inútiles y abusivos y para nada necesarios. (109)

[day after day, she plays the role of heroic and tormented housewife, a role that does not fit her at all, overwhelmed by tasks that she has always performed without any apparent effort, surly and hostile, making them all feel, even Clara, useless and abusive and good for nothing.] (109)

Motherhood, never an aspiration of Eva's, is something that has been imposed on her from a young age. Even her name links her to the first biblical mother Eve, highlighting her inability to escape the societal pressures of motherhood. Eva's initiation into selfless motherhood begins when, as a child, her parents pushed her to take care of her brothers and sisters, as well as managing the family store, as soon as she returned from school. Eva is burdened by this maternal responsibility and the fear of not living up to her parents' expectations, knowing that "todo se apoya en ella … esto la fatiga y la asusta y siente tentaciones de abandonar … y se afianza en Eva la desagradable sensación de que le han hecho trampa" ["everything depends on her … that fatigues and scares her, and she feels the temptation to abandon it all … and the disagreeable sensation that she has been tricked grows in Eva"] (129). This maternal pressure follows her into adulthood, where she is expected to be the all-knowing, all-powerful mother. Elia and the children take her maternal presence for granted, bringing her homeless dogs or cats to care for throughout the summer, an act that assuages their own sense of guilt (86). Meanwhile, they promptly forget about the existence of the strays, since they know that Eva will care for them, as motherhood is assumed to be a role that Eva will fulfil.

The way in which Elia describes the childlike nature of everyone in Eva's life highlights Eva's loneliness, stemming from being the only responsible adult in the house. Pablo and Elia are like needy children, requiring as much of her time and attention as does Clara. Eva's constant impulse to associate herself with and care for dependent individuals – likely an unconscious response to an internalized gender script – frustrates Pablo, who would like Eva to dedicate more time exclusively to him. As Eva attempts to perform the maternal role, she isolates herself from Pablo, who is

aburrido y fatigado, molesto incluso, ante el hecho de que su mujer le dedique poca atención y menos tiempo … harto Pablo a veces … de adolescentes desorientados, de drogadictos en vías de rehabilitación, de mujeres abandonadas o expulsadas o perseguidas o violadas por maridos o amantes o jefes de oficina … incapaz Eva de rechazarlos y ni siquiera de ponerles límites. (51)

[bored and exhausted, even annoyed, by the fact that his wife dedicates little attention and less time to him ... Pablo is fed up sometimes ... by disoriented adolescents, by drug addicts on the way to rehabilitation, by abandoned or thrown out or stalked women or women raped by husbands or lovers or bosses ... Eva incapable of rejecting them or even of setting up boundaries.] (51)

Pablo appreciates Eva's caring impulses, so long as they are directed at him. When her attention is on other people, regardless of whether they need her more, Pablo feels rejected and unloved.

Just as Eva feels isolated by the maternal role that society imposes on her, Elia experiences a similarly disorienting reaction to – and almost a rejection of – motherhood upon the birth of her first child. When Elia reflects on giving birth to her son, she recalls how she was disconcerted by the diverse range of people who insisted on calling her "mother," effectively relegating and narrowing her identity to that single role. She remembers that "todos, médicos, monjas, enfermeras y hasta los amigos, obstinados en llamarla mamá, un mamá que debiera halagarla y que la pone sin embargo incómoda, quizás sea sólo que le da vergüenza, o que le resulta, a pesar de los interminables meses de embarazo, inesperada y ajena la maternidad" ["everyone, doctors, nuns, nurses and even friends, persistent in calling her mom, a mom that should have flattered her, which instead made her uncomfortable, maybe only from shame, or because, in spite of the unending months of pregnancy, motherhood seemed unexpected and foreign to her"] (15). Her words express a taboo sentiment for societies invested in reprosexuality, namely, that not all biological mothers feel comfortable or "natural" within the confines of motherhood. Religious institutions, the medical community, and society at large work to maintain Elia in this role, emphasizing her maternal difference or identity.

Jorge's reaction to their son's birth highlights the different roles prescribed to mothers and fathers. Jorge is "feliz, desmesuradamente feliz, incomprensiblemente feliz, maravillosamente feliz, 'es una criatura preciosa, Elia, al mirarla he pensado que ya he hecho todo lo que tenía que hacer en la vida, que ahora ya podría morir'" ["happy, excessively happy, marvellously happy, 'she is a precious creature, Elia, looking at him, I have thought that now I have done everything I had to do in life, that now I could die'"] (15). Jorge considers his duties as a father to have been completed; he has "fathered" a child, or rather, put forth the genetic material necessary to bring a child into existence. He is not subject to – as is Elia – the pressure of being defined by one's parenthood or the incipient multitude of tasks and responsibilities that a newborn implies for a mother.

Varada presents examples of characters enacting stereotypically gendered parental roles; at times, characters (like Jorge) fulfil them, while in other instances, they challenge them. Eva is not the stereotypical maternal figure, exhibiting a mixture of traditionally labelled masculine and feminine traits that cause others to both adore her and, to some extent, fear her. Elia elaborates upon the many identities that members of the household impose upon Eva, saying that everyone in the house is

> un poco enamorados de nuestra madre abadesa, nuestra sacerdotisa de las misas negras, tan ingenuas, venerándote, admirándote, deseándote, temiéndote, todos girando a tu alrededor como niños perdidos o como perritos sin amo, mientras tú nos gobiernas y nos amparas con la abnegación de una madre amantísima o con las veleidades perversas e inocentes de una reina loca. (53)

> [a little in love with our mother abbess, our priestess of the black mass, so naive, worshipping you, admiring you, wanting you, fearing you, everyone revolving around you like lost children or like ownerless dogs, while you govern us and protect us with the self-denial of a well-loved mother or with the perverse and innocent whims of a crazy queen.] (53)

Eva is trapped in "su papel de mujer fuerte (papel que otros inventaron para ella y en el que la encerraron como en una coraza, como en una mortaja)" ["her role of strong woman (a role that others invented for her and in which they trapped her like in a breastplate, like in a shroud)"] (130), feeling that she must be strong and tough in order to support the many individuals who depend on her, despite her insecurities. Eva has a "feminine consciousness ... overrun by a masculine un-relatedness and aloofness towards others, in particular those who are most in need of her empathy and nurturance" (Dolgin Casado 167). Thus, Eva espouses the stereotypically masculine concept of love as a competition and exertion of power, as opposed to the all-suffering, selfless maternal love modelled by Alberto. Eva believes that, in her personal life, "el amor ha sido algo a conseguir trabajosamente, algo que se conquista en el combate, que se impone tal vez a los demás" ["love has been something achieved laboriously, something that one conquers in combat, that perhaps is imposed on others"] (232). Beneath her tough exterior, Eva is truly desperate for love, which pushes her to strive to be the mother figure for whom everyone clamours. At the same time, Eva's fear of rejection causes her to maintain an emotional barrier between herself and those she cares about the most, isolating herself and augmenting her "pavor incontrolable a la soledad, un miedo terrible a que ellos la abandonen, su amiga y su marido, y la dejen sola, al margen, para siempre ya sola y abandonada y sin amor" ["uncontrollable terror of loneliness, a terrible fear that they will abandon her, her friend and her husband, and leave her alone, on the margins, forever alone and abandoned and without love"] (242). At her core, much like Clara, Eva exhibits a childlike craving for acceptance and security from her loved ones, looking for the certainty that she will never be abandoned.

The Role of the Doppelgänger in Parent/Child Relationships

Eva and Alberto experience non-normative parenthood in ways that other parental figures in these texts do not. In addition to their fluid understanding of parenthood along a spectrum of experiences and enactments, another concept key to understanding the parent/child relationships represented in these works is that of the doppelgänger, which I use to explore emotional similitude between characters in this chapter. A pervasive figure within world literature, the doppelgänger generally symbolizes a split in one's psyche, a division between reality and fantasy, a vision of oneself in the body of another (Webber 1–3). Castro's and Tusquets's works repeatedly display a doubling of characters, themes, and the narrative itself. Through their doubling and queering of the parental identity, Alberto and Eva play with a definition of parenthood outside of heteronormativity's limits. The concept of "doubleness" easily aligns itself with queer theory because it is often seen as:

> a strategy for negotiating differences between and within male and female, center and margin, inside and outside, public and private, realism and romance. To be "double" is to resist categorization as one thing or the other; to invoke "doubleness" is to address binary oppositions without resting comfortably in either of the two terms being opposed. (Warhol 857)

Among the characters themselves, there are many instances of doubling, or appearances of the doppelgänger. Although *Varada* contains several characters who could be labelled as doppelgängers, I will focus on Fidelia's conversion into Alberto's doppelgänger, as well as the doubling relationship between Eva and Clara (and, to some extent, Elia). Like a queered subject, "the doppelgänger is an interrogation of the limit and on the limit – its interruptive power consists in the necessity of the limit as well as its equally necessary delimitation or transgression" (Vardoulakis 10). While aware of the confines of heteronormative society, these characters play with the boundaries of the performance of parenthood and child/parent relationships.

As Alberto "transforms" into a father figure, Fidelia becomes his doppelgänger, taking his place as the stereotypical selfless maternal figure. Watching Fidelia play with their son in the park, Alberto

> se dio cuenta de que aquella mujer enamorada era él mismo, era su misma expresión y su mismo deseo de entonces, el tiempo sólo había hecho una mudanza en todos estos años: había permitido que el amor de ella ocupara su lugar, un lugar que había custodiado celosamente al lado de las mujeres a las que había amado durante todos aquellos años y que ahora, gracias a Fidelia, le convertían finalmente en un hombre. Un hombre como otro cualquiera. (144–5)

> [realized that the woman in love was him, was his very expression and his same desire from back then, time alone had moved in all those years: it had allowed her love to occupy his place, a place that he had guarded jealously alongside the women he had loved during all those years and now, thanks to Fidelia, had finally converted him into a man. A man like any other.] (144–5)

Fidelia will now be the one to care for an infant, neglecting her own needs to provide for her son, just as Alberto once did for her. Readers are never privy to Fidelia's thoughts, but she seems to accept her motherhood, choosing to keep the baby despite the sacrifice implied for her as a young single mother. Formed in Alberto's self-abnegating image, Fidelia even takes her son to the same park that she and Alberto frequented years ago. Curiously, the end of the story reveals that the baby is three months old, the same age as Fidelia when Alberto began to have romantic feelings for her. This detail, which could easily have been omitted in such a brief story, allows for the possibility that Fidelia might begin to feel romantically attached to her son, potentially passing through the same parental stages as did Alberto, continuing an incestuous circle of parent/child relationships. Castro's work "consistently question[s] how human beings imagine and practice relationships, and how much 'intersubjectivity' articulates ethical responsiveness and responsibility," considering "the ways in which female subjects approach, perceive, and grapple with others and the discourses of otherness" (Molinaro, "Looking for" 137). Therefore, as Fidelia takes on a parental role, the similarities and differences between her parental performance and Alberto's are displayed, creating a doppelgänger.

In *Varada*, Clara intentionally constructs a skewed double narrative of her relationship with Eva that imposes yet another identity on Eva. Similar to the way in which Elia "la ha mitificado siempre [a Eva]" ["has always mythologized (Eva)"] (21), Clara is "desarrollando como siempre otra historia" ["developing another history, like always"] (120), establishing a fantasy world where Eva is her godlike mother and she is the princess daughter who has been rescued from "esta ciudad inmunda de reptiles pegados a la tierra, doblados sobre el suelo" ["that filthy city of reptiles stuck to the earth, doubled over the ground"] (66). For Clara, Eva is "la madre blanca, la mujer pájaro de plumaje nevado" ["the white mother, the bird mother with white plumage"] (65) who has come to rescue her "hija de la luz" ["daughter of the light"] (65) from her denigrating surroundings. Clara idealizes Eva, ascribing to her a level of perfection that Eva can never achieve. In Clara's fantasy world, "no ha figurado nunca un padre, y piensa ahora que no lo tuvo nunca, hija sólo de esta madre hermosa y resplandeciente, suavidad de plumas, dulce sabor a miel, que la lleva consigo hacia su reino" ["a father never belonged, and she thinks now that she never had one, daughter only of that beautiful and dazzling mother, softness of plumes, sweet flavour of honey, who takes her back to her kingdom"] (67). In this narrative, based on reality but certainly not an accurate representation of it, Clara hopes to find the maternal love to which she has never been exposed. Her fantasy world excludes men through an expression of the desire for an empowering, woman-centred, and possibly lesbian relationship.

When Eva sends Clara back to her uncle and aunt's house, Clara realizes that the image of Eva that she fabricated is a false reflection of her identity, and their relationship was never as Clara imagined it to be. Clara – as well as Elia, who is undergoing the dissolution of her marriage – is shipwrecked in time, living her life as if "el tiempo la hubiera exiliado de su devenir y ella quedara por fin detenida en la orilla, varada al margen de las cosas, varada entre los restos del naufragio, expulsada del tiempo, vomitada del tiempo y de la vida" ["time had exiled her from her future and she would finally stay detained on the shore, stranded on the margin of things, stranded among the remains of the shipwreck, expelled from time, vomited out by time and life"] (29). In reality, the shipwreck represents both women's isolation from the experience of love. Clara was on the verge of experiencing love in her relationship with Eva, but never truly was able to be fulfilled by love.

The problem from which all of *Varada*'s characters suffer is their inability to receive the type of love that they desire, a uniquely and ubiquitously human predicament. Each one of them – Eva, Elia, Pablo, and Clara – crave a redemptive love that was not afforded to them in their childhood. Ironically, however, each of them has the opportunity to be loved, but as they are so "encerrada cada una en sí misma" ["locked up in themselves"] (103), they selfishly either do not realize the opportunities for love that are being presented to them or reject them because they are seeking love from a different individual. In the mother/daughter relationship between Eva and Clara, Clara represents "the ideal of total love, total surrender, innocence always betrayed" (Mazquiarán de Rodríguez 177), the individual who exposes all her vulnerabilities in the hope of being loved. She is ultimately rejected by Eva, who cannot appreciate Clara's love due to her incessant fear that Pablo has stopped loving her. Simultaneously, while Pablo craves Eva's love and validation, he initiates an affair with another woman, partially because Eva is not being overwhelmingly attentive toward him. Finally, Elia wallows in self-pity after losing Jorge's love, never pausing to consider how much her son loves her and needs her presence in his life.

Although Eva cannot reciprocate Clara's feelings, it was Clara's intense desire to be loved that initially drew Eva to her. Clara is Eva's doppelgänger, representing a doubling of Eva, a mirror that reflects her past and a reminder of her neglected childhood.[8] In Clara, Eva sees her own unrequited search for parental love, on some level desiring to nurture Clara in order to rewrite her own past. Eva represents a parental figure for Clara; she also views a reflection of her childhood in Clara. Acknowledging that Eva is powerful, Clara simultaneously realizes that Eva has never been able to overcome the feelings of rejection she experienced as a child. Clara "la ve [a Eva] como una niñita que juguetea inocente con la pistola que ha olvidado su papá, un revólver cuyo mecanismo y cuyo alcance no comprende pero con el que puede infligir a otros, infligirle a ella, un daño irreparable" ["sees [Eva] as a little girl who plays the innocent with the pistol that her dad has forgotten, a revolver whose mechanism and whose range she does not understand but with which she can inflict on others, inflict on herself, an irreparable damage"] (159–60). Clara knows that Eva has a dual capacity to heal or harm those around her.

While Eva does at times exhibit care for Clara, at other times their relationship is defined in terms of master and slave instead of mother and daughter, a duality often encountered in the doppelgänger relationship (Webber 5). Clara is willing to do anything to earn even a scrap of Eva's love, debasing herself to the point of desiring to become an object for Eva's personal use. Clara thinks that "sería magnífico que Eva la utilizara ... como cenicero, como cepillo de las uñas, como prendedor, como cualquiera de estos objetos familiares que maneja ya sin prestarles apenas atención" ["it would be magnificent if Eva used her ... as an ashtray, as a nail brush, as a brooch, as any of those familiar objects that she handles without paying any attention to"] (140). Their relationship can be "a sort of masochistic slave-master relation in which Clara ... clinging to the female role of merger as an escape from the demands of autonomous selfhood, is willing to debase herself to the lowest level to gain Eva's love" (Ichiishi 148). Taken to this extreme, the mother/daughter relationship formed between Eva and Clara highlights a degradation of the relationship.

Clara's doppelgänger connection with Eva is broken by a third party. The doppelgänger narrative is often terminated either when characters become narcissistically enamoured by their doppelgängers or when a third party intervenes. According to Webber, "In *Doppelgänger* stories the dyadic scheme is typically undone by a triangle of desire, the potential of which apparently lies in the rivalry of host and double over a female third party" (18). In *Varada*, the third party is Pablo, although the triangle of desire does not follow the typical pattern. Clara and Eva do not fight for his affection; rather, Clara and Pablo vie for Eva's love and attention. Clara bears such hatred and jealousy toward Pablo that she wants to kill him: "Clara se sabe capaz de asesinar, estremecida en el odio con una intensidad que sólo conocía en el amor, con un ansia feroz de saltarle a la garganta, de hundirle el cuchillo del pan en el corazón" ["Clara knows she is capable of killing, shaken by her hate, whose intensity she previously knew only in love, with a ferocious longing to leap at his throat, to bury the bread knife in his heart"] (121). Pablo senses Clara's desire for Eva and responds in a way that goads on her jealousy. His sexual exploits factor into the ultimate separation between the two women, as Eva chooses Pablo over Clara, unable to forgive her non-biological daughter for the revelations she exposes about the couple's marriage.

Eva's failed attempt to parent her own doppelgänger can be interpreted as a warning against trying to recreate or duplicate oneself in one's child. While parents often seek immortality through a repetition of their identity in their offspring, this impulse does not bring Eva any satisfaction. Rather, it simply reminds her of her own insecurities and fervent desire to be loved, aspects of her childhood that she has never been able to suppress. Clara's final expulsion from the fantasy home she has imagined for herself comes after confiding in Eva that she witnessed Pablo having sex with another woman in the couple's bed. Eva unleashes all her rage on Clara instead of Pablo in this moment: "Eva no puede soportarla, incapaz de perdonar que fuera ella quien formulara en palabras lo que todos sabían" ["Eva can't stand her, incapable of forgiving her for formulating the words to express what everyone already knew"] (246). Eva's impulses toward mothering are overcome by her own insecurities, and Clara will always symbolize her failures. Eva's reaction to Clara is complicated, as she is "both drawn to and repulsed by Clara (as most of us are in the presence of someone who stirs within us negative aspects of our own shadow), whose visible lack of self-confidence and self-esteem is so like Eva's when put to the test by Pablo's indiscretion" (Dolgin Casado 166). Before Clara leaves the house, Eva attempts suicide, converting herself into a reflection of Clara (and Elia) through her troubled actions. After her failed suicide attempt, Eva sends Clara away to distance herself from painful reminders of what Eva considers to be her own inadequacies.

The Cyclical Parent/Child Relationship

Although the parent/child relationships in both texts ultimately dissolve, they provide an alternative perspective on this familial connection, describing its cyclical nature. In "El amor inútil," the cyclical nature of parenthood is expressed through the setting of the park, which appears at the beginning and end of the story. Alberto begins his parent/child relationship with Fidelia there, as they take their weekly walks and establish their relationship, both in Alberto's mind and in the eyes of passersby in the park, who observe Alberto and understand him to be Fidelia's father. The short story concludes in the park, ending with Fidelia as the parent who brings her child there. For each parent/child relationship, the park is the setting in which Alberto and Fidelia establish an emotional connection with their child. In the first paragraph of "El amor inútil," the narrator discusses the at times fleeting nature of love, comparing the emotion to leaves in the wind, always blowing "en la misma dirección" ["in the same direction"] (137). This image evokes the inevitability of love's ephemeral qualities, as well as its cyclical nature. Just as leaves fall from the trees every autumn, love comes to an end, at times to be resuscitated in a new configuration or relationship, just as trees regain their leaves in the spring. As the love explored in this story is parental love, the narration frames the encounter between Fidelia and Alberto that produces their son as the next iteration of a cyclical, wandering love.

Varada offers a thematically cyclical vision of motherhood, where Eva, Clara, and even Elia at times offer skewed reflections of one another. Eva notes a "similitud muy especial" ["very special similarity"] (88) between Elia and Clara, such as their affinity for creating fantasy worlds, although their jealousy of each other does not permit them to get along. Furthermore, Eva and Elia maintain a decades-long friendship; Eva is described as a "desdoblamiento de Elia" ["split personality of Elia"] (38); as their similar names might suggest, the two women are "fundidas ambas ... en una realidad en cierto modo indivisible y única" ["both united ... in a reality that, in a certain way, is inseparable and unique"] (41). The many links between Clara, Eva, and Elia facilitate the formation of a circular relationship wherein they fluctuate between fulfilling both mother and daughter roles for one another. While Eva mainly occupies the strong, maternal role toward Clara and Elia, Clara at times feels "orgullo" ["pride"] and "ternura" ["tenderness"] toward Eva, "como si un hijo suyo hubiera sacado diez en todas las asignaturas y hasta banda de honor" ["as if a child of hers had received As in all their assignments and even made honour roll"] (138–9). Although more removed from the maternal role, Elia at times is both mother and child to Clara. When she comes into Clara's room at night to comfort her, Elia speaks with "la voz de otro niño, acaso tan asustado y doliente como ella misma" ["the voice of another child, perhaps as scared and hurt as Clara herself"] (164). Pablo recognizes the three women's fluid capacity to care for or accept care from one another, to "aliarse entre sí por medio de un vínculo en el que Pablo como hombre no participa, moviéndose las tres en un círculo pernicioso y enrarecido, densamente mujeril, al que no puede él tener acceso" ["join forces through a connection in which Pablo, as a man, could not participate, the three moving in a dangerous and congested circle, densely feminine, to which he could not have access"] (103). The mother/daughter relationship in *Varada* has a cyclical, interchangeable nature, allowing the women to alternately mother and be mothered – a concept that appears in *El mismo mar de todos los veranos*, as well.

The cyclical mother/daughter bond in *Varada* is foregrounded by the pervasive image of the sea – a constant within Tusquets's trilogy – that reiterates this fluid connection. The exact symbolism of the sea differs in each novel, but many critics have linked the sea to identity formation and eroticism. Laura Parau argues that the sea plays a cathartic role in Tusquets's trilogy, becoming "una presencia que acompaña, potencia y finalmente aplaca las vibraciones internas de los personajes" ["a presence that accompanies, strengthens, and finally placates the characters' internal vibrations"], linked to the emotional states of the protagonists (156). While Parau argues that the sea in *Varada* is "embravecido" ["enraged"] (156), an angry space of conflict that reflects the turmoil of Eva and Pablo's marital problems, the sea also symbolizes the union of women, a space from which Pablo is excluded. Cornejo-Parriego writes of the power of the sea to form identity, arguing that "el mar, con su fluidez y su falta de fronteras rígidas, simboliza, ante todo, la identidad de los personajes, inaprehensible, ambigua, y en continuo proceso de cuestionamiento" ["the sea, with its fluidity and lack of rigid borders, symbolizes, above all, the identity of the characters, incomprehensible, ambiguous, and in a continuous process of questioning"] (53). For Roberta Johnson, Tusquets's sea can be both positive and negative, as it is a link to the past. Johnson explains that the sea is "all-encompassing: it is both the past and the present; it facilitates memory and the construction or reconstruction of self" ("On the Waves" 66). The aspects of identity that characters discover about themselves while in the sea often occur simultaneously with discoveries about their sexuality. In Tusquets's body of work, the sea has been linked to the vagina (García Villalba 138), birth, fertility, and a "positive vision of female erotic energy" (Bellver, "The Language of Eroticism" 25). In *Varada*, Elia's time in the water "no tiene nada de ejercicio o de deporte ... es un gesto ritual, la invocación, la comunión acaso de una mujer acuática y sacrílega" ["has nothing to do with exercise or sports ... it is a ritual gesture, the invocation, perhaps the communion of an aquatic and sacrilegious woman"] (26). This communion or union with the sea is a feminine one, the sea representing a space filled with potential connections among the three women who are already linked in Tusquets's narrative. By connecting the sea and motherhood, Tusquets references Cixous, who also extrapolates on the interchangeable relationship between mother and daughter symbolized in the sea, writing that "We ourselves are sea, sands, corals, seaweeds, beaches, tides, swimmers, children, waves ... seas and mothers" (160). From the sea, Elia learns of fluidity and the potential to eschew identity borders in order to form new types of relationships with Clara and Eva.

While powerful in its unification of all women, Tusquets's and Cixous's representation of cyclical motherhood is to a certain extent essentialist. By focusing on women's connection to the sea as the generator of life, extreme importance is placed upon the power of women's reproductive capabilities, continuing to relegate women to the maternal role. In her theory of hydrofeminism, Astrida Neimanis proposes queries and ideas that move beyond essentialist or reductionist definitions of motherhood and womanhood. Neimanis acknowledges that water and other liquids (breast milk, menstrual blood, semen) can provide an empowering perspective that unifies not only women, but men as well, whose bodies are likewise regulated by fluids. Patriarchal society does not wish to acknowledge this concept, as fluidity blurs the boundaries between masculinity and femininity. Neimanis's statements suggest the possibility of establishing a fluid, cyclical understanding of masculinity and fatherhood, another way of establishing an alternate performance of fatherhood that takes into account the potential unifying force of their semen, just as breast milk and menstrual blood have been proposed to bring women together. As liquids do not adhere to boundaries, permeating whatever space they are found in, Neimanis affirms their ability to allow us to reflect on the delineations between self and other. She questions

> What sort of ethics and politics could I cultivate if I were to acknowledge that the unknowability of the other nonetheless courses through me – just as I do through her? To say that we harbor waters, that our bodies' gestation, sustenance, and interpermeation with other bodies are facilitated by our bodily waters, and that these waters are *both* singular *and* shared, is far more literal than we might at first think. (90)

Hydrofeminism lays the foundation for a fluid understanding of parenthood whose acceptance of blurred borders between parent and child may lead to new ways of experiencing these identities, which exist along a diverse spectrum of possible enactments of the parent/child relationship and roles.

The Limitations of Parenthood

While both texts present unique perspectives on potential ways of enacting parenthood, Alberto and Eva ultimately reject their parental roles and responsibilities for their non-biological children. In "El amor inútil," Alberto abandons Fidelia twice, once at two years old so that she will be able to meet him later in life and feel a romantic connection to him, and again after their sexual encounter. While Alberto was invested enough to return from Palma de Mallorca in order to watch Fidelia with their son at the end of the story, he does not approach her. Instead, Alberto "se levanta del banco, que cruza el parque, que hace su viaje errático como una hoja seca, pero encuentra al final su agujero y huye" ["gets up from the bench, crosses the park, makes his erratic journey like a dry leaf, but finally finds his hole and escapes"] (144–5). Alberto did form a non-normative familial connection with Fidelia when she was an infant, but he chooses not to pursue their connection once she is grown, either as a parental figure to her or as romantic partners.

Varada ends with Clara's realization that she will not be awarded with the love she so desires. Just as the doppelgänger can never truly return home (Webber 53), Clara attempts to commit suicide after Eva expels her from the house; for her, this option is preferable to returning to the town of reptiles. Yet, like her love for Eva, Clara's suicide attempt is unsuccessful, as she throws herself in front of a motorcycle instead of a larger, more lethal vehicle. Injured and confused but alive, she is returned to the home of her biological relatives, scarred on multiple levels by her encounter with Eva, which ultimately symbolizes maternal rejection for Clara. Despite her aversion toward her aunt and uncle, Clara comes to believe that her uncle is the only person who has ever loved her: "solo la ha querido – una pobre variedad de amor, pero amor de todos modos – el hombre sapo" ["only he, the toad man, has loved her – a poor variety of love, but love in any case"] (67). Although it is implied that he molests her, Clara views this manipulative, broken relationship as her last chance at a parent/child relationship where she might experience love.

The dissolution of Eva and Clara's relationship raises the question of whether Tusquets has elaborated a rejection of motherhood in *Varada*. While it would be difficult to assert that Eva completely renounces mothering – given that she has biological children – she certainly rejects her relationship with Clara. Initially compelled to fulfil a maternal role for her needy doppelgänger, Eva soon finds Clara's intense affection annoying and suffocating, "un amor que a Eva le causa un fastidio sin límites y que hace incluso se arrepienta algunas veces de haberse metido a esta chica en la casa" ["a love that causes Eva an annoyance without limits and that, at times, even makes her regret having brought that girl to the house"] (88). Ironically, although Eva feels a great sense of panic at the thought of losing Elia and Pablo's love, when she is presented with Clara's unconditional love, she is not able to accept it. In a way, then, Eva's decision to end her relationship with Clara is a rejection of motherhood, her way of overcoming imposed maternity that demands all women to constantly perform mothering for others. However, her action cannot be labelled as a complete subversion of heteronormativity and fixed gender roles, as Eva makes this choice to help herself forget Pablo's infidelity and attempt to repair her marriage.[9] Regardless of how the relationship with Clara ends, it reveals the danger of imposing the traditional motherhood role on all women and the failure and pain to which such enforced identities can lead.

Elia is another character who eschews the traditional motherhood role, and her relationship with her son further informs the vision of motherhood presented in *Varada*. The novel begins with Elia's description of typical mothers at the beach with their children, mothers whose lives are incomprehensible to her because they revolve solely around their children. At the novel's end, Elia retrieves her son from summer camp, falling prey to fixed maternal roles by choosing to devote her identity and personal sense of worth to motherhood. This ending to the novel forms a cyclical narration, linking *Varada*'s beginning to its conclusion. Elia chooses to embrace motherhood while Eva rejects her non-biological mother/child connection with Clara, presenting two alternatives along the spectrum of parenthood. Of course, Eva still has biological children whom she will most likely continue to parent in some form. *Varada* demonstrates that performances of parenthood can vary, not only from parental figure to parental figure, but within one parental figure's relationship to the various children for whom they perform parenthood. An examination of Eva and Clara's relationship in *Varada* leads to a unique perspective on a novel that offers no easy or clear-cut conclusions about motherhood. *Varada* has been called "the most positive and up-lifting of the three" (Gould Levine, "Reading, Rereading, Misreading" 212) novels in Tusquets's trilogy, as well as being designated a novel that purportedly "heralds the triumph of the feminine maternal principle in the universe" (Dolgin Casado 172). These interpretations, of course, stem from an analysis focused on Elia, not the failed mother/daughter relationship between Eva and Clara. Even analyses centred on Elia's motherhood have problematic elements. Nina Molinaro asserts, "It is noteworthy that Elia as narrator directs herself to an absent male receiver, a son instead of a daughter. When she finally reappropriates her own story, she consigns her future to the joys of motherhood, a role that has inspired no narrative attention until the conclusion" (*Foucault, Feminism and* 68). While some critics might find a reaffirmation of motherhood in *Varada*, Elia's enactment of motherhood, as well as Eva and Clara's relationship, clearly exposes the negative pressures of stereotypical motherhood that are imposed on many women.

In these texts, Castro and Tusquets develop thought-provoking characters that reach beyond the confines of traditional, heteronormative definitions of parenthood. The affective bonds that Alberto and Eva form with their non-biological children, as well as the unhealthy connections those children have with biological relatives, demonstrate that biological links are not necessary in familial formation. Alberto and Eva create cyclical parent/child relationships with Fidelia and Clara that at times suggest incestuous connections and the parental figures' desire to create alternative versions of themselves in their non-biological children. These parental figures question the limits of parenthood, incorporating a mixture of stereotypically maternal and paternal elements into their performances. These non-normative families, which ultimately dissolve, pinpoint additional performances of parenthood along the spectrum of possible Spanish family formations.

Chapter Six

A Family in All Senses

Fernando León de Aranoa's 2010 film *Amador* blurs geographic, economic, and cultural borders while questioning the constructs of family and even happiness itself. The eponymous title character is an elderly, bedridden Spaniard whose family has entrusted his care to Marcela, an undocumented, pregnant woman from Peru. Along with Puri, a Spanish sex worker who visits Amador once a week, Marcela cares for Amador and develops an emotional connection to him, while his biological family constructs their dream home across the country. Presenting Marcela's experience through the visceral lens of the five senses, León de Aranoa's film questions normative familial constructions to establish an affective familial bond between Marcela and Amador. With touch and taste, two senses crucial to Marcela's caregiver role as she must physically assist Amador and prepare food for him, the two create an exclusive connection of care. Amador teaches Marcela to use sight as a tool for seeking out positive signs about the future, and by the end of the film, Marcela begins to use her voice to gain agency by speaking back against the sounds of others' agendas. Smells – rotting flowers in particular – alert Marcela to the false promises presented to her in her romantic situation and her position as an immigrant in Spain. Through her rebellion against situations and relationships that are typically understood to cause happiness, Marcela rejects the heteronormative script of pregnancy and romantic relationships as all-fulfilling roles for women. Despite the complexities of their relationship – muddied by economic exchange, colonial legacy, and the power dynamics of the caregiver role – Marcela and Amador care for each other in ways that members of their established families cannot. Amador and Marcela (and to some extent, Puri) form a non-normative family through the five senses and affective ties only possible through a disavowal of the purported happiness to be found through participating in traditional, heteronormative familial roles. Without minimalizing the struggles of women from marginalized groups, *Amador* depicts female characters who embrace their otherness, looking beyond superficial happiness to claim emotional support and meaning through alternative affective ties, creating an example of a non-normative family that exists within the diverse spectrum of Spanish familial formation.

Throughout the film, Marcela (played by Magaly Solier) must make a series of decisions about her life, often confronting a range of unappealing options. She decides to take the caretaker job to help her boyfriend, Nelson (played by Pietro Sibille), raise money for a refrigerator needed for his flower business. Nelson, whose dream is to open a legitimate flower shop, organizes a group of fellow immigrants who sell flowers stolen from dumpsters. Marcela and Nelson refurbish the flowers, wrapping them in plastic and ribbon, spraying them with perfume, and preserving them in the fridge until they can be sold. Marcela is not invested in Nelson's dream, her dissatisfaction with her life evident at the opening of the film, as she tearfully writes Nelson a letter explaining why she is leaving him, packs a suitcase, and makes it as far as the bus stop. She faints while waiting for the bus, waylaying her journey to an unknown destination away from Nelson and leading to the discovery that she is pregnant. Nelson never realizes that she is pregnant, but Amador (played by Celso Bugallo) guesses her secret early on during their time together and immediately feels connected to her fetus. Amador dies shortly after Marcela begins to care for him, leaving her with a moral dilemma, as she needs to complete a month's work to receive the money needed for the fridge that she and Nelson have already bought on credit. Marcela continues to visit Amador's apartment daily, confiding the truth to Puri while doing her best to conceal Amador's death from his neighbours and family, until one day she arrives at the apartment to find Amador's daughter and her husband waiting for her.

León de Aranoa's focus on three marginalized characters – an undocumented immigrant, a frail older man, and a prostitute – is representative of the types of characters on which his work is centred (Black 73). Part of the *cine social* [social issue cinema] genre (Triana-Toribio 16),[1] León de Aranoa's films frequently address various social crises (Black 74). Produced in 2010, *Amador* is a reflection of the economic crisis that began in Spain in 2008, affecting both citizens and immigrants to Spain. As a way of examining social crises, León de Aranoa's oeuvre in general – and *Amador* in particular – emphasizes empathy, emotion, and sympathetic connections between audiences and protagonists (78). While many critics praise this style, his "[d]etractors argue that León de Aranoa's films resort to affective manipulation, relying on emotive soundtracks, character identification, and carefully plotted narratives to achieve little more than 'maudlin melodrama' (Lee 2006)" (Cameron 58).[2] However, Isolina Ballesteros writes about the function of melodrama in film, positing that, within such movies, the family becomes a tool for discussing larger social issues and provoking emotional reactions from audiences, while the use of marginalized characters bolsters a film's political message ("Embracing the Other" 4, 10). The heightened emotional awareness and use of marginalized characters in *Amador*, therefore, positions the film well to be analysed through the lens of affect theory.

Amador uncovers the home lives of two families – Marcela and Nelson's relationship against that of Amador and his biological family – and examines the assumption that the family is an institution meant to bring happiness to its members. However, neither Amador's nor Marcela's families offer them emotional fulfilment or comfort. In *The Promise of Happiness*, Sara Ahmed reasons that happiness can be a tool to maintain individuals in roles of oppression (the "happy" housewife, for example), thereby perpetuating certain configurations of people, such as the family unit (2, 11). Individuals who do not experience or exhibit signs of happiness in situations or groups that have been socially construed as happy become affect aliens, those who "are affected in the wrong way by the right things" or who "affect others in the wrong way: your proximity gets in the way of other people's enjoyment of the right things" (67). In *Amador*, Marcela is an affect alien, someone who "converts good feelings into bad, who as it were 'kills' the joy of the family" (Ahmed, *The Promise of* 49). One of the main ways in which Marcela divulges her status as an affect alien is through her lacklustre response to her pregnancy. While Marcela does not debate whether to continue with her pregnancy, she also does not tell anyone, especially Nelson, that she is pregnant. When Amador guesses her secret, her eyes fill with tears and her mouth forms a tight line. In many ways, Marcela embodies the storyline of a "successful" immigrant who is living the "European dream," which is described by Vega-Durán in *Emigrant Dreams, Immigrant Borders* as the motivation to relocate to Europe driven by the desire for economic stability or even prosperity, characterized by a prioritization of modernity and consumerism (34, 39–40). Marcela has a place to live, an employer, and a romantic partner who is focused on upward mobility and with whom she is about to start a family. None of her familial relationships or economic steps toward achieving the "European dream" affect Marcela as they "should," however, striking a discordant blow to audience assumptions about what an immigrant should desire. Marcela emanates a passive dissatisfaction throughout most of the film, her method of pushing back against normative expectations.

Marcela's lack of happiness when faced with imminent motherhood and forming a family with Nelson is juxtaposed against Amador's relationship with his family. On the surface, they represent a perfect Spanish family. They are economically stable enough to hire domestic help, they have the security of citizenship, and they occupy the privileged role of a multigenerational heteronormative family. As Ahmed asserts, the "face of happiness" can often look "rather like the face of privilege" (*The Promise of* 11); members of Amador's family should more easily be able to experience happiness than Marcela and Nelson, as their privilege has cleared many obstacles to happiness. Amador enjoys many privileges that Marcela cannot – including whiteness and masculinity – but he is marginalized by his age and his loneliness. His daughter Yolanda and her husband do not appear to have a strong affective relationship with Amador. Rather than grief, their primary emotion after Amador's death is fear that they will no longer receive his pension benefits. In Amador's crumbling relationship with his children, the film exposes contemporary Spanish anxieties about the future of the family, an institution that cannot live up to the idealized standard of the traditional nuclear family.

Numerous contemporary Spanish films have questioned the stability of the Spanish nuclear family, showing decay and disintegration of the family unit through death, abandonment of family members, physical abuse, or incest. In several films, one or both parents have either died or abandoned their children. In *Héctor* (2003, directed by Gracia Querejeta), the protagonist is abandoned as a baby by his father and loses his mother, who was addicted to pills and alcohol, to a car accident. In *Rastros de Sándalo* [*Traces of Sandalwood*] (2014, directed by María Ripoll), the film centres on the loss of childhood suffered by two sisters who are violently separated from each other in their youth. Young protagonists often lose a parent: the young protagonist in *Estiu 1993* [*Summer 1993*] (2017, directed by Carla Simón) is orphaned after losing her parents to AIDS; in *El viaje de Carol* [*Carol's Journey*] (2002, directed by Imanol Uribe), the mother dies and the father is persecuted after the Spanish Civil War; in *El laberinto del fauno* [*Pan's Labyrinth*] (2006, directed by Guillermo del Toro), another film about the Spanish Civil War, the child protagonist suffers at the hands of a cruel stepfather after her father has died. In *Ismael* (2013, directed by Marcelo Piñeyro), a father has long been separated from his son because he was unaware of his birth. In *Biutiful* (2010, directed by Alejandro González Iñárritu), a father struggles to keep his family together as they deal with economic hardship, the mother's addiction issues, and the father's terminal disease. In *La mosquitera* [*The Mosquito Net*] (2010, directed by Agustí Vila), the family is fragmented by both parents, who engage in sexual activities with people other than their partner. In *Azuloscurocasinegro* [*Dark Blue Almost Black*] (2006, directed by Daniel Sánchez Arévalo), a man asks his brother to impregnate his wife after being unable to do so himself, leading to familial conflict and fracturing.

Many other films indicate that the Spanish family is rotten, not only due to death or absence, but because of incest or other forms of sexual or physical violence that parents perpetrate on their children. Domestic violence (against women and children, respectively) is a central topic in *Te doy mis ojos* [*Take My Eyes*] (2003, directed by Icíar Bollaín) and *El bola* [*Pellet*] (2000, directed by Achero Mañas). In *Cuando vuelvas a mi lado* [*When You Return to My Side*] (1999, directed by Gracia Querejeta), three daughters are raised in a loveless home, learning later that their mother killed their father due to his incestuous behaviour. In *Elisa, vida mía* [*Elisa, My Life*] (1976, directed by Carlos Saura), a father abandons his daughters only to reconnect with them as adults and engage in incestuous behaviour with one of them. In *La isla interior* [*The Island Inside*] (2009, directed by Dunia Ayaso and Félix Sabroso), three adult children struggle with an emotionally unavailable mother and a schizophrenic father who consistently sexually abused one of the daughters. Of course, Pedro Almodóvar is the best-known Spanish director whose films often focus on some aspect of the dysfunctional Spanish family, like *Todo sobre mi madre* [*All about My Mother*] (1999), in which the son dies, never having met his father, who has become a trans woman working as a prostitute; and *Volver* [*To Return*] (2006), which deals with familial fragmentation and incest.

The future of both families (Marcela's and that of Amador's children) is uncertain at the end of the film. Like many contemporary Spanish families, Amador's family members find themselves pulled away from each other as individuals need to work outside the home to meet the economic and lifestyle demands of sustaining the middle-class family. Yolanda and her husband have pinned their future happiness on Amador's economic potential to contribute to the family, not only in order to guarantee the family's survival, but to maintain a lifestyle replete with vacations and other consumeristic pursuits. To this end, the family outsources care work for their eldest member while using Amador's pension to build their dream house. The film explores the importance of economic support versus emotional support within the familial unit, questioning what truly brings happiness to family members or whether the fostering of happiness can even be one of the functions of the family.

Yolanda hopes to keep Amador's death a secret so the family can continue to collect his pension, although it is questionable how long that plan will be sustainable.

Marcela's future is also uncertain, but open to the possibility that she will find happiness or contentment, possibly even within a new familial construction. At the very least, Marcela's unhappiness is a symbol of resistance; as she rejects an unappealing life with Nelson, she opens herself to an alternative future. Ahmed argues that suffering can be productive, "a way of doing something" and expressing one's "disagreement with what has been judged as good" (*The Promise of* 210). Those who are unhappy seek out ways to ease their suffering, often changing their circumstances, surroundings, or relationships that are causing the negative emotion. Suffering, therefore, is an active response, while happiness "can be a way of going along with what you are being asked to do" (Ahmed, *The Promise of* 210). Instead of feigning happiness, Marcela acknowledges her discomfort; by the end of the film, she realizes that she does not have to stay with Nelson. The flower shop is his dream alone, and even though she accepted the caretaker job to pay for the fridge, she ultimately tells Nelson that the money is not his. Marcela has decided what she does not want for her future, even though she does not appear to have a concrete plan for a new life. Regardless, to "narrate unhappiness can be affirmative; it can gesture toward another world, even if we are not given a vision of the world as it might exist after the walls of misery are brought down" (Ahmed, *The Promise of* 107). *Amador*'s conclusion, of course, cannot and should not be read as an unambiguously happy ending. Marcela refuses to find happiness where she "should," her resistance opening new possibilities for her, but the film offers no guarantee that Marcela will find happiness. As *Amador* ends with Marcela and Puri, sitting together on a bench alongside Marcela's suitcase and awaiting an unknown future, Marcela still does not have a plan for employment, childcare, or an established living situation.

Relationship Building through Touch

In *Amador*, Marcela, Amador, and Puri utilize various types of physical touch to establish and build relationships between themselves. The first instance of touching is between Marcela and Amador; as his caretaker, she must physically touch him to help him navigate the apartment. Domestic or caregiver work in Spain, often done by immigrants from Latin America or Africa, exposes a complicated relationship between economic and affective ties, "as a singular type of labor that reveals the dynamic interplay of gender difference, coloniality, and global supply chains in democratic Spain" (Murray 14). Since the 1980s, Spain has seen a drastic rise in immigration, which now totals over 10 per cent of the country's population, although Spain's 2008 economic crisis caused a reverse flow of immigration wherein many Latin American immigrants returned to their countries of origin, often followed by Spaniards seeking economic opportunities abroad (Murray 19–20). The relationship between Marcela and Amador begins as a purely economic one. Amador's daughter Yolanda meets with Marcela in a coffee shop across from Amador's apartment, where Yolanda explains the position as mostly keeping her father company. She offers Marcela the job after a brief conversation, remarking that Marcela does not need any qualifications for the position, a statement that minimizes the importance of the role despite the fact that Yolanda's elderly father will be completely in Marcela's care. At the end of their meeting, Yolanda asks, "¿Le he dicho ya cómo se llama?" ["Have I told you his name yet?"] (13:57–8), having omitted personal details in favour of discussing her father's physical needs as she might talk about any job that could be outsourced. Marcela responds to Yolanda with another question – "¿Puede ser 150?" ["Can it (the advance) be 150 euros?"] (13:59) – showing that her investment in this relationship is also financial. Although she views the arrangement as purely economic, Marcela will quickly develop affective ties, in part due to the nature of care work, a vulnerable act that "is not about letting an object go but holding on to an object by letting oneself go, giving oneself over to something that is not one's own" (Ahmed, *The Promise of* 186). Amador does not acknowledge Marcela's presence in the apartment until Marcela must touch him to help him urinate (Portillo 359), a highly private and intimate moment where Amador chooses to ask Marcela's name, realizing that a stranger is seeing him in a state of vulnerability. Amador may only be comforted or relieved of the need to urinate with Marcela's assistance, her physical labour of holding him up a reality that they would both rather have avoided or hidden. Ahmed writes of "the burden of concealment," the idea that some bodies may be made comfortable only through the physical work of others (such as domestic workers), but workers and recipients of such work may prefer to conceal the labour itself, enjoying the benefits of another's effort without acknowledging the person who exerted herself to make someone else comfortable (Ahmed, *The Cultural Politics* 149). In such an intimate situation, the reality of Marcela's labour cannot be concealed. This physical touch, however, facilitates the beginning of a relationship that will expand beyond the purely economical, although financial issues remain a concern and motivation for Marcela.

Through physical touch, emotional investment, and paid labour, Marcela begins to take the place of Amador's family. She alternately performs the role of parent and daughter: Marcela cares for Amador's physical needs, but she also listens to Amador's advice and is economically provided for by the money he pays her. As Marcela performs the role of caregiver/mother figure for Amador, a rehearsal for her upcoming biological motherhood, the repetition of motherly acts shapes Marcela's subjectivity in a way that connects her emotionally to Amador. Judith Butler asserts that we all are born into "gendered, racial, national" (Reddy and Butler 117) norms that limit how we may perform our identities, but as subjects, we maintain the agency to craft our performance from within those restrictions. Marcela's repeated performances of care transform her relationship with Amador into a familial one.

The affective ties between Marcela and Amador provide a commentary on Spanish perceptions of Latin American women, who are often seen as "ideal" nannies, housekeepers, or caretakers for older Spaniards, due to a shared language, as well as stereotypes that perceive Latin American women as submissive, long-suffering mother figures whose attributes include "a denial of their own subjectivity, suffering and sacrifice, moral superiority, nurturing" (Flesler and Shepherd 252). Murray compares Marcela to a flower, a prevalent symbol throughout the film, stating that she is "immersed in gender expectations that hearken back to a problematic, essential womanhood predicated on weakness and beauty" (143). No one in the film, apart from Amador, expects much from Marcela, reading her as weak and passive. This stereotype of the Latin American mother figure found in many Spanish films[3] has been critiqued as a misogynistic model meant to serve as a guide for Spanish women whose natality rates are low (Flesler and Shepherd 252). Latin American women are also attractive as care workers due to their economic vulnerabilities and precarious residency status. A study by Fundació Surt found that "immigrant worker women are exploited by long hours, sudden dismissal without compensation, threats of reporting their legal status, low wages or non-payment" (Murray 15). Yolanda most likely sees Marcela as an attractive candidate to care for her father because of her "perceived kindness, simplicity, and precarious financial situation" (Murray 143), the last of which will keep Marcela from making excessive demands on her employer.

While the care relationship can be mutually beneficial, as it can mean "upward mobility for many poor and working-class women" (Murray 14), these women are at the mercy of the families whose children and elderly they care for. Latin American immigrant women occupy an uncanny place in Spain, a country that is both home and not home.

Due to Spanish colonization, with its echoes of sexual conquest, Latin American women are "seen as highly assimilable through their roles as potential sexual partners, wives, and future mothers of Spanish children" (Flesler and Shepherd 246), and Spain perhaps sees it as a "moral duty" (Lutz 117) to take in immigrants from its former colonies. In Marcela's relationship with Amador, there is always a power and privilege imbalance. Reflecting this imbalance, Ahmed's concept of conditional happiness suggests a set of conditions for happiness, or an order in which people may achieve happiness. Certain individuals must wait for their happiness as secondary, only after another's happiness has been achieved. According to Ahmed:

> Citizenship provides a technology for deciding whose happiness comes first. What is at stake in citizenship is the differentiation between those who *are* and who are *not yet* citizens (what I call "would-be citizens"), where the "not yet" is offered as promise of what is to come. If the promise of citizenship is offered as a promise of happiness, then you have to demonstrate that you are a worthy recipient of its promise. (*The Promise of* 133)

In their relationship, Marcela has the promise of happiness – the 500 euros that she will ultimately keep for her own future with her unborn child – but it can only be achieved as long as Amador and Yolanda are happy with her services.

While Marcela connects with Amador through a caretaker's motherly touch, Puri is a Spanish prostitute who visits once a week to engage in sexual touching with Amador.[4] When Puri first appears at the apartment, Marcela asks her what she does with Amador for an hour every Thursday. Puri responds that, just like Marcela, she is taking care of Amador. Marcela is surprised to learn that Puri makes more in an hour (30 euros) than she does all day, but Puri reasons, "Mi trabajo necesita una especialización y el tuyo no" ["My job needs specialization and yours doesn't"] (1:03:03–4). A long shot from earlier in the film affirms the notion that much of Marcela's job is sitting, waiting, and simply being a presence within the apartment. In the shot, Marcela sits alone at Amador's kitchen table. She had been working on some sewing, but her hands now rest inactive on her lap as she stares into the distance. The long shot reveals Marcela's place within the apartment and Amador's life, and speaks to the isolation and loneliness of both characters. Marcela and Amador physically share the space of the apartment, but they are each trapped within their own minds. Through physical and sexual touch, Puri breaks through Amador's isolation, connecting to him and caring for him sexually and emotionally for the past four or five years. Puri tells Marcela that they used to have sex, a relationship that shifted to hand jobs, although lately Amador has not shown interest in this sexual activity. Puri continues to visit and presumably engage in some sort of sexual touching, although her company is clearly as important as the sexual acts. Puri and Marcela "forman un vínculo de entendimiento mutuo, casi maternal, en su cuidado de Amador debido a su coexistencia en este mundo de invisibilidad de profesiones que aún siguen sin mucho reconocimiento oficial" ["form a bond of mutual understanding, almost maternal, in their care of Amador due to a coexistence in this world of invisibility of professions that still continue without much official recognition"] (Black 89). Even after Amador dies, Puri continues to visit Marcela at the apartment, and the two of them pray for Amador's soul. While emotional ties have clearly been formed between the three characters, both women began their relationships with Amador on the basis of economic necessity. Sex and care work are both types of "[c]ommodified intimacy or intimate labor" (Stehle and Weber 94), establishing economic and power differentials between Amador and the women. Although he is currently marginalized due to his age and infirmity, Amador has lived as a privileged member of his society. His relationship with Puri can be viewed as another affirmation that he belongs, that he has a "right" to occupy space in Spain. Amador receives pleasure from Puri, which "involves not only the capacity to enter into, or inhabit with ease, social space, but also functions as a form of entitlement and belonging. Spaces are claimed through enjoyment, an enjoyment that is returned by being witnessed by others" (Ahmed, *The Cultural Politics* 164–5). Puri and Marcela both witness Amador's pleasure without questioning his right to receive pleasure and care from them. Although she avoids Amador's bedroom when Puri visits, Marcela knows what they are doing. When she enters his room for the first time after Puri's visit, Marcela smiles slyly, notable because she rarely smiles or appears animated in any way. Marcela and Puri provide different physical services for Amador, but physical touch facilitates emotional intimacy and relationship building between all three characters.

Arguably the most important type of touch in the film comes when Amador asks to feel Marcela's stomach in hopes of noting movement by the fetus within, solidifying the non-normative familial bond between all three through this performance of familial care expressed through touch. This request comes after Amador realizes that Marcela is pregnant as he watches her organize his bedroom. With certainty, Amador states, "Estás embarazada" ["You're pregnant"] (30:26). Marcela nods in affirmation, tears in her eyes. Amador then asks what she will call the baby; when she admits that she is unsure, he tells her she needs to have

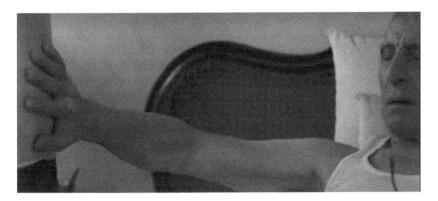

Figure 6.1 Amador touching Marcela's stomach

a name. Amador asks, "¿Puedo tocarlo?" ["Can I touch it?"] (30:56), so Marcela comes closer to the bed.

Amador places his hand on her stomach and closes his eyes. He moans several times, noises that could be interpreted as sexual, manifestations of pain, or simply an overabundance of emotion. Amador asks permission to speak to the fetus, saying, "Llegas tarde. Nos vamos a cruzar. Aquí no hay sitio para nadie. Pero yo me voy ya y te dejo mi sitio. Tu madre lo va a guardar para ti. Es tuyo. Acuérdate. Que nadie te lo quite" ["You're arriving late. We're going to miss each other. Here there isn't room for anyone. But I am leaving already, and I will leave you my spot. Your mother is going to save it for you. It's yours. Remember. Don't let anyone take it from you"] (31:41–32:04). Amador feels a connection to the fetus, strong enough to promise that he will leave his spot in Spain and in life for the newcomer. Marcela, in ways a mother figure to Amador, is further linked to the Spaniard through his connection with the fetus. Even so, after this emotionally moving moment, the next shot shows Marcela literally waiting in line, not for her child's place in the world, but for the 150 euros from Yolanda, reminding viewers that, despite the construction of affective ties, their relationship is demarcated by economic demands. When Puri finds out that Marcela is pregnant, she also asks to touch Marcela's stomach and inquires if she has chosen a name. These are the only two people beside the doctor to know about Marcela's pregnancy, and the emotional connections Marcela and the fetus have with each of them stand in contrast to the relationship that Marcela has with people in her normative familial construction. Nelson never realizes that Marcela is pregnant; at one point, he touches her stomach and comments that she has gained weight. Marcela lives with Nelson and has conceived a child with him; while she is expected to create a family with him, their relationship does not fulfil her emotional needs. This juxtaposition of Nelson's touch to Puri's and Amador's physical interactions with Marcela illustrates the concept that biological connection is not necessarily the most meaningful indicator of familial affinity. Nelson's touch does not increase his intimacy with Marcela, nor does it allow him to better understand her. When Amador and Puri touch Marcela's stomach, however, they convey love and acknowledgment of who she is, establishing a familial bond between them.

Amador's acceptance of Marcela's baby, ceding his spot in Spain for the child to come, is both a symbol of their formation of a non-normative family and a reflection on the concept of the nation as family. By giving his spot to a Latin American immigrant's future child, Amador, a Spanish man, signals his acceptance of a new, multiracial and multicultural Spain, providing an alternate construction of family, wherein parenthood is performed by a Spanish man who welcomes immigrant members into a multicultural family. The skin of Marcela's body represents a border that her fetus will cross to enter into Spanish society. Although Amador welcomes Marcela's child, the film reflects social anxieties about the presence of immigrants in Spain. Ahmed writes about "soft touch," the concept that a nation is akin to a body vulnerable to attack by others. Ahmed affirms that

> the metaphor of "soft touch" suggests that the nation's borders and defences are like skin; they are soft, weak, porous and easily shaped or even bruised by the proximity of others. It suggests that the nation is made vulnerable to abuse by its very openness to others. The soft nation is too emotional, too easily moved by the demands of others, and too easily seduced into assuming that claims for asylum, as testimonies of injury, are narratives of truth. (*The Cultural Politics* 2)

Marcela and her unborn child push against the soft, human borders of Spain, a country whose literature and film have long conflated symbols of family with those of nation. Many contemporary cinematic and literary representations of the Spanish family address the panic that "[i]ncorporating migrants into the family could destabilize nationalist hierarches" (Murray 39), presenting immigrants as a source of contamination or pollution within the home (134). However, just as the Spanish family faces the anxiety of societal and racial changes, "of becoming 'less white,' by allowing those who are recognized as racially other to penetrate the surface of the body" (Ahmed, *The Cultural Politics* 3), several depictions of the Spanish family in recent films reveal that the institution was rotten or in decay before the influx of immigration that brought with it the fears of outside contamination. This familial disintegration is manifested within *Amador* by the fact that Amador's biological family has left him in the care of a near-complete stranger to build their dream house on the coast, suggesting "the breakdown of family bonds among Spanish nationals" (Murray 146), and indicating that the concept of the traditional Spanish family never fully existed as a functional affective unit. Rather than an idealized, fictional construction of the family, *Amador* demonstrates that Spanish families have always existed along a diverse spectrum of lived experiences and familial configurations.

Even if the wholesomeness of the traditional Spanish family is a myth, nationalist impulses resist the concept of any type of reconfiguration of the family unit. Ahmed considers love within the family to be the urge to reproduce sameness, to create "future generations in the image I have of myself and the loved other, who together can approximate a 'likeness,' which can be bestowed on future generations" (*The Cultural Politics* 129). In such a description of love, immigrants and other nonnormative or marginalized figures would be seen as a threat to the family and the nation (144). *Amador*, however, offers a more positive view of immigrants, as individuals who might be able to mend and unify the broken Spanish family. While immigrant domestic workers are often not seen as real members of the Spanish families they serve (Murray 135), Marcela and Puri, by the end of the film, seem to be more closely affectively linked to Amador than his biological family.

Reconfiguring Family Ties through Taste

Taste is another point of connection between Marcela and Amador, strengthening their relationship, even as it reveals the weaknesses in Amador's link to his biological family. Associated with food, taste falls under the caregiver's purview, as a caregiver or mother figure is often responsible for food preparation. One of Marcela's first actions in Amador's apartment is to prepare him a soup, which he ignores while she remains in the apartment. When Marcela returns the next day, the soup bowl is empty, foreshadowing Amador's acceptance of her presence and the development of their affective relationship. Through consumption, Amador indicates his willingness to accept Marcela as a caregiver, an openness that facilitates their non-normative familial formation.

Marcela's consumption, as it only occurs once throughout the film despite having access to food and drink at various points, solidifies her connection to Amador. The only time Marcela ingests something onscreen is when she drinks a coffee, sitting in the café across from Amador's apartment the day after he has died. While debating about what she should do next, Marcela pauses to drink coffee and ruminate on her affective connection with Amador. She is visibly upset by his death, and the coffee creates a symbolic connection between the two of them based on consumption. While she thinks, a woman in a wheelchair passes by outside. Amador and Marcela had watched the woman from his window, Amador telling her that she was a mermaid who hid her legs under the blanket on her lap. As I will later argue, mermaids and the sea are symbols of hope in *Amador*. As Marcela watches the woman pass, she decides to continue visiting Amador, maintaining the ruse that he is alive, a choice that allows Amador to continue caring for her economically.

While Marcela drinks a coffee in the café where she feels close to Amador, she never consumes food or drink with Nelson, emphasizing the lack of connection between the two of them. When she goes on a date with Nelson and later when she attends a block party, food and drink are available to her, but Marcela does not partake in either situation. Early in the film, when Marcela and Nelson are surrounded by the chaos of flower sellers in their apartment, Marcela comments, "Me duele la barriga" ["My stomach hurts"] (8:26–8). Nelson asks her if she has eaten, to which she shakes her head. As food symbolizes connection in the film, Marcela indicates her lack of connection to Nelson in this scene, caused in part by their incompatible desires for the future. Nelson forges ahead with his flower-selling plans while Marcela quietly and disapprovingly sits at the centre of his machinations.

Just as with Nelson, Marcela does not consume any food or drink in either of her meetings with Yolanda, evidence that her affective link with Amador does not extend to other members of his biological family. In the first and last meeting with Yolanda, which occur in the same café where Marcela drinks her coffee, two glasses of water sit on the table, but neither woman drinks. Although Yolanda appears kind enough to Marcela, her family stands to be threatened by Marcela's symbolic status as a pregnant immigrant, an anxiety-provoking marker of a changing, multicultural Spain. Just as Ahmed writes about the soft borders of a nation, vulnerable to invasion by outsiders, immigrants performing

> domestic work within Spanish homes render national boundaries fuzzy. Indeed, the concepts of inside/outside, self/Other, native/foreigner become blurry when these women enter Spanish homes and engage in care work that aims to preserve the home – customarily depicted as a site

of tradition and a microcosm of the nation – and to perpetuate the national population and culture through social reproduction. (Murray 133–4)

While Yolanda and her husband depend on Marcela's cheap labour, they may also worry about how she will alter Amador's home or the image of family they have constructed for themselves. In a way, Marcela does invade Amador's home. After his death, she fills his apartment with red and white flowers, colours reminiscent of the Peruvian flag. One bouquet of flowers is even arranged into the stripes of the Peruvian flag – red, white, and red – alluding to Spanish anxieties about invasion of the home country. Immigrants and the domestic work they provide might be allowed into Spain, but only insofar as they play by the rules of Spanish culture. Ahmed asserts that multiculturalism offers happiness only through assimilation to established cultural norms, offering happiness "in return for loyalty to the nation, where loyalty is defined in terms of playing its game" (*The Promise of* 122). Marcela seems to understand the need to carefully navigate her position as someone who occupies an in-between cultural space. Her keepsake box, which appears twice in the film, symbolizes her cultural identity. The box has a false bottom, under which Marcela guards photos and her Peruvian passport, the only concrete identifier of her home country. Marcela opens the box to examine the contents or add something for safekeeping, but the false bottom is a reminder that she cannot allow too much of her cultural identity to show in the foreign environment in which she now lives.

Whether Yolanda and her husband are conscious of these anxieties of cultural invasion, they are certainly keeping a vigilant eye on Marcela. After Amador's death, there are several moments when Marcela returns to his apartment and notices that things are not as she had left them: the fan is rotating when she had left it stationary, and she finds a mysterious candy wrapper on the floor. Marcela suspects that Amador's unhappy spirit remains in the apartment. One day, she returns to see that the door to the apartment is open, Yolanda and her husband waiting inside. Yolanda and Marcela go to the café across the street to talk, where Yolanda tells her that they are very content with her work. They would like her to keep coming to air out the house, get the mail, and keep Amador company, noting that "las casas, si no, se deterioran" ["otherwise, houses deteriorate"] (01:43:33). Yolanda explains that they are overbudget with the construction of their new house, and Amador was helping with his pension. Essentially, Yolanda asks Marcela to do the dirty work of hiding Amador's death until the construction can be completed, a proposal that is economically beneficial for them all. Yolanda's affective response to Amador's death, motivated primarily by economic concerns, is another indicator of the decay of the Spanish family. As Yolanda proposes this arrangement, Marcela watches Yolanda's husband unwrap a candy across the street. As the wrapper floats to the ground, she recognizes it as the same candy wrapper she found in Amador's apartment. Every time she was worried about a ghostly presence, it was really Amador's family checking in on the apartment. While Marcela was wracked with grief and guilt over her deception surrounding Amador's death, his biological family had already known about his death, involved in the betrayal in an even more convoluted way. Yolanda ends her conversation with Marcela by saying that Amador is like a flower, beautiful even in death, lamenting the "hueco grande" ["large hole"] (01:44:39) that his death has left in their lives. Marcela responds, "No se preocupe. Pronto se va a llenar" ["Don't worry. It will soon be filled"] (01:44:43–6), referencing the imminent birth of her baby, although Yolanda is unaware of her meaning or of Amador's belief that he was cosmically linked to Marcela's unborn child.

Smelling the Flowers: Love, Death, and False Promises

While Marcela feels emotionally connected to Amador, she remains sceptical about romantic love, as well as the promises of a better life to be found through immigration. Nelson insists that Spain will provide a stable future for them both, boasting that his flower business will never fail, as people commemorate the three most important life events (love, birth, and death) with flowers. He comments that while the majority of the flowers sold in Spain previously came from Holland, they now arrive from Latin American countries, a changing pattern that reflects current migratory movements. For Nelson, the flower is a symbol of the immigrant, resilient and able to survive. The movie opens with the shot of a single flower, growing alone on a hillside. Soon, immigrant flower sellers run past as they hurry to scavenge discarded flowers from nearby dumpsters. The flower remains upright, unharmed, embodying "both fragility and strength as it survives the trampling" (Murray 143), a reflection of how Nelson sees himself.

For Marcela, however, Nelson's flowers represent death and decay, the negative underside of both the immigrant experience and her affective relationships. Marcela's job caring for Amador represents the economic promise of a better future, until his death leaves her in an impossible predicament. Marcela brings flowers to Amador's apartment after his death, a common ritual performed for the deceased. In this case, Marcela intends for the flowers to mask the smell of Amador's decaying body. Smells in the film alert the audience to situations in Marcela's life that are not as they appear – in this case, both immigration's false promise of a better life that disappears with Amador's death and the illusion of the perfect Spanish family. Like the flowers that Nelson sells, whose appearances have been designed to deceive purchasers, the Spanish traditional nuclear family presents itself as a beautiful flower. Upon closer inspection, the family reveals itself to be rotten, diseased by economic concerns that cause stress and familial fragmentation. Yolanda and her husband profess their love for Amador, but it is a conditional affective relationship complicated by their desire for Amador's pension, and they willingly leave Amador in his depressing apartment under Marcela's care. Economic and emotional ties bind Marcela to Amador, whose death threatens an end to economic upward mobility for Marcela and Nelson, revealing the harsh reality of the immigrant experience in Spain. Marcela cannot move Amador's body, nor report his death to Yolanda, because then she would not complete the month of service required to receive the 500 euros she and Nelson need to pay for the fridge they have already purchased (and upon which their livelihood depends). As Madrid summer temperatures continue to rise, Marcela is desperate to keep the smell from reaching Amador's suspicious neighbour. She brings armfuls of bouquets, filling Amador's room with flowers in various stages of death and decay. The flowers alone cannot mask the smell of death, partly because they have already lost much of their smell by the time Nelson procures them. When Marcela asks why Nelson sprays the flowers before selling them, he replies with no hint of irony, "Para que huelan a flores" ["So they smell like flowers"] (16:32–4). Marcela, whose questioning attitude is appreciated much more by Amador than by Nelson, responds, "¿Las flores no huelen a flores?" ["The flowers don't smell like flowers?"] (16:38–9). This deception mirrors Marcela's experience of being an immigrant in Spain. She imagined that Spain would offer her a better life, but she has found little about which to be happy. Marcela complains that the perfume used on the flowers makes her sick, most likely due to the pregnancy that she has not revealed to Nelson. Her aversion to the smell of the perfume is a commentary on her relationship with Nelson, much like the dying flowers he attempts to market as markers of romance.

Marcela's relationship with Nelson leaves her desiring something less superficial, especially after comparing their relationship with an epistolary courtship between Amador and a woman whose identity is unknown to her. After Amador's death, Marcela reads a letter he had written but never had the chance to send to the woman, where he finally admits that he loves her, "con toda mi alma" ["with all my soul"] (01:11:18–21). The woman will never read Amador's words, as she dies around the same time as Amador. Marcela sends the letter, but it is returned to the apartment with a note that the recipient is deceased. In the letter, Amador had written that his words were worthless kept within himself, but in his beloved "quizá florezcan" ["maybe they would flower"] (01:11:13–15). The image of words blooming into a flower symbolizes love's promise of beauty, health, and life, in this case offered too late. When Marcela returns to her apartment after reading the letter, she asks Nelson if there is anything he would like her to know in case something unforeseen, like sudden death, should happen to one of them. Nelson can't think of anything, failing another test she has quietly set for him. While on the surface Nelson seems to adore her, telling her that he will open a flower shop with her name and spelling out "Flores Marcela" ["Marcela's Flowers"] in magnets on the fridge, Nelson is completely out of touch with her emotions and desires. Furthermore, *Amador* provides evidence of Nelson's "indiscreet infidelities" (Reuben Muñoz 1162), calling into question Nelson's happiness and affective ties to Marcela. In several instances, Marcela lies alone in bed, unable to sleep, while Nelson is nowhere to be seen. Once, audiences see him outside drinking and loudly chatting with one of the Latin American flower sellers, Gladis, and her friends. Marcela and Nelson's relationship resembles the flowers they try to revive enough to sell; the promise of freshness and vitality is little more than an illusion, the flower's perfumed smell a distant memory. Marcela's unhappiness with her romantic relationship and current economic situation is understandable and even productive, as it allows her to analyse her life and think critically about which aspects of her life she must push back against. Reuben Muñoz criticizes scholars who complain about Marcela's silences and glum life prospects, calling this type of analysis patronizing. He asserts that such a perspective "harbours the false assumption that fear and introversion are negative or unrealistic traits to impose on Marcela's character, when really, they offer a glimpse into part of the experience of the precarious, female immigrant" (1162). *Amador* does not offer viewers the upbeat and scrappy immigration story they might expect or desire. Rather, Marcela's character reflects the harsh reality of a woman marginalized by intersecting identity categories.

Sight, Hope, and Visions of the Future

Sight, both in reference to what Marcela can and cannot see, functions as a promise of future happiness in the film, a complicated vision for Marcela to accept. Marcela spends most of her time either in the apartment she shares with Nelson or in Amador's home, neither location an inspiring sight. Often considered a refuge, a shelter from the rest of the world, particularly for older people who have spent many years there (Ness et al., 1), Amador's home instead represents life's stagnation. His apartment's colour palette is composed of tones of brown, including the curtains, the floor, the bedspread, and the walls. Puri suggests that Amador's biological family has left him there, "muerto de asco" ["dead from disgust"] (1:04:20). The state of Amador's apartment reflects Spanish anxieties about the changing formation of the family. The home, the centre of the family, has "visibly disintegrated, a form of decay that suggests the death of an old way of life and the nation's inability to negotiate the cultural diversity central to its tenuous modernity. Domestic servants are hired to keep entropy at bay" (Murray 140–1). In this instance, sight provides Marcela with the knowledge that Amador's biological family has neglected him, proving that his affective connection with them is damaged. Marcela does her best to compensate for this familial neglect, maintaining order and tidiness within the apartment; it is not until after Amador's death, however, that she brings colour to the apartment with the red and white flowers meant to disguise the smell of decay.

The only other splash of colour in Amador's apartment is his puzzle, filled with blue tones of the ocean and sky, set against white, puffy clouds. The sea in *Amador* symbolizes both connection and separation. On the one hand, "the sea functions as a spectral reminder of the struggles already endured by those migrants whose journeys are successful" (Noble 645). As Fiona Noble establishes, the characters in *Amador* and the audience never see the water; rather, it is evoked through conversations and the puzzle (645). The absence of the sea positions Marcela's journey of immigration as an experience belonging to the past, something that Marcela has already overcome. As part of the immigrant journey, the sea both creates a border between Latin America and Spain (and Marcela and Amador) and becomes a point of connection, something that must be traversed to end the separation between the two cultures (Noble 647). When Amador asks Marcela if there is sea in her country, she shakes her head, even though Peru has an extensive coast along the Pacific Ocean. Marcela's motivations behind the misguiding shake of the head are unclear. She may come from an interior part of Peru, where she would not have seen the sea regularly. Marcela could simply wish to be agreeable, or the film might be making a tongue-in-cheek commentary on Amador's perceptions (as a Spaniard) of Latin America and immigrants.

I propose that Marcela's tiny lie is connected to the symbolism of the sea as the promise of hope, the enticement of a journey that will lead to a better life. Marcela may have denied the presence of the sea in Peru because she felt there was no hope for her there. Amador asks if she left her country because there was no sea, and she again lies with a nod of the head, although it remains to be seen if Spain will offer her the potential for a better life. Amador is a man who finds signs of the sea everywhere, maintaining an abundance of hope despite his depressing apartment and the fact that his biological family has left him behind. Amador may hope that he will be reunited with his family after the beach house is constructed, as Yolanda states that she was saving a room for him with a sea view in the house they were building. Amador's puzzle choice expresses a desire for connection with his biological family that will never come to fruition. Nonetheless, the sea is a hopeful image for Amador, one he associates with those he cares about, including Puri, whom he calls a mermaid. Amador sees hidden mermaids everywhere, telling Marcela that the woman they watch from his bedroom window is a mermaid, too, who uses a wheelchair so that she can hide her tail under a blanket.[5] Marcela teases him, calling him crazy, but Amador replies that Marcela's problem – a problem shared by all women, as well as people from her country, he clarifies – is the inability to believe in what she cannot see, or her lack of foresight. If the sea represents hope for the future, Amador must know that his earthly future is limited, but his understanding of life is cyclical. He knows that he will die, but he believes that Marcela's child will take his place, or even that he will be born again as Marcela's child. For Amador, the hope of the sea and the journey to which it refers is the transition between life and death, a voyage that connects all people, regardless of nationality.

For Amador and Marcela, the puzzle symbolizes a way of interpreting one's place in life, each life an individual puzzle affected by unique cultural and economic factors. Amador views life as a series of steps, like putting together a puzzle: through coming to know oneself and understanding the puzzle pieces of life, a person gains agency and helps them to make the best decisions for their future. Marcela's puzzle, however, is complicated in ways that Amador's is not, by the effects of immigration and postcolonialism in Spain. Despite his kindness toward Marcela, Amador demonstrates his privileged perspective when he tries to explain life to Marcela as a puzzle. He theorizes, "Antes de nacer, te dan todas las piezas. Tú no sabes que las tienes, pero te las dieron, y a ti, te toca ir colocándolas en su sitio. Eso es la vida" ["Before being born, they give you all the pieces. You don't know that you have them, but they gave them to you, and it's your responsibility to put them in their place. That's life"] (22:53–23:04). Marcela is quick to respond that she was not given anything to help her through life.

Without much reflection, Amador insists, "A ti te las dieron también. Lo que pasa es que no lo sabes. Pero las tienes. Y es responsabilidad tuya saber dónde va cada una" ["They gave them to you, too. What happens is that you don't know it. But you have them. And it's your responsibility to know where each piece goes"] (23:17–25). Amador does not pause to think that the pieces of gender, race, colonialism, and geography have shaped their two puzzles very differently. Because he has led a privileged life, Amador can insist on the importance of individualism, effort, and determination in shaping one's life course, while Marcela has struggled with factors that Amador knows nothing about.

Ahmed explains that, for immigrants to be assimilated into their new countries, they must pass a happiness test for citizenship (*The Promise of* 130) and "accept empire as the gift of happiness, which might involve an implicit injunction to forget or not to remember the violence of colonial rule" (*The Promise of* 131). If Marcela wishes to succeed in Spain, she must put the difficulties of the journey behind her, out of mind just like the sea is out of sight, and not focus too intently on the ways in which her life is affected by postcolonialism. As an affect alien, Marcela struggles to conjure up the appropriate emotional reactions to situations that should make her happy. Nelson is much more eager to unquestioningly assimilate into Spanish society, unbothered by being

> bound by the happiness duty not to speak about racism in the present, not to speak of the unhappiness of colonial histories, or of attachments that cannot be reconciled into the colorful diversity of the multicultural nation. The happiness duty for migrants means telling a certain story about your arrival as good, or the good of your arrival. The happiness duty is a positive duty to speak of what is good but can also be thought of as a negative duty not to speak of what is not good, not to speak from or out of unhappiness. (Ahmed, *The Promise of* 158)

Nelson consciously distinguishes himself from other Latin American and African immigrants, whom he characterizes as lazy, scornfully describing how one of the flower sellers tried to "jugarse el inmigrante conmigo" ["play the immigrant with me"] (27:24–6), describing him as a "negro cabrón" ["Black asshole"] (27–3). Nelson, who sees himself as an entrepreneur, has plans that include expanding the flower business into a shop, moving into a better apartment, travelling with Marcela, and having a child in the near future.

However, Marcela cannot share this positive vision of a future together. In fact, Nelson's "optimism, hope, and happiness can be technologies of control" (Ahmed, *The Promise of* 188). With his upbeat attitude, Nelson encourages Marcela to look past all the points of dissatisfaction in her life and simply accept her reality. Marcela's unhappiness in her relationship with Nelson is a tool she uses to think critically about her life and the aspects of it she would like to change. Although her pregnancy upsets her plans to leave Nelson, she does not consider ending the pregnancy, despite her lack of enthusiasm. Through a conversation between Marcela and Nelson, audiences learn that he convinced her to abort a fetus two years ago that Marcela would have been happy to have kept. Marcela's biggest issue with Nelson is that she cannot imagine a future with him, saying, "Cierro los ojos y no veo nada" ["I close my eyes and I don't see anything"] (34:06–8). Her lack of vision or imagination for the future stems from her past experiences that have taught her not to put faith in something she cannot see. When she has her first sonogram, Marcela asks the doctor if the fetus looks like her. The doctor smiles and responds that it's too soon to know such things. At a later sonogram, Marcela repeats the question, and the doctor affirms that the fetus looks just like her. Marcela can rest assured that this is a future she can see, deciding to leave Nelson (whom she just can't see in her future) to embark on a new journey that includes only herself and her child.

The Sound of Agency

In *Amador*, Marcela's journey is chronicled through sound; she begins the film a quiet individual overpowered by the noises around her but slowly finds her voice (although she never becomes verbose) as her personal agency grows. Marcela rarely speaks at the beginning of the film, her expressions – ranging from frowns to the tiniest of smiles – too timid to make much of an impact on those around her. Marcela's silence is contrasted with the film's overwhelming diegetic sound. In early scenes, Marcela seems to shrink into the apartment she shares with Nelson, chaotically filled with immigrant flower sellers who argue loudly about quantities and prices of the flowers they sell. In Amador's apartment, the noises of domesticity overtake her: the whirring of the blender, the clink of Amador's pills as they pop out of their packaging onto the plate, the advertisements on the radio about money orders to Latin America. Other sounds represent the vigilance of Spaniards who are suspicious about her intrusion into Amador's home. Yolanda calls on the telephone to check on her, and the neighbour rings the doorbell while demanding to speak with Amador, both noises jarringly interrupting Marcela's work.

Marcela's relationship with Amador begins in silence, as she embodies the stereotype of "immigrant women as caring automatons who remain largely mute or monosyllabic" (Ryan, "Maternal Identities" 406). Her relationship with Amador grows, and Marcela begins to find her voice, arguing with Amador and questioning him in a playful way. After Amador claims that he doesn't believe she has a boyfriend because no one calls the apartment, Marcela carries on a loud, fake phone conversation about going dancing in an attempt to convince Amador. However, just because Marcela becomes more vocal with Amador, her personality does not completely change. In many ways, Marcela never follows the stereotypical path of the immigrant success story. In her refusal to blindly accept happiness, Marcela demonstrates that what she wants for herself, and what she is able to attain, does not reflect what society might imagine as her aspirations. Toward the end of the film, as she and Puri hang Amador's puzzle of the sea that they have completed and framed, Marcela reflects on the value of silence in a voiceover, sharing, "En mi tierra se dice solo cuando todo esté en silencio, entonces escucharéis de verdad" ["In my country, they say that only when everything is in silences will you truly hear"] (01:45:09–14). While Marcela finds agency through reclaiming her voice, her earlier silence also had purpose. Others may interpret Marcela's silence as weakness, much as Rafa's quiet demeanour in *La buena estrella* (chapter 3) can be read as weakness. For both Marcela and Rafa, however, silence equates not to weakness but rather a reflective stillness that allows them to observe and process the world around them. Marcela uses her silence to listen to Amador, which allows her to understand him in a way that no one else does. By listening to Amador, she grows close to him, forming the familial bond that gives her the strength of voice that will ostensibly allow her to guide her child, much in the way that Amador performs a parental role for Marcela by giving her advice and life lessons.

In the cyclical nature of the film, Amador, Marcela, and her fetus become a non-normative family. Marcela is a mother figure, both expecting a biological child and caring for Amador, who has many of the same needs as a child and accepts her care, affirming the psychic link he feels with her fetus. In other ways, Amador is a father figure for Marcela, providing her with the economic support she needs to re-envision her life, as well as the gift of acceptance. As a symbolic representative of the Spanish people, Amador creates a space in Spain for Marcela and her child. Ahmed asserts that to "inherit the family is to inherit the demand to reproduce its form. The family also becomes a pressure point, as being necessary for a good or happy life, which in turn is how we achieve a certain orientation toward something and not others as good" (*The Promise of* 46). While Marcela accepts Amador's spot for her son, a decision recognized through her completion of his puzzle (Domingo Amestoy 123), the family Marcela forms with her son will not be a recreation of the stereotypical, traditional Spanish family, but rather an alternate family formation that exists along a diverse spectrum of familial relationships and performances, one that blends cultures and experiences to create a unique unit. Amador believes that he will live on through Marcela's son, who will be a new type of Spanish citizen, a cultural mixture that has provoked so much anxiety. While many fear what Ahmed calls the "cannibalistic fantasy" (*The Cultural Politics* 64) of otherness, the threat that a person or group will be subsumed within the body of the other, Amador is not afraid. In fact, he has the opposite reaction, eager to be incorporated into Marcela's life through the birth of her child. In the letter he writes to the mysterious woman he loves, Amador tells her that he does not have much time left, asking, "¿No escuchas por la noche las sirenas al otro lado de la pared? No estoy triste. Será solo un rato a oscuras, y pronto otra mujer me dará a luz" ["At night, don't you hear the mermaids on the other side of the wall? I am not sad. It will be dark for only a little while, and soon another woman will give birth to me"] (1:09:37–10:03). Amador's words are a confirmation that he feels connected to the fetus, that he believes in some way his spirit will be reincarnated in Marcela's baby. As Amador speaks these words, Marcela (and perhaps the fetus) hears his message, the sound of Amador's voice reinforcing their non-normative familial connection and emboldening Marcela toward greater agency through a belief that she and her child belong in Spain.

At the end of the film, Marcela's future is uncertain, but she has gained agency and taken control of her performance of parenthood and configuration of family, her relationship with Amador suggesting that Spain is open to the construction of more diverse, multicultural families. In the final scene, Marcela has left Nelson and is waiting on a bench with Puri, alongside her suitcase.

As they wait on the bench, Puri asks Marcela if she has decided on a name for her child. Marcela smiles and nods, ostensibly meaning that she has decided to name her baby Amador, reaffirming their non-normative familial connection. However, *Amador* ends with no guarantee or indication that Marcela is no longer an affect alien or that she will search out stereotypical happiness as part of the typical immigrant success story. Often happiness implies "living a certain kind of life, one that reaches certain points, and which, in reaching these points, creates happiness for others" (Ahmed, *The Promise of* 48). If she were to adhere to the "European dream," described by Vega-Durán as economic accumulation and participation in a consumerist society, Marcela would have stayed with Nelson and subscribed to his dream of a flower shop,

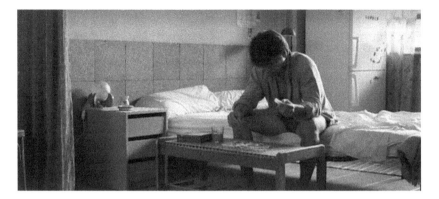

Figure 6.2 Nelson examining the torn-up letter

earning more money, moving into a nicer place, and having children when the time was right. Instead, Marcela has proven that she will act according to her own impulses, as her dream cannot be contained within a migratory script, demonstrating that immigrants' motivations and desires are just as diverse and unique as constructions of the family and performances of familial roles. She remains an affect alien, a killjoy who cannot "pin hopes on the future" because she cannot "imagine happiness as what lies ahead" (Ahmed, *The Promise of* 160). By accepting her own unhappiness and not trying to construe her negative situation as a positive one, Marcela can "make room for life, to make room for possibility, for chance" (20). Marcela has chosen a different future, but her vision is not clouded by false hope or happiness.

Amador begins by documenting one of Marcela's unsuccessful journeys. She tearfully writes Nelson a letter stating that they don't love each other anymore, packs her bag, and leaves their shared apartment. She passes out waiting for the bus, waking up to a sonogram where she learns that she is pregnant. Marcela chooses to return to their apartment, tear up the letter, and unpack her bag. At the end of *Amador*, Marcela is making a similar journey, and while audiences might be tempted to feel hopeful for her, Marcela's problems are no more resolved than they were at the beginning of the film. She is still pregnant, alone, without a plan, and economically vulnerable. Spectators are not sure whether Marcela is returning to Peru or merely moving to a new apartment in Madrid. Either way, this is not a tidy or uplifting immigrant success story. Before leaving her apartment, Marcela removes the magnets from the fridge that spelled her name, making it clear to Nelson that the flower shop is his dream alone. Her decision highlights the fact that Marcela has decided to prioritize emotional connections over economic ones. While her relationship with Amador began as an economic relationship, the two received great affective benefits from their connection. Conversely, while her relationship with Nelson was intended as a romantic one, it became economic and transactional, as the couple directed their energies to surviving and making enough money to pay for the fridge. Marcela leaves the letter she had written him at the beginning of the film, torn into pieces for him to reassemble.

This letter-turned-puzzle evokes Amador's explanation for why he completed puzzles, stating that it was just different (better) when you figured something out for yourself. Every person must solve the puzzle of their own identity, including how one's individual identity fits within the larger puzzle of a familial identity. At the very least, Marcela's life is now a puzzle that she will be figuring out on her own. It is possible to "read these moments of 'leaving' as defiance [...] Defiance does not merely reject but also performs possibilities for other futures, if elsewhere" (Stehle and Weber 94). While Marcela has no guarantees of a more positive future, she has used her unhappiness to fight back against a life that she did not design or want for herself.

In *Amador*, a focus on the five senses shows how Marcela breaks free from societal and familial constraints that do not make her happy in order to establish new familial connections with Amador and Puri. Touch and taste – both important senses in a caretaker/patient relationship – foster a meaningful affective relationship between Marcela and Amador, highlighting the exclusivity of this relationship by clearly separating Marcela from Nelson and Yolanda, with whom she does not engage in consumption or affirming moments of touch. Through sound, Marcela finds her voice and agency, accepting Amador's verbal statement that she and her child belong in Spain and may occupy his place. Finally, Marcela uses the smell of rotting flowers to examine the false promises that have been made to her, finding agency in her unhappiness as an affect alien. Her negative emotions allow her to reconsider and reject those parts of her life that do not fulfil her. Amador feels a strong connection with Marcela and her unborn child with the help of the five senses, partly because the affective ties with his own biological family are unsatisfactory. Although Marcela and Puri first feel connected to Amador by financial motives, this does not obviate the emotional ties that later develop between them. *Amador* is a reconsideration of the family on a personal and national scale, demonstrating an alternate method of establishing exclusion or inclusion within the family, and leading to another example of enactments of family that exist along a broad spectrum of possibilities.

Conclusion

Throughout the analysis of contemporary Spanish families in this book, my aim has been to show the wide range of ways in which families are constructed and parental roles are performed in literature and film. Despite the pervasive image of the patriarchal, traditional family promulgated under Franco's dictatorship, Spanish families have always existed along a broad spectrum of realities. Although this book examines Spanish families from a cinematic and literary perspective, much of the sociological research on Spanish families demonstrates shared themes between artistic representations of Spanish families and their societal counterparts. Akiko Tsuchiya, in her discussion of the Spanish nineteenth-century realist novel, reflects on the cultural truths that literature can reveal. Tsuchiya states that while fiction might attempt to contain deviance, it also "betrays an equally powerful impulse to resist normativity, opening up new spaces of subjectivity (if not always of agency) and redefining the limits of what the dominant culture takes for granted as 'reality'" (5). The contemporary Spanish literary texts and films in this book do just that, calling for a redefinition of the reality of Spanish families by making space for an entire spectrum of non-normative performances of parenthood and alternative familial constructions.

While the idea of the traditional, patriarchal Spanish family – in existence long before, but solidified by, Franco's National Catholicism – lingers in current societal messages about gender roles and family construction in Spain, I argue that the ubiquitousness of the traditional family model is a myth, as examples of alternate families in literature and film prove. Some Spanish families may adhere to certain characteristics of this traditional configuration of family, but it is a concept that is impossible to fully live up to at all times, and it often may not be in the best interest of parents to attempt to live up to this hegemonic model. Instead, what may often look like failure to live up to hegemonic, patriarchal family standards can be the basis for creating an alternative and more authentic construction of family. Rafa in *La buena estrella* and Leo in *Todo lo que tú quieras* perform their parenthood in ways that at times align them with hegemonic expectations of fatherhood, but ultimately they establish alternative families outside of these limitations. Lluís in *El mal francés* and Constancito in *¿Por qué me comprasteis un walkie talkie si era hijo único?* also look to non-normative definitions of masculinity and family when heteronormative expectations are too limiting. In these examples, characters become more realized versions of themselves as individuals and as parents when they deviate from the hegemonic, heteronormative script, revealing the positive potential of failing to live up to these standards.

Rather than attempting to measure individuals or families by hegemonic standards, however, parenthood and family in contemporary Spain should be understood along a spectrum of changeable performances and identities, a concept rooted in Judith Butler's description of the fluidity of gender. In *Performing Parenthood*, I acknowledge that certain chapters focus on motherhoods or fatherhoods, rather than parenthood in general, because patriarchal Spanish society still ascribes certain traditional gender roles to enactments of motherhood or fatherhood. With the idea of parental performances as a spectrum, however, I hope we may move to a conceptualization of parenthood in which parental enactment is not tied directly to gendered expectations for mothers or fathers, while not ignoring the importance that an individual's sexual orientation may have for the ways in which they perceive and perform their parenthood. In many films and literary texts in *Performing Parenthood*, sexuality and sexual identity are significant aspects of characters' personalities that do not disappear with parenthood, often informing their performances of parenthood. In *El mal francés*, Lluís must understand his sexual orientation before he can construct a parental identity or perform his parenthood. Chapters 2, 4, and 6 highlight the importance of physical touch in family formation, both between parent and child and between parents, for whom sensuality can be a pivotal tool in maintaining family unity. Chapter 5 investigates the limitations of sexuality in the parent/child relationship, through a focus on two potentially incestuous relationships between parental figures and children. These examples show that sexuality can be expressed in healthy and unifying ways for some families, while for other families, sexuality can be enacted in harmful ways.

In general, the alternative or non-normative families that I analyse show that the family unit can have a positive or negative impact on its members; most often, the family unit fulfils both positive and negative functions for family members at different times and within a variety of circumstances. The mother in "La niña sin alas" who bites off her daughter's wings performs her parenthood in a way that both shelters and limits her child. In *Varada tras el último naufragio*, Eva alternately nurtures and ignores her non-biological daughter Clara. In "El amor inútil," Alberto at times fulfils a caregiving role for his non-biological daughter and at other times represents an incestuous threat to her. The shifting nature of the family shows that performances of parenthood are not just part of a spectrum based on different individuals. Rather, one individual may perform their parenthood in a variety of ways according to different situations, and motivations behind enactments of parenthood may be complicated and at times contradictory.

In almost all examples of non-normative families in this book, parenthood is shown to be a performance that must be repeated, much like gender; in several cases, the roles between parent and child can alternate with a great sense of fluidity. In *Tras la pared*, mothers and daughters create an intergenerational community of care, wherein parents and children alternate between caregiver and care recipient roles. In *Amador*, Marcela and Amador form a non-normative family in which they alternately receive and accept different types of care (financial, physical, and emotional) from each other. In various instances, characters view parenthood as a mimetic act, seeking out a model on which to base their own parenthood (like Lluís in *El mal francés*) or attempting to create doppelgängers of themselves in their children (Eva in *Varada tras el último naufragio* and Alberto in "El amor inútil"). These texts and films demonstrate parenthood to be a role sustained through a repetition of acts, this repeated performance more important than a biological connection.

While the examples of family in *Performing Parenthood* are literary and cinematic, not faithful reproductions of actual Spanish families, these cultural representations reveal many truths about the society in which they were produced and Spanish perspectives on family. Non-normative enactments of Spanish families in these examples reflect the lived experiences of characters rather than any intentional agenda on the part of characters to create an alternative family structure. However, these texts and films are influenced by Spanish society's fluctuating relationship with immigration, women's changing economic roles, which impact evolving expectations for men within the family and childcare roles, and the growing number of non-biological families and families with same-sex parental figures, to name only a few social factors that impact contemporary Spanish families. When seen in conversation with one another, these representations of Spanish families present a diverse spectrum of familial configurations and parental performances, demonstrating the impossibility of arriving at any one definition of the Spanish family. Rather than attempting to limit contemporary Spanish families to any specific set of expectations or classifications, scholars of the Spanish family and all those who wish to understand Spanish familial constructions should embrace the plurality of parenthoods present in Spanish culture and society, which leads to a wide and diverse spectrum of Spanish families.

Notes

Introduction

1 In a book about non-normative literary and cinematic representations of the contemporary Spanish family, readers might (rightly so) expect to read more about Pedro Almodóvar's oeuvre, as his films focus on alternative constructions of Spanish families. Although I acknowledge the great debt that scholars of the Spanish family owe to Almodóvar's groundbreaking works, I have chosen not to analyse his films in greater detail in this book because a robust body of scholarship on Almodóvar already exists.

2 The concept of "two Spains" reflects the idea that Spain is deeply ideologically divided into politically conversative and liberal groups. Poet Antonio Machado espoused this idea in an untitled poem (number LIII) published in 1909, while essayist Mariano José de Larra discussed the concept in his 1836 essay "Día de difuntos de 1836" ["All Souls Day 1836"], although the concept may well pre-date these authors (Manganas 19–20).

3 Roberta Johnson provides an excellent analysis of how the equality/difference debate among Spanish feminists has continued to evolve in contemporary times in her chapter "The Spanish Equality/Difference Debate Continues" in the 2018 *A New History of Iberian Feminisms*, edited by Silvia Bermúdez and Roberta Johnson.

4 While the Transition provided a path to modernization for Spain, it was not a perfect reimagining of the country, nor a completely linear path to progress. Sarah Thomas writes of the "continuance of dictatorship institutions and individuals in the governance of the new democratic state" (10). Although Spanish women gained more rights overall, the after-effects of nearly forty years of dictatorship lingered. For a more complete understanding of *la Movida*, please see Francisco Fernández de Alba's *Sex, Drugs, and Fashion in 1970s Madrid* (2020).

5 Illegal under Franco's dictatorship, abortion has been a controversial topic in Spain since the Transition, with popular opinion divided and the reality of lived experiences for Spanish women often differing from the law. In 1985, abortion was legalized only in the case of rape, fetal abnormalities, or risk to the mother. Spanish Parliament passed a law in 2010 that granted women the right to abortion for any reason during the first fourteen weeks, while abortions after that date could occur only in particular circumstances (Lete et al. 75). The 2010 law, which passed by only six votes, eliminated imprisonment as a potential repercussion for women who received abortions that fell outside of legal restrictions. Spanish society remained divided on abortion rights, with Catholic groups protesting the passing of the law and the conservative political party Partido Popular [Popular Party] asserting their goal to repeal the law (Lago 559). While the 2010 law seemed progressive on paper, the reality for Spanish women in need of abortions was far from ideal. Doctors who identified as "conscientious objectors" were allowed to refuse this health care to their patients, often forcing women to travel great distances to find clinics and providers that would help them (Casey). In May of 2022, a new law regarding women's health passed, stating that women will be able to access abortions in the nearest public hospital, "conscientious objector" doctors must be publicly listed as such, and girls of sixteen years or older may receive an abortion without parental permission. Among other reforms, the law also offers free birth control and paid time off for severe menstrual pain ("Así queda la ley").
6 This, of course, was altered by the Spanish economic crisis (2008–2014) that caused many families to depend upon one another for economic survival yet again. The crisis, combined with the bursting of the Spanish housing bubble beginning in 2008, meant that it was common for Spaniards to live with their parents well into their thirties.
7 Sara Cooper's 2004 *The Ties That Bind: Questioning Family Dynamics and Family Discourse in Hispanic Literature* addresses positive and negative aspects of the Hispanic family, instances of abuse and trauma juxtaposed against examples of familial support. Yeon-Soo Kim extends the narrative of the Spanish family as both "restrictive and regenerative" (32) through a study of visual mediums in *The Family Album: Histories, Subjectivities, and Immigration in Contemporary Spanish Culture* (2005).
8 However, the decade following the Spanish Civil War also produced many traditional and conservative novels aligned with the dictatorship that offered a vision of the "ideal" Spanish family, including Rafael García Serrano's *La fiel infantería* [*The Faithful Infantry*] (1943), Gonzalo Torrente Ballester's *Javier Mariño* (1943), José Antonio Giménez Amau's *La cueva de ladrones* [*The Cave of Thieves*] (1949), and José María Alfaro's *Leoncio Pancorbo* (1942).

9 Paul Begin writes about domestic violence in Spain in his chapter "Picking a Fight with Domestic Violence: New Perspectives on Patriarchy in Contemporary Spanish Cinema," featured in Tiffany Trotman's 2011 *The Changing Spanish Family: Essays on New Views in Literature, Cinema and Theater*.

10 The United Nations 2020 global estimates on numbers of women and girls who are killed by partners or family members provide the sombre perspective that gender violence is not only a Spanish problem. Worldwide in 2020, the United Nations report finds that a girl or woman is killed by a family member or partner every 11 minutes, for a total of approximately 47,000 deaths (*Killings of Women* 7). In a comparison of intimate partner homicide from 2014 to 2020 in six European countries, Spain ranked lowest at nearly 0.3 per 100,000, while Belarus ranked highest with 1.1 per 100,000. While Spain's numbers may not look concerning when compared with other European countries, any gender violence is problematic. Gender violence has been the topic of contemporary cinema in Spain, including the film *Te doy mis ojos* [*Take My Eyes*], directed by Icíar Bollaín in 2003.

11 Spanish society tends to view immigrants from certain cultures as more threatening than others, which is often reflected in Spanish immigration policies. In "Cuban Exceptionalism: Migration and Asylum in Spain and the United States," Maryellen Fullerton discusses the special treatment given to Cuban asylum seekers in Spain, which the Spanish government began to modify in the early 2000s. While Cuban immigrants have generally been fairly welcome in Spain, Spanish society in general has a history of perceiving immigrants from other countries in a less favourable light. For example, in *The Return of the Moor: Spanish Responses to Contemporary Moroccan Immigration*, Daniela Flesler describes Spanish social anxieties related to Moroccan immigration to Spain.

12 In Spanish literature and film, lesbian motherhood is a small but growing topic. While Mila Martínez's *Tras la pared* portrays lesbian motherhood in an overwhelmingly positive light, several cultural representations of lesbian motherhood tend to be negative. In the film *A mi madre le gustan las mujeres* [*My Mother Likes Women*], directed by Daniela Fejerman and Inés París in 2002, the protagonist Sofía's adult children react negatively when their divorced mother comes out as gay. Although the children eventually come around to Sofía's new relationship, Jackie Collins's analysis of the film asserts that the protagonist avoids "the label of bad mother" (156) only through the support of her ex-husband, which allows Sofía and her partner to establish their lesbian relationship as "acceptable" (156) in the eyes of her family. In "Transitions and Representations of Lesbianism in the Spanish Media," Raquel Platero Méndez discusses Spanish television

shows like *Hospital Central* [*Central Hospital*] and *Aquí no hay quien viva* [*No One Could Live Here*] that show lesbian characters getting married and having children, but still "suffering lesbophobia" (71). In *101 Reykjavik*, directed by Baltasar Kormákur, Lola is a Spanish lesbian teaching a flamenco class in Reykjavik, who becomes pregnant after sleeping with a man. She later begins a romantic relationship with that man's mother, leading to "critiques of family dysfunction" (Perriam 68) and casting the lesbian mother character in a negative light.

1 Writing Fatherhood

1 Todó published *El mal francés* in Catalan first (2006) and then in Spanish (2009), as is his pattern for most novels he publishes. Todó comments that, as a bilingual person, he writes interchangeably between Catalan and Spanish (Jerónimo and Todó 121). *¿Por qué me comprasteis un walkie talkie si era hijo único?* has been published only in Spanish.
2 *El mal francés* is a title that has several layers of meaning. The literal interpretation can mean either the bad French national or the bad French language. Lluís goes to France during the novel, both to study the language and to have some physical distance from his life in Spain, which allows him to process his homosexuality and incipient fatherhood. The phrase can also refer to syphilis, perhaps a humorous connection to Lluís's desire to experiment sexually.
3 While Franco relished projecting an image of himself as the ideal Spanish man and father, his personal and family life frequently contradicted the ideology he espoused. Although the regime asserted the importance of large families to create a new generation of patriotic citizens, Franco and his wife produced only one child. Furthermore, Franco's message of austerity was directly contrasted by his immediate family's social climbing and desire to accumulate wealth (Perriam et al. 73).
4 While the Nationalists did establish a definition of ideal masculinity during the Spanish Civil War, upon which Franco's regime expanded, this was not the only prevalent version of Spanish masculinity circulating at the time. In "The Battle to Define Spanish Manhood," Nerea Aresti offers an insightful explanation of the different types of masculinity that developed at the beginning of the twentieth century and during the Spanish Civil War. While fundamental differences exist between these conceptualizations of masculinity, both groups prized self-control.
5 Two classic examples in Greek mythology of children born from male pregnancy are Athena, who was born from her father's head, and Dionysus, who was born from his father's thigh (Leitao 2).
6 Throughout the novel, the topic of incest is addressed in a humorous manner. The narrator invents different names to define the relationship

between the incestuous pair, such as "hermarido" (a combination of "hermanos" ["siblings"] and "maridos" ["spouses"]) and "maranos" (a mixture of "maridos" ["spouses"] and "hermanos" ["siblings"]) (125).

7 Don Juan's sexual orientation has been contested by scholars who suggest that he may well have been a homosexual or bisexual character. The work of Spanish critic and scholar Gregorio Marañón – including his book *Don Juan: Ensayos sobre el origen de su leyenda* [*Don Juan: Essays about the Origin of His Legend*], published in 1940 – was one of the first to address this topic.

8 The relation between literature and identity formation is a common topic among gay writers, one notable example being Terenci Moix, a Catalan author whom Todó claims as a major source of inspiration. The tendency to link identity to literature can be seen in Moix's *Memorias* [*Memoirs*], *El Peso de la Paja* [*The Weight of Straw*], and *Extraño en el paraíso* [*Stranger in Paradise*], among others of his works.

9 Although he does not do so in *El mal francés*, Lluís Maria Todó uses footnotes in his 1994 novel *El juego del mentiroso* [*The Liar's Game*], with the goal of obscuring the text's authenticity.

10 Although not the focus of this chapter, it is important to note that both Todó and Balmes are Catalan authors who write from a peripheral rather than centrist position within the Spanish literary sphere. Catalan identity is a strong theme in both novels. While Todó's work does not manifest itself in favour of nationalism of any kind, he exposes it as a powerful type of mimesis. According to Todó in *El mal francés*, "es sabido que el nacionalismo … es una de las formas más extendidas, más interesantes y más insidiosas de gregarismo, y por tanto de mimetismo" ["it is known that nationalism … is one of the most extended, most interesting and most insidious forms of gregariousness, and therefore of imitation"] (29). Balmes writes about the devaluation of the Catalan language in modern society. Manolo is the character who embodies the strongest aversion to all things Catalan. Balmes compares this rejection of Catalan culture to betrayal, writing that "Manolo negó su catalanidad tres veces como San Pedro" ["Manolo denied his Catalan identity three times like Saint Peter"] (219).

11 The title *Héroes del Cilicio* [*Cilice Heroes*] may also be a reference to Héroes del Silencio [Heroes of Silence], a famous Spanish rock band.

2 M(other)hood and Disability

1 The protagonist's bodily autonomy and unquestioned right to make decisions about her pregnancy may seem like a more fantastic element of the story than the fact that humans have wings. Spanish women have long received the message that motherhood is a biological imperative, and especially during Franco's dictatorship, women's bodies were policed by the establishment of "una estrecha relación de poder sobre el cuerpo

femenino, con claras intervenciones tanto en términos de sanciones legislativas como de control normativo" ["a tight relationship of power over the feminine body, with clear interventions as much in terms of legislative sanctions as in regulatory control"] (Nash, "Turismo, género" 43).

2 While societal and individual views on pregnancy and sexuality vary greatly, the infantilization of pregnant women is documented both universally and in Spain. Francisca Fernández Guillén, a Spanish lawyer who specializes in reproductive and sexual health, has written and co-written various articles advocating against the "dehumanization of childbirth and pregnancy" (Villarmea Requejo and Fernández Guillén 213) in Spain, denouncing a record of forced sterilizations, the medical community's paternalist attitude toward pregnant individuals, and doctors' refusal to share pertinent information with their pregnant patients (Villarmea Requejo and Fernández Guillén 218). A study of obstetric violence (OV) in Spain, which is described as "any medical practice or attitude [that] ignores women's and infants' rights, desires, decisions, needs, emotions and/or dignity" (Mena-Tudela et al. 1) found that 38.3 per cent of Spanish women participating in the study reported experiencing OV, compared with 18.3 per cent of women in Brazil, and 75.1 per cent of women in Ethiopia (Mena-Tudela et al. 2). Spanish study participants cited various forms of infantilization from the medical community, including the use of childish diminutives to address them, lack of informed consent and refusal to answer patients' questions or resolve their medical concerns, and even unnecessary medical interventions (Mena-Tudela et al. 3). At the same time, Western societies also sexualize and fetishize pregnant bodies, evident in the abundance of pregnancy pornography available online. In her 2000 article "Sexing the Belly," Rebecca Huntley notes that a keyword search using the terms "pregnant" and "pleasure" came up with 126,657 sites offering corresponding pornographic material (351). In the article "From 'Madonna' to 'Whore,'" Jennifer Musial explains the social dichotomy of perceiving pregnant women as either asexual or hypersexual, while the existence of various types of pornography related to pregnancy – lactation porn, pregnant schoolgirl porn, etc. – "is fascinating because it features women who are clearly adult and maternal" (405). Whether fetishized or infantilized, such views of pregnant individuals obscure their voice and agency.

3 While maternity leave in Spain is covered under Spanish labour laws, in many other countries, maternity leave or other workplace accommodations related to pregnancy are covered under disability laws or policies. For example, in the United States, maternity leave is part of the 2008 Americans with Disabilities Act Amendments Act (Williams et al. 99). In Spain, some women workers have been subject, without their knowledge, to pregnancy

tests by their employers, and women's health concerns during pregnancy have been used by employers as a justification for their dismissal (Ryan, "All Turbulent on" 42).

4 While the inclusion of the Icarus myth in "La niña sin alas" teaches social conformity and obedience, it can also be interpreted as a warning for parents. Depending on how they interact with their children, the children may decide to disobey and act according to their own desires.

5 Perhaps it is telling that the earliest and most notable example of Spanish *jouissance* comes from Saint Teresa, religious mother figure and mystic portrayed in the throes of exquisite agony by Bernini's statue. Monitored by the Inquisition, Saint Teresa represented a threat to the Catholic Church because she achieved an ecstatic (erotic) connection with God free from masculine intercession.

6 Foucault asserts that sexuality has always been part of the family and that children are sexual individuals, even though sexuality outside of the monogamous husband/wife scenario is often considered taboo. In the nineteenth century, children's sexuality was heavily monitored and repressed by the education system, religion, and medical authorities. Regardless of these efforts at control, Foucault elucidates upon the connections between pleasure and power, describing the home as a "network of pleasures and powers linked together at multiple points and according to transformable relationships" (46).

7 Paloma Díaz-Mas's highly autobiographical novel *Lo que olvidamos* [*What We Forget*] (2016) touches on the role a mother or daughter may play in the other's construction of identity. The novel's protagonist is a daughter who recounts her perspective of adjusting to life with her mother's dementia. Like much of Díaz-Mas's work, the relationship between the two is complicated, sometimes positive while at other times causing frustrations for the daughter. Díaz-Mas reflects on the importance of shared memories in identity formation, explaining that "es un poco un juego de espejos: lo que la hija olvida, lo que la madre olvida que suscita recuerdos de la hija, los recuerdos compartidos, lo que la hija recuerda a raíz del olvido de la madre. Construimos, de alguna manera, nuestra identidad por esos recuerdos selectivos" ["it is a little bit a game of mirrors: what the daughter forgets, what the mother forgets that stirs up the daughter's memories, shared memories, that the daughter remembers based on the mother's forgetfulness. In a way, we build our identity through those selective memories"] (Jerónimo and Díaz-Mas 184).

8 Laura Freixas addresses this issue in the prologue to her collection of short stories *Madres e hijas* [*Mothers and Daughters*], which includes "La niña sin alas." Freixas writes that certain critics view the label of "woman writer" or "feminine literature" as a crutch for female writers, a way of accessing

unmerited accolades. Freixas asserts that "la mera expresión *literatura femenina* pone incómodo a todo el mundo. Los varones parecen sospechar que las mujeres se escudan en ella para obtener algún privilegio. A menudo se oye murmurar que a calidad igual, es más fácil publicar, o ganar un premio, para una mujer que para un hombre" ["the mere expression *feminine literature* makes everyone uncomfortable. Men seem to suspect that women use it as an excuse to obtain some privilege. Often you hear it murmured that with works of equal quality, it is easier for a woman than a man to publish or win a prize"] (13).

3 The Shifting Face of Fatherhood

1 Compulsory hetero-parenting differs from compulsory parenting, which is a term related to the issue of abortion. In his book *Compulsory Parenthood: The Truth about Abortion*, Wendell W. Watters argues that neither men nor women should be forced against their will to be parents. Compulsory parenting requires pregnancies to be carried to term, regardless of individuals' feelings or desires toward parenthood.
2 While Spanish masculinities are complex and constantly evolving, the field of masculinity studies has only recently begun to produce scholarship focused on Spain. In the introduction to *Casting Masculinity in Spanish Film*, Mary T. Harston provides an excellent review of the history of masculinity studies that exist within a Spanish context, asserting that very little was produced on the topic before the 1990s, and that much of the existing scholarship has a cultural studies focus.
3 For additional resources on the diverse definitions of contemporary masculinities in Spain and Latin America, please refer to "Memorias de las masculinidades disidentes en España e Hispanoamérica," a database that compiles literary, artistic, and audiovisual pieces with autobiographical elements that speak to non-heteronormative examples of masculinities.
4 Various studies have shown that engaging in paid work is a crucial factor in identity formation for many men in Western cultures. In the article "Male Hegemony in Decline? Reflections on the Spanish Case," Borràs Català et al. provide an extensive review of studies that connect men's identity formation with the paid labour in which they engage: "In contemporary Western culture, paid work is one of the main elements that identifies men and allows them to be defined as such. Therefore, men who are separated from productive activity because of retirement, inactivity, or unemployment are no longer the men they were: the lack of paid work in their lives discredits them as men (Guasch 2003). Lack of work and the loss of a job threaten men's identity and men's dignity (Corbiére 2005), as is pointed out in the excellent work by Merla (2007) referring to men engaged

in housework and childcare outside the labour market. These men pay a high price of social and familiar stigma: their identity as men is challenged because they do not engage in paid work" (408–9).
5 The idea of a man being able to perform womanhood and motherhood more effectively than biological women has been developed in iconic movies such as *Tootsie* (1982), *Kramer vs. Kramer* (1979), and *Mrs. Doubtfire* (1993), to name a few.
6 Within the field of literary criticism, a well-established body of scholarship describes Dracula as a homosexual or bisexual character, often linking the topic of sexuality in *Dracula* to the concept of monstrosity. While there are too many works to mention here, Christopher Craft's *Another Kind of Love: Male Homosexual Desire in English Discourse, 1850–1920* and Damion Clark's chapter "Preying on the Pervert: The Uses of Homosexual Panic in Bram Stoker's *Dracula*" in the edited anthology *Horrifying Sex: Essays on Sexual Difference in Gothic Literature* are two notable examples of literary criticism that discusses homosexuality in *Dracula*. In her article "'A Wilde Desire Took Me': The Homoerotic History of *Dracula*," Talia Schaffer argues that *Dracula* "explores Stoker's fear and anxiety as a closeted homosexual man during Oscar Wilde's trial" (381). Barry McCrea, in the article "Heterosexual Horror: Dracula, the Closet, and the Marriage-Plot," asserts that *Dracula* describes the "exotic foreign world" of heterosexuality, as "viewed from inside the gay closet" (253).

4 Lesbian Maternal Community Formation

1 *No voy a disculparme* relates the beginning of Mel and Carla's relationship and the obstacles they face as a couple due to their age difference and Mel's friendship with Carla's mother, Álex. As they begin their romantic relationship, Álex struggles with the guilt associated with falling in love for the first time after her husband's death, trying to decide how to share this news with Carla. *Autorretrato con mar al fondo* follows multiple story lines, including Mel and Carla's experience of raising their daughter and the resolution of Sara and Patricia's storyline as they return from Mozambique and repair their relationship. The novel furthermore narrates the story of Eva, one of Mel's friends, who returns home to find her partner María murdered, leading Eva to search for answers to her death.
2 Studies of maternal sexuality among lesbian couples might reveal a completely different characterization of the maternal body; however, sociological studies about lesbian sexual behaviours during pregnancy are non-existent or extremely difficult to find. Research about lesbian motherhood often focuses on the division of parenthood responsibilities, effects of gender and racial diversity between lesbian mothers and adopted

children (Biblarz and Savci), and relationship satisfaction after becoming parents (Goldberg and Sayer). Jacqui Gabb investigates how lesbian sexual identity is impacted by motherhood, but she does not study how pregnancy affects the sexual behaviours of lesbian partners. More research is needed to show how lesbian sexual behaviours are impacted by pregnancy.

3 Warranted or not, literary critics and members of academia have ordinarily responded negatively to contemporary Spanish lesbian narrative. Although Spain is currently the largest producer of lesbian and gay literature in the Spanish-speaking world, it remains a literary production that claims a small readership and even smaller critical public, evidenced by the lack of scholarship in this area (Foster 462; Rodríguez Pérez 87). The lesbian production that does exist – including the establishments that support it, such as the publishing house Egales (started in 1995 in Barcelona) and the gay and lesbian bookstore Berkana (opened in 1993 in Madrid) – has been harshly criticized for its literary quality and its supposed inability to break away from the heterosexist discourse. In reference to Egales's "Salir del armario" ["Coming Out of the Closet"] book collection, Jill Robbins said, "The lesbian novels in the 'Salir del armario' ['Coming out of the Closet'] series in fact represent the lesbian women as 'normal citizens,' often with children and eventually 'married' to other lesbians, thus reaffirming the norms of the heterosexist public sphere" (113). As is often the case with "women's literature," critics tend to either consider lesbian literature a representation of "low culture" or associate it with erotic or pornographic literature. Therefore, although the publication of novels that deal with lesbian motherhood (such as *Tras la pared*) indicates progress, Spanish (and international) authors and publishers of lesbian literature still face many prejudices and stereotypes about the genre.

4 Various feminist theorists have proposed concepts similar to Rich's lesbian continuum. For example, Mary Daly's notion of gyn/ecology urges women to draw strength from one another, proposing "the re-claiming of life-loving female energy" (355). In her biomythography *Zami: A New Spelling of My Name*, prominent African American feminist Audre Lorde highlights the importance of female relationships in her life, renaming herself Zami, which is "a Carriacou name for women who work together as friends and lovers" (255). Although Rich published "Compulsory Heterosexuality and Lesbian Existence" decades before the advent of queer theory, the fluidity of her lesbian continuum is a helpful point of reference for the notion of parental performance I establish in this book.

5 Álex's unquestioned enthusiasm for Carla and Mel's relationship and motherhood demonstrates a crucial form of emotional support that many lesbian couples do not receive from their biological families. In a study of lesbian motherhood in Australia, Du Chesne and Bradley found that

an experience often shared by lesbian mothers is a negative, heterosexist reaction to announcements of the addition of children to lesbian families. Such responses from extended families posit "lesbian mothers as most deviant, and as bad for children" (Du Chesne and Bradley 29).

5 Beyond the Biological Family

1 Although it is not as common to use the concept of the doppelgänger to analyse emotional similarities between characters, other literary scholars have done so, such as Lynda Koolish in her 2001 article in *MELUS*, "'To Be Loved and Cry Shame': A Psychological Reading of Toni Morrison's *Beloved*." In this article, Koolish argues that Beloved is a "doppelgänger, an alter ego, a shadow, a darker and more authentic version of the self" for Sethe, who uses Beloved as a mirror to understand her own emotions (170). An emotional doppelgänger can serve as a mirror for another character, allowing them to explore their own thoughts and feelings or envision themselves as they would have been had some aspect of their life been different. In their article "The Other Self: Psychopathology and Literature," Javier Saavedra Macías and Rafael Velez Núñez discuss the history of the literary term doppelgänger, or double. They explain that doppelgänger is a term coined in 1796 in a German novel, *Siebenkäs*, written by Jean Paul, used to describe "the paradox of encountering oneself like another" (Saavedra Macías and Velez Núñez 260). In this chapter, the shared likeness of the doppelgänger connection is focused on emotional rather than physical connection.

2 *Varada tras el último naufragio* is often viewed by critics such as Linda Gould Levine, Catherine G. Bellver, and Mary S. Vásquez as the final novel in a rather unconventional trilogy beginning with *El mismo mar de todos los veranos* [*The Same Sea Every Summer*] (1978) and followed by *El amor es un juego solitario* [*Love Is a Solitary Game*] (1979). Other critics (Stacey Dolgin Casado, Pablo Gil Casado, and Nina Molinaro) consider these three works a tetralogy, along with Tusquets's collection of short stories titled *Siete miradas en un mismo paisaje* [*Seven Views of the Same Landscape*] (1981). Regardless of its classification, *Varada* has been subject to a paucity of critical attention in comparison with Tusquets's overarching body of work. The infrequent mentions of *Varada* typically analyse the novel's function in relation to the trilogy or tetralogy (Dolgin Casado 148). *Varada*'s literary value merits greater investigation, as does the relationship between secondary characters Eva and Clara.

3 Analyses of *Varada* largely focus on the "life-death-rebirth drama of Elia's psyche" (Dolgin Casado 159), while any critical evaluation of the other characters is linked to how their roles impact Elia's experience. Stacey

Dolgin Casado asserts a prevalent belief about *Varada*, writing, "The novel is about Elia, and only about Elia, whose psychological trials and tribulations are a fictional projection of those of her demiurge" (162). While the novel's main plot clearly revolves around Elia, it is a fallacious argument that *Varada*'s meaning can be resumed exclusively through her transformative search for personal identity.

4 The mother/daughter relationship between Clara and Eva has potential for valuable critical interpretation, even though various critics have written Clara off as a minor character, a symbol of childhood whose "gradual degrading and eventual elimination" from the narrative "implies a progressive disengagement from a childlike, immature world view" (Ichiishi 216). Nina Molinaro and Stacey Dolgin Casado share similar perspectives about Clara's one-dimensionality and limited importance in *Varada*. Moreover, an investigation of the mother/daughter relationship in *Varada* substantiates Clara's significance as more than a token of lost childhood. A character named Clara appears in all three novels of Tusquets's trilogy, arguably as different manifestations of the same individual. In *El mismo mar de todos los veranos*, Clara is a young student with whom the narrator has a brief affair. In *El amor es un juego solitario*, Clara is used by the narrator as a sexual pawn.

5 While contemporary instances of non-biological parenthood are usually voluntary, Spain's recent history is marred by the forced removal of babies from their mothers during Francisco Franco's dictatorship. The "systematic" theft of 300,000 newborns occurred throughout Franco's regime (Escudero 71). Babies were taken from mothers considered undesirable by the regime (like single mothers or Republican women), who were told the babies had not survived childbirth, and given to families supportive of the regime to raise as their own.

6 Tusquets reflects upon her challenging relationship with her mother in "Carta a la madre" (1996), although she describes the satisfying experience of being a mother in the essay "Ser madre" (2000).

7 The blurring of gender lines in *Varada* can even be said to extend to a narrative level. Tusquets's stream-of-consciousness style creates a level of confusion when trying to decipher which character is speaking at any given moment. According to Barbara F. Ichiishi, Tusquets's style causes all the voices to sound similar, even leading to a "feminizing" of Pablo's voice (160). Tusquets plays with gender roles to create a blurring of identity and perhaps a challenge to the patriarchal norm.

8 In *Varada*, there are many characters that could be described as doppelgängers, but for the purposes of this analysis, only the relationship between Eva and Clara will be discussed. Clara also holds symbolic meaning for Pablo and Elia, as well: "For Pablo, Clara represents the erotic

potential of youth, but she refuses to elaborate upon his unfinished past. Clara also embodies a younger version of Elia, acting as a metaphorical link between the past and the present Elia; and, although their stories may be different, the two women share a similar faith in the transformative power of fantasy" (Molinaro, *Foucault, Feminism and* 66).

9 The protagonist in *El mismo mar de todos los veranos* makes a similar choice, returning to her husband instead of truly exploring the potential of a lesbian relationship.

6 A Family in All Senses

1 See chapter 3 for a definition of *cine social* [social issue cinema], a genre that grew increasingly popular immediately following the start of Spain's economic crisis in 2008, as the crisis itself "became unavoidable; dissatisfaction permeated everything, and changed cultural agendas gradually from 2008 to 2011" (Triana-Toribio 16). Ángel Quintana has suggested that, more than *cine social* [social issue cinema], León de Aranoa's work constitutes *realismo tímido* [timid realism], a film genre that attempts to reflect the reality of the world without investigating its complexities (254).

2 *Amador* has received extremely mixed reviews and has not been as fully embraced as many of León de Aranoa's other films. Jonathan Holland's review describes *Amador* as "a project that's not up to his best," noting the emotional buy-in (or manipulation) the director asks of the audience. Holland adds that *Amador* is "a well-intentioned if diffuse slice of urban poetry that can't decide whether it wants us to laugh, cry or just feel guilty."

3 Many contemporary Spanish films present the Latin American immigrant woman as an idealized mother figure. Notable examples include Fernando León de Aranoa's *Princesas* (2005) and Icíar Bollaín's *Flores de otro mundo* (1999), where Latin American immigrant women are brought to a small town in Spain with the hope that they will marry Spanish men and start families with them. Though not as prevalent, contemporary Spanish film also perpetuates the stereotype of the self-sacrificing immigrant mother figure from African countries as well. Marcelo Piñeyro's *Ismael* (2013) features an undocumented African mother figure who is dedicated to her child. In Alejandro González Iñárritu's *Biutiful* (2010), protagonist Uxbal leaves his children in the care of an immigrant mother from Africa at the end of the film.

4 In many contemporary Spanish films, including León de Aranoa's *Princesas* (2005), prostitution is presented increasingly as the work of immigrant women. These films reflect statistics that show that around 90 per cent of prostitutes in Spain at the beginning of the twenty-first century were from other countries, around half from Latin America (Flesler and Shepherd 243).

When Marcela asks Puri if she makes a lot of money, she replies that she used to, but now she relies on long-term clients, as "girls from Marcela's country" have hurt her business.

5 León de Aranoa's 1994 short film *Sirenas* [*Mermaids*] clarifies Amador's fascination with the sea and mermaids. In this film, an older deaf man was the only one of his companions to survive a shipwreck, according to him because his deafness did not allow him to hear the siren's song. After this incident, he is no longer allowed to live alone and must alternate between his children's homes, an uncomfortable arrangement for everyone. He dies at the end of the film, believing that sirens and the sea have guided him on through the next stage of his journey.

Bibliography

Ahmed, Sara. *The Cultural Politics of Emotion*. Routledge, 2004.
– *The Promise of Happiness*. Duke UP, 2010.
Alberdi, Inés. *La nueva familia española*. Grupo Santillana de Ediciones, 1999.
Álvarez, Pilar. "In Spain, International Adoptions Plunge while Surrogacy Grows." *El País*, 30 Jan. 2019. https://english.elpais.com/elpais/2019/01/30/inenglish/1548835396_594194. html. Accessed 8 Aug. 2022.
– "Spain Sees Worst Year for Gender Violence Deaths since 2015." *El País*, translated by Simon Hunter, 2 Jan. 2020, https://english.elpais.com/elpais/2020/01/02/ inenglish/1577951554_688193.html. Accessed 11 Sept. 2021.
Álvarez Pérez, Antonio. *Enciclopedia intuitiva, sintética y práctica: Tercer grado*. Miñón, 1964.
Amador, directed by Fernando León de Aranoa. Reposado Producciones, 2010.
"Así queda la ley del aborto: fin al permiso paterno a partir de los 16 años, registro de objetores y salud menstrual." *RTVE*, 17 May 2022. www.rtve.es/noticias/20220517/fin-permiso-paterno-objetores-conciencia-salud-menstrual-asi-queda-ley-aborto/ 2349386.shtml. Accessed 21 June 2022.
Aresti, Nerea. "The Battle to Define Spanish Manhood." *Memory and Cultural History of the Spanish Civil War: Realms of Oblivion*, edited by Aurora G. Morcillo. Brill, 2014, pp. 147–78.
Ballesteros, Isolina. *Cine (ins)urgente: Textos fílmicos y contextos culturales de la España postfranquista*. Editorial Fundamentos, 2001.
– "Embracing the Other: The Feminization of Spanish 'Immigration Cinema.'" *Studies in Hispanic Cinemas*, vol. 2, no. 1, 2005, pp. 3–14.
Balmes, Santi. *¿Por qué me comprasteis un walkie talkie si era hijo único?* Principal de los libros, 2012.
Barnes, Diana M. "Recovering Gender: Motherhood and Female Identity in *El pájaro de la felicidad* and *Gary Cooper que estás en los cielos*." *The Changing*

Spanish Family: Essays on New Views in Literature, Cinema and Theater, edited by Tiffany Trotman. McFarland & Company, 2011, pp. 109–25.

Baudrillard, Jean. *Simulacra and Simulation*. Translated by Sheila Faria Glaser. U of Michigan P, 1994.

Beauvoir, Simone de. *The Coming of Age*, translated by Patrick O'Brian. Norton & Company, 1972.

Begin, Paul. "Picking a Fight with Domestic Violence: New Perspectives on Patriarchy in Contemporary Spanish Cinema." *The Changing Spanish Family: Essays on New Views in Literature, Cinema and Theater*, edited by Tiffany Trotman. McFarland & Company, 2011, pp. 126–40.

— "When Victim Meets Voyeur: An Aesthetic of Confrontation in Hispanic Social Issue Cinema." *Hispanic Research Journal*, vol. 9, no. 3, 2008, pp. 261–75.

Bell, Shannon. *Reading, Writing & Rewriting the Prostitute Body*. Indiana UP, 1994.

Bell, Vikki. *Interrogating Incest: Feminism, Foucault and the Law*. Routledge, 1993.

Bellver, Catherine G. "Intertextuality in *Para no volver*." *The Sea of Becoming: Approaches to the Fiction of Esther Tusquets*, edited by Mary S. Vásquez. Greenwood P, 1991, pp. 103–22.

— "The Language of Eroticism in the Novels of Esther Tusquets." *Anales de la literatura española contemporánea*, vol. 9, no. 1/3, 1984, pp. 13–27.

Benet, Juan. *Volverás a Región*. Ediciones Destino, 1996.

Biblarz, Timothy J., and Evren Savci. "Lesbian, Gay, Bisexual, and Transgender Families." *Journal of Marriage and Family*, vol. 72, no. 3, 2010, pp. 480–97.

Bieder, Maryellen. "Carmen de Burgos: Modern Spanish Woman." *Recovering Spain's Feminist Tradition*, edited by Lisa Vollendorf. The Modern Language Association of America, 2001, pp. 241–59.

Biutiful. Directed by Alejandro González Iñárritu. Focus Features International, 2010.

Black, Kyle K. "La inmigración y la labor inmaterial en *Amador* (2010) de Fernando León de Aranoa." *Transmodernity: Journal of Peripheral Cultural Production of the Luso-Hispanic World*, vol. 7, no. 2, 2017, pp. 73–96.

Bloom, Harold. *The Anxiety of Influence: A Theory of Poetry*. 2nd ed., Oxford UP, 1997.

Bordo, Susan. *Unbearable Weight: Feminism, Western Culture, and the Body*. U of California P, 1993.

Borràs Català, Vicent et al. "Male Hegemony in Decline? Reflections on the Spanish Case." *Men and Masculinities*, vol. 15, no. 4, 2012, pp. 406–23.

Bourland Ross, Catherine. *The Changing Face of Motherhood in Spain: The Social Construction of Maternity in the Works of Lucía Extebarria*. Bucknell UP, 2015.

— "Left Behind: Cultural Assimilation and the Mother/Daughter Relationship in Najat El Hachmi's *La hija extranjera* (2015)." *Hispanófila*, vol. 183, 2018, pp. 351–65.

- "Why We Are All in the Club: *El club de las malas madres.*" *The Changing Spanish Family: Essays on New Views in Literature, Cinema and Theater*, edited by Tiffany Trotman. McFarland & Company, 2011, pp. 9–23.
Brooksbank Jones, Anny. *Women in Contemporary Spain.* Manchester UP, 1997.
Butler, Judith. *Bodies That Matter: On the Discursive Limits of Sex.* Routledge, 1993.
- *Gender Trouble.* Routledge, 1990.
- "Imitation and Gender Subordination." *The Lesbian and Gay Studies Reader*, edited by Henry Abelove, Michèle Aina Barale, and David M. Halperin. Routledge, 1993, pp. 307–20.
- "Performative Acts and Gender Constitution: An Essay in Phenomenology and Feminist Theory." *Theatre Journal*, vol. 40, no. 4, 1988, pp. 519–31.
Cameron, Bryan. "Documenting Podemos and the Rise of DIY Politics in Fernando León de Aranoa's *Política, manual de instrucciones* (2016)." *Hispanic Research Journal*, vol. 20, no. 1, 2019, pp. 58–72.
Carrón, C. David. "Achero Mañas: 'Era humillante trabajar en películas que no me gustaban.'" *La Razón*, 14 Aug. 2010. https://www.larazon.es/historico/3797-achero-manas-era-humillante-trabajar-en-peliculas-que-no-me-gustaban-GLLA_RAZON_301396/. Accessed 25 May 2021.
Casas Aguilar, Anna. "Espectros de la paternidad y disolución de fronteras en *Biutiful* de Alejandro González Iñárritu." *Journal of Spanish Cultural Studies*, vol. 16, no. 2, 2015, pp. 179–91.
Casey, Nicholas. "In Spain, Abortions are Legal, but Many Doctors Refuse to Perform Them." *New York Times*, 21 Sept. 2021. www.nytimes.com/2021/09/21/world/europe/spain-abortion-doctors.html. Accessed 21 June 2022.
Castro, Luisa. "El amor inútil." *Páginas amarillas*, edited by Sabas Martín. Lengua de Trapo, 1997, pp. 137–45.
- "Los hijos como propiedad." *El País*, 11 June 2008. http://elpais.com/diario/2008/06/11/opinion/1213135205_850215.html. Accessed 18 July 2013.
Chodorow, Nancy. *The Reproduction of Mothering: Psychoanalysis and the Sociology of Gender.* U of California P, 1978.
Cixous, Hélène. "Sorties: Out and Out: Attacks/Ways Out/Forays." *The Logic of the Gift: Toward an Ethic of Generosity*, edited by Alan D. Schrift. Routledge, 1997, pp. 148–73.
Clare, Eli. *Exile and Pride: Disability, Queerness, and Liberation.* Duke UP, 2015.
Clark, Damion. "Preying on the Pervert: The Uses of Homosexual Panic in Bram Stoker's *Dracula.*" *Horrifying Sex: Essays on Sexual Difference in Gothic Literature*, edited by Ruth Bienstock Anolik. McFarland & Company, 2007, pp. 167–76.
Collins, Jackie. "Challenging the Rhetorical Oxymoron: Lesbian Motherhood in Contemporary European Cinema." *Studies in European Cinema*, vol. 4, no. 2, 2007, pp. 149–59.

Connell, R.W. *Masculinities*. U of California P, 2005.
— *The Men and the Boys*. U of California P, 2000.
Cooper, Sara E. *The Ties That Bind: Questioning Family Dynamics and Family Discourse in Hispanic Literature*. UP of America, 2004.
Cornejo-Parriego, Rosalía V. "Mitología, representación e identidad en 'El mismo mar de todos los veranos' de Esther Tusquets." *Anales de la literatura española contemporánea*, vol. 20, no. 1/2, 1995, pp. 47–63.
Craft, Christopher. *Another Kind of Love: Male Homosexual Desire in English Discourse, 1850–1920*. U of California P, 1994.
Crisp, Thomas. "From Romance to Magical Realism: Limits and Possibilities in Gay Adolescent Fiction." *Children's Literature in Education*, vol. 40, 2009, pp. 333–48.
Daly, Mary. *Gyn/ecology: The Metaethics of Radical Feminism*. Beacon Press, 1978.
Daniels, Cynthia R. *Exposing Men: The Science and Politics of Male Reproduction*. Oxford UP, 2006.
Davis, Stuart. "Que(e)rying Spain: On the Limits and Possibilities of Queer Theory in Hispanism." *Reading Iberia: Theory/History/Identity*, edited by Helena Buffery, Stuart Davis, and Kirsty Hooper. Peter Lang, 2007, pp. 63–78.
Díaz-Mas, Paloma. "La niña sin alas." *Madres e hijas*, edited by Laura Freixas, Anagrama, 1996, pp. 159–68.
Delphy, Christine. "The Main Enemy." *Feminist Issues*, vol. 1, no. 1, 1980, pp. 23–40.
Dolgin Casado, Stacey. *Squaring the Circle: Esther Tusquets's Novelistic Tetralogy (A Jungian Analysis)*. Juan de la Cuesta, 2002.
Dolor y gloria. Directed by Pedro Almodóvar, El Deseo, 2019.
Domingo Amestoy, Susana. "Postmodern Realisms: Memory, Family and the Collapse of the Nation in Fernando León de Aranoa's Films." *Collapse, Catastrophe and Rediscovery: Spain's Cultural Panorama in the Twenty-First Century*, edited by Jennifer Brady, Ibon Izurieta, and Ana-María Medina. Cambridge Scholars Publishing, 2014, pp. 113–34.
Döring, Tobias. "Edward Said and the Fiction of Autobiography." *Wasafiri*, vol. 21, no. 2, 2006, pp. 71–8.
Du Chesne, Louise, and Ben Bradley. "The Subjective Experience of the Lesbian (M)other: An Exploration of the Construction of Lesbian Maternal Identity." *Gay & Lesbian Issues and Psychology Review*, vol. 3, no. 1, 2007, pp. 25–33.
"El líder de Love of Lesbian, Santi Balmes, se ríe del fracaso en su debut como novelista." *20 Minutos*. 18 Dec. 2012. www.20minutos.es/noticia/1680398/0/lider-lov-of-lesbian/santi-balmes-rie-fracaso/debut-como-novelista/. Accessed 11 March 2013.

Encinar, Ángeles. "En busca del secreto de la narrativa de Luisa Castro." *La pluralidad narrativa: escritores españoles contemporáneos (1984–2004)*, edited by Ángeles Encinar and Kathleen M. Glenn. Biblioteca Nueva, 2005, pp. 149–61.

Engels, Frederick. *The Origin of the Family, Private Property, and the State*. Resistance Books, 2004.

Engelstein, Stefani. "The Father in Fatherland: Violent Ideology and Corporeal Paternity in Kleist." *Contemplating Violence: Critical Studies in Modern German Culture*, edited by Stefani Engelstein and Carl Niekerk. Editions Rodopi, 2009, pp. 49–66.

Escudero, Carolina. "From Trauma to Resilience: Reparation through Artistic Mediation. Stolen Babies Families from Spain, the 'Bus Experience.'" *Journal of Liberal Arts and Humanities*, vol. 1, no. 2, 2020, pp. 71–6.

"Familia." *Diccionario de Autoridades*, Diccionario histórico de la lengua española, 1732, https://apps2.rae.es/DA.html. Accessed 21 June 2022.

"familia." *Diccionario de la lengua española*, Real Academia Española, 2021, https://dle.rae.es/familia. Accessed 21 June 2022.

Faucheux, Amandine H. "Race and Sexuality in Nalo Hopkinson's Oeuvre; or, Queer Afrofuturism." *Science Fiction Studies*, vol. 44, no. 3, 2017, pp. 563–80.

Ferguson, Ann. "Motherhood and Sexuality: Some Feminist Questions." *Hypatia*, vol. 1, 1986, pp. 3–22.

Fernández de Alba, Francisco. *Sex, Drugs, and Fashion in 1970s Madrid*. U of Toronto P, 2020.

Ferrán, Ofelia. "La escritura y la historia: Entrevista con Paloma Díaz-Mas." *Anales de la literatura española contemporánea*, vol. 22, no. 1, 1997, pp. 327–45.

Finnerty, Deirdre. "The Republican Mother in Post-Transition Novels of Historical Memory: A Re-Inscription into Spanish Cultural Memory?" *Memory and Cultural History of the Spanish Civil War: Realms of Oblivion*, edited by Aurora G. Morcillo. Brill, 2014, pp. 213–45.

Flesler, Daniela. *The Return of the Moor: Spanish Responses to Contemporary Moroccan Immigration*. Purdue UP, 2008.

Flesler, Daniela, and N. Michelle Shepherd. "Domesticity, Motherhood, and Transnational Reproductive Work in Contemporary Latin American Immigration to Spain." *Theorising the Ibero-American Atlantic*, edited by Harald E. Braun and Lisa Vollendorf, Brill, 2013, pp. 241–63.

Flores de otro mundo. Directed by Icíar Bollaín, La Iguana, 1999.

Foster, David William. "Lesbigay Publishing in Spain." *Hispania*, vol. 90, no. 3, 2007, pp. 462–9.

Foucault, Michel de. *The History of Sexuality: Volume I An Introduction*, translated by Robert Hurley. Vintage Books, 1980.

Freccero, Carla. "Queer Times." *After Sex? On Writing since Queer Theory*, edited by Janet Halley and Andrew Parker. Duke UP, 2011, pp. 17–26.

Freixas, Laura. "Prólogo." *Madres e hijas*, edited by Laura Freixas, Anagrama, 1996, pp. 11–20.
Freud, Sigmund. *The Interpretation of Dreams*. Translated by A.A. Brill, Turnbull & Spears, 1922.
– "The Medusa's Head." *The Standard Edition of the Complete Psychological Works of Sigmund Freud*, edited by James Strachey. Hogarth Press, pp. 273–4.
– *The Schreber Case*. Translated by Andrew J. Webber. Penguin Group, 2002.
Fullerton, Maryellen. "Cuban Exceptionalism: Migration and Asylum in Spain and the United States." *Inter-American Law Review*, vol. 35, no. 3, 2004, pp. 527–75.
Gabb, Jacqui. "Locating Lesbian Parent Families." *Motherhood and Space*, edited by S. Hardy and C. Wiedmer. Palgrave Macmillan, 2005.
Gallop, Jane. *Sexuality, Disability, and Aging: Queer Temporalities of the Phallus*. Duke UP, 2019.
– *The Daughter's Seduction: Feminism and Psychoanalysis*. Cornell UP, 1982.
García Villalba, Miriam. "Maternidad, ficción y apología de la sexualidad lésbica: entramado de símbolos en la narrativa de Esther Tusquets." *Siglo XXI. Literatura y Cultura Españolas*, vol. 17, 2019, pp. 125–53.
Garland Thomoson, Rosemarie. *Extraordinary Bodies: Figuring Physical Disability in American Culture and Literature*. Columbia UP, 2017.
Gil Casado, Pablo. *La novela deshumanizada española (1958–1988)*. Anthropos, 1990.
Gilbert, Sandra M., and Susan Gubar. *The Madwoman in the Attic: The Woman Writer and the Nineteenth-Century Literary Imagination*. Yale UP, 1979.
Goldberg, Abbie E., and Aline Sayer. "Lesbian Couples' Relationship Quality across the Transition to Parenthood." *Journal of Marriage and Family*, vol. 68, no. 1, 2006, pp. 87–100.
Gould Levine, Linda. "Reading, Rereading, Misreading and Rewriting the Male Canon: The Narrative Web of Esther Tusquets's Trilogy." *Anales de la Literatura Española Contemporánea*, vol. 12, no. 1/2, 1987, pp. 212–17.
– "The Female Body as Palimpsest in the Works of Carmen Gómez-Ojea, Paloma Díaz-Mas, and Ana Rossetti." *Indiana Journal of Hispanic Literatures*, vol. 2, no. 1, 1993, pp. 181–206.
Griswold, Robert. "Introduction to the Special Issue on Fatherhood." *Journal of Family History*, vol. 24, no. 3, 1999, pp. 251–4.
Grosz, Elizabeth. *Volatile Bodies: Toward a Corporeal Feminism*. Indiana UP, 1994.
Halberstam, Jack. *The Queer Art of Failure*. Duke UP, 2011.
Hartmann, Heidi I. "The Unhappy Marriage of Marxism and Feminism: Towards a More Progressive Union." *Capital & Class*, vol. 3, no. 2, 1979, pp. 1–33.
Hartson, Mary T. *Casting Masculinity in Spanish Film: Negotiating Identity in a Consumer Age*. Lexington Books, 2017.

Harvey, Robert. *Search for a Father: Sartre, Paternity, and the Question of Ethics*. U of Michigan P, 1991.
Hawkes, Gail L. "Dressing-Up – Cross-Dressing and Sexual Dissonance." *Journal of Gender Studies*, vol. 4, no. 3, 1995, pp. 261–70.
Heredero, Carlos. "New Creators for the New Millennium: Transforming the Directing Scene in Spain." *Cinéaste*, vol. 29, no. 1, 2003, pp. 33–7.
Holland, Jonathan. "Amador." Review of *Amador*, directed by Fernando León de Aranoa. *Variety*, 25 Oct. 2010, p. 40.
Homans, Margaret. "Adoption and Essentialism." *Tulsa Studies in Women's Literature*, vol. 21, no. 2, 2002, pp. 257–74.
Huntley, Rebecca. "Sexing the Belly: An Exploration of Sex and the Pregnant Body." *Sexualities*, vol. 3, no. 3, 2000, pp. 347–62.
Ichiishi, Barbara F. *The Apple of Earthly Love: Female Development in Esther Tusquets's Fiction*. Peter Lang, 1994.
Irigaray, Luce. *This Sex Which Is Not One*, translated by Catherine Porter. Cornell UP, 1985.
Ismael. Directed by Marcelo Piñeyro, Antena 3 Films, 2013.
Jagose, Annamarie. *Queer Theory: An Introduction*, NYU P, 1996.
Jerónimo, Heather. "Angels or Monsters? Motherhood in the Dystopian World of Paloma Díaz-Mas's 'La niña sin alas'." *Letras Femeninas*, vol. 41, no. 2, 2015, pp. 56–66.
Jerónimo, Heather, and Lluís Maria Todó. "'En Cataluña hay una gran tradición de respeto a la diferencia.' Conversación con el escritor Lluís Maria Todó." *Arizona Journal of Hispanic Cultural Studies*, vol. 17, 2013, pp. 121–35.
Jerónimo, Heather, and Paloma Díaz-Mas. "'Somos lo que recordamos, pero también somos lo que olvidamos': Conversación con Paloma Díaz-Mas." *Anales de la literatura española contemporánea*, vol. 44, no. 1, 2019, pp. 181–201.
Johnson, Roberta. "On the Waves of Time: Memory in *El mismo mar de todos los veranos*." *The Sea of Becoming: Approaches to the Fiction of Esther Tusquets*, edited by Mary S. Vásquez. Greenwood P, 1991, pp. 65–78.
– "The Spanish Equality/Difference Debate Continues." *A New History of Iberian Feminisms*, edited by Silvia Bermúdez and Roberta Johnson. U of Toronto P, 2018, pp. 359–67.
Johnson, Roberta, and Olga Castro. "First-Wave Spanish Feminism Takes Flight in Castilian-, Catalan-, and Galician-Speaking Spain." *A New History of Iberian Feminisms*, edited by Silvia Bermúdez and Roberta Johnson. U of Toronto P, 2018, pp. 221–35.
Kafer, Alison. *Feminist, Queer, Crip*. Indiana UP, 2016.
Karpin, Isabel, and Kristin Savell. *Perfecting Pregnancy: Law, Disability, and the Future of Reproduction*. Cambridge UP, 2012.

Killings of Women and Girls by Their Intimate Partner or Other Family Members: Global Estimates 2020. 2021, www.unodc.org/documents/data-and-analysis/statistics/crime/UN_BriefFem_251121.pdf.

Kim, Yeon-Soo. *The Family Album: Histories, Subjectivities, and Immigration in Contemporary Spanish Culture*. Bucknell UP, 2005.

Kimbrell, Andrew. *The Masculine Mystique: The Politics of Masculinity*. Ballantine Books, 1995.

Kimmel, Michael. *Manhood in America: A Cultural History*. 4th ed., Oxford UP, 2018.

– "Masculinity as Homophobia: Fear, Shame, and Silence in the Construction of Gender Identity." *Theorizing Masculinities*, edited by Harry Brod and Michael Kaufman. Sage Publications, 1994, pp. 119–41.

Koolish, Lynda. "'To Be Loved and Cry Shame': A Psychological Reading of Toni Morrison's 'Beloved.'" *MELUS*, vol. 26, no. 4, 2001, pp. 169–95.

Kosofsky Sedgwick, Eve. *Epistemology of the Closet*. U of California P, 2008.

Kristeva, Julia. *The Portable Kristeva*, edited by Kelly Oliver. Columbia UP, 1997.

Kristeva, Julia, and Arthur Goldhammer. "Stabat Mater." *Poetics Today*, vol. 6, no. 1/2, 1985, pp. 133–52.

Kukla, Rebecca. *Mass Hysteria: Medicine, Culture, and Mothers' Bodies*. Rowman & Littlefield, 2005.

La buena estrella, directed by Ricardo Franco. Enrique Cerezo Producciones Cinematográficas, 1997.

La gran familia, directed by Fernando Palacios, Pedro Masó Producciones Cinematográficas, 1962.

La gran familia española, directed by Daniel Sánchez Arévalo, Mod Producciones, 2013.

Labanyi, Jo. *Gender and Modernization in the Spanish Realist Novel*. Oxford UP, 2000.

Lago, María de. "Spain Changes Law to Allow Abortion on Demand Up to 14 Weeks and without Parental Consent." *BMJ: British Medical Journal*, vol. 340, no. 7746, 2010, p. 559.

Lauster, Nathanael T. "Housing and the Proper Performance of American Motherhood, 1940–2005." *Housing Studies*, vol. 25, no. 4, 2010, pp. 543–57.

Leitao, David D. *The Pregnant Male as Myth and Metaphor in Classical Greek Literature*. Cambridge UP, 2012.

Lete, Iñaki et al. "Is There a Need for a New Abortion Law in Spain?" *European Journal of Contraception and Reproductive Health Care*, vol. 19, 2014, pp. 75–7.

Lévi-Strauss, Claude. *The Elementary Structures of Kinship*. Beacon P, 1971.

Lorde, Audre. *Sister Outsider: Essays & Speeches by Audre Lorde*. Crossing Press, 1984.

– *Zami: A New Spelling of My Name*. Crossing Press, 1982.
Lutz, Helma. *Migration and Domestic Work: A European Perspective on a Global Theme*, Ashgate, 2008.
Mabrey, María Cristina C. "Pilar Miró y Ricardo Franco: Un tributo póstumo a dos atrevidos cineastas del cine español de los setenta." *CiberLetras*, no. 9, 2013. www.lehman.cuny.edu/ciberletras/v09/mabrey.html.
"Madrid Bans Catholic Group's Anti-Transgender Bus." *BBC News*, 1 March 2017, www.bbc.com/news/world-europe-39125187. Accessed 11 Sept. 2021.
Makomè, Inongo vi. *Natives*, translated by Michael Ugarte. *Phoneme Media*, 2015.
Manganas, Nicholas. *Las dos Españas: Terror and Crisis in Contemporary Spain*. Sussex Academic P, 2016.
Mangini, Shirley. *Memories of Resistance: Women's Voices from the Spanish Civil War*. Yale UP, 1995.
Mar, María del and Martín Aragón. "Framing LGBT-Phobic Incidents in Spain: Beyond Hate Crimes." *Revista de Criminología, Psicología y Ley*, vol. 3, 2020, pp. 57–93.
Marañón, Gregorio. *Don Juan: Ensayos sobre el origen de su leyenda*. Espasa-Calpe, 1940.
Marder, Elissa. *The Mother in the Age of Mechanical Reproduction: Psychoanalysis, Photography, Deconstruction*. Fordham UP, 2012.
Márquez Rodríguez, Alexis. *Lo barroco y lo real-maravilloso en la obra de Alejo Carpentier*. Siglo Veintiuno Editores, 1982.
Martínez, Mila. *No voy a disculparme*. Egales S.L., 2009.
– *Tras la pared*. Egales S.L., 2010.
Mazquiarán de Rodríguez, Mercedes. "Talking with Tusquets." *The Sea of Becoming: Approaches to the Fiction of Esther Tusquets*, edited by Mary S. Vásquez. Greenwood P, 1991, pp. 173–88.
McCrea, Barry. "Heterosexual Horror: Dracula, the Closet, and the Marriage-Plot," *NOVEL: A Forum on Fiction*, vol. 43, no. 2, 2010, pp. 251–70.
McRuer, Robert. "Compulsory Able-Bodiedness and Queer/Disabled Existence." *The Disability Studies Reader*, edited by Lennard J. Davis. Taylor & Francis Group, 2013, pp. 369–78.
Mena-Tudela, Desirée et al. "Obstetric Violence in Spain (Part III): Healthcare Professionals, Times, and Areas." *International Journal of Environmental Research and Public Health*, vol. 18, no. 3359, 2021, pp. 1–17.
Messina, Roberta, and Salvatore D'Amore. "Adoption by Lesbians and Gay Men in Europe: Challenges and Barriers on the Journey to Adoption." *Adoption Quarterly*, vol. 21, no. 2, 2018, pp. 59–81.
Molinaro, Nina L. *Foucault, Feminism, and Power: Reading Esther Tusquets*. Bucknell UP, 1991.

- "Looking for the Other: Peninsular Women's Fiction after Levinas." *Women in the Spanish Novel Today: Essays on the Reflection of Self in the Works of Three Generations*, edited by Kyra A. Kietrys and Montserrat Linares. McFarland, 2009, pp. 133–51.
Morman, Mark T., and Kory Floyd. "A 'Changing Culture of Fatherhood': Effects on Affectionate Communication, Closeness, and Satisfaction in Men's Relationships with Their Fathers and Their Sons." *Western Journal of Communication*, vol. 66, no. 4, 2002, pp. 395–411.
Mulvey, Laura. "Visual Pleasure and Narrative Cinema." *Contemporary Literary Criticism: Literary and Cultural Studies*. 4th ed., edited by Robert Con Davis and Ronald Schleifer. Addison Wesley Longman, 1998, pp. 448–56.
Murray, N. Michelle. *Home Away from Home: Immigrant Narratives, Domesticity, and Coloniality in Contemporary Spanish Culture*. U of North Carolina P, 2018.
Musial, Jennifer. "From 'Madonna' to 'Whore': Sexuality, Pregnancy, and Popular Culture." *Sexualities*, vol. 17, no. 4, 2014, pp. 394–411.
Nash, Mary. "Experiencia y Aprendizaje: La Formación Histórica de los Feminismos en España." *Historia Social*, vol. 20, 1994, pp. 151–72.
- "Turismo, género y neocolonialismo." *Historia Social*, no. 96, 2020, pp. 41–62.
- "Un/Contested Identities: Motherhood, Sex Reform and the Modernization of Gender Identity in Early Twentieth-Century Spain." *Constructing Spanish Womanhood: Female Identity in Modern Spain*, edited by Victoria Loree Enders and Pamela Beth Radcliff. SUNY P, 1999, pp. 25–49.
Neimanis, Astrida. "Hydrofeminism: Or, On Becoming a Body of Water." *Undutiful Daughters: New Directions in Feminist Thought and Practice*, edited by Henriette Gunkel, Chrysanthi Nigianni, and Fammy Soderback. Palgrave Macmillan, 2012, pp. 85–100.
Ness, Tove M., Ove Hellzen, and Ingela Enmarker. "'Embracing the Present and Fearing the Future': The Meaning of Being an Oldest Old Woman in a Rural Area." *International Journal of Qualitative Studies in Health and Well-Being*, vol. 9, 2014, pp. 1–11.
Newton-Jackson, Elizabeth. "Overlooked, Forgotten, Avoided: The LGBT Community and Public Art." *Women's Studies Journal*, vol. 34, no. 1/2, 2020, pp. 92–106.
Noble, Fiona. "Beyond the Sea: Seascapes and Migration in Contemporary Spanish Cinema." *Bulletin of Hispanic Studies*, no. 95, 2018, pp. 637–56.
Oliver, Kelly. "Julia Kristeva's Feminist Revolutions." *Hypatia*, vol. 8, no. 3, 1993, pp. 94–114.
- "Motherhood, Sexuality, and Pregnant Embodiment: Twenty-Five Years of Gestation." *Hypatia*, vol. 25, no. 4, 2010, pp. 760–77.
Olson, Gary A., and Lynn Worsham. "Changing the Subject: Judith Butler's Politics of Radical Resignification." *JAC*, vol. 20, no. 4, 2000, pp. 727–65.

Parau, Laura. "Espacios terapéuticos en la trilogía de Esther Tusquets." *Hispanic Research Journal*, vol. 18, no. 2, 2017, pp. 146–58.
Park, Shelley M. "Adoptive Maternal Bodies: A Queer Paradigm for Rethinking Mothering?" *Hypatia*, vol. 21, no. 1, 2006, pp. 201–26.
— *Mothering Queerly, Queering Motherhood: Resisting Monomaternalism in Adoptive, Lesbian, Blended, and Polygamous Families*. SUNY P, 2013.
Pérez-Sánchez, Gema. "One Big Queer European Family? Immigration in Contemporary Spanish Gay and Lesbian Films." *Twenty-First-Century Gay Culture*, edited by David A. Powell. Cambridge Scholars Publishing, 2008, pp. 157–82.
Perriam, Chris. *Spanish Queer Cinema*. Edinburgh UP, 2013.
Perriam, Chris et al. *A New History of Spanish Writing: 1939 to the 1990s*. Oxford UP, 2000.
Platero Méndez, Raquel. "Transitions and Representations of Lesbianism in the Spanish Media." *Lesbian Realities/Lesbian Fictions in Contemporary Spain*, edited by Nancy Vosburg and Jacky Collins. Bucknell UP, 2011, pp. 60–103.
Portela Jordi Antón, Lino. "Santi Balmes: 'Por favor, ¿podéis cambiar eso de que tengo problemas de erección?'" 25 Oct. 2012. http://rollingstone.es/noticias/view/santi-balmes-por-favor-podeis-cambiar-eso-de-que-tengo-problemas-de-ereccion. Accessed 17 Dec. 2013.
Portillo, Aurelio del. "La visibilidad de los marginados en el cine de Fernando León de Aranoa." *Los derechos humanos en el cine español*, edited by Juan Antonio Gómez García. Dykinson, 2017, pp. 323–71.
Poveda, David et al. "Professional Discourses on Single Parenthood in International Adoptions in Spain." *Political and Legal Anthropology Review*, vol. 36, no. 1, 2013, pp. 35–55.
Queipo, Alan. "Achero Mañas: Realidad o ficción." *Notodo.com*, 8 Aug. 2010. Accessed 4 Aug. 2013.
Quintana, Ángel. "Fernando León de Aranoa: *Princesas* (2005) y el realismo tímido en el cine español." *Foro Hispánico: Revista Hispánica de Flandes y Holanda*, vol. 32, 2008, pp. 251–63.
Radcliff, Pamela Beth. "Imagining Female Citizenship in the 'New Spain': Gendering the Democratic Transition, 1975–1978." *Gender & History*, vol. 13, no. 3, 2001, pp. 498–523.
Ragan, Robin R. "La monogamia y sus descontentos: el amor y el deseo en el cine español contemporareo." *Los hábitos del deseo: formas de amar en la modernidad*, edited by Carme Riera Guilera, vol. 1, no. 1, 2005, pp. 121–6.
Ramiro-Fariñas, Diego, Francisco J. Viciana-Fernández, and Víctor Montañés Cobo. "Will Highly Educated Women Have More Children in the Future? In Southern Europe, It Will Largely Depend on Labour Market Conditions." *Vienna Yearbook of Population Research*, vol. 15, 2017, pp. 49–54.

Reddy, Vasu, and Judith Butler. "Troubling Genders, Subverting Identities: Interview with Judith Butler." *Agenda: Empowering Women for Gender Equity*, African Feminisms vol. 2,1: Sexuality in Africa, no. 62, 2004, pp. 115–23.

Reuben Muñoz, Lindsey. "The Biopolitics of Domesticity in Fernando León de Aranoa's *Amador* (2010)." *Bulletin of Spanish Studies*, vol. 96, no. 7, 2019, pp. 1153–75.

Reynolds, Alberta L., and Sandra L. Caron. "How Intimate Relationships Are Impacted When Heterosexual Men Crossdress." *Journal of Psychology & Human Sexuality*, vol. 12, no. 3, 2000, pp. 63–77.

Rich, Adrienne. "Compulsory Heterosexuality and Lesbian Existence." *The Lesbian and Gay Studies Reader*, edited by Henry Abelove, Michele Aina Barale, and David M. Halperin. Routledge, 1993, pp. 227–54.

Richmond, Kathleen J.L. *Women and Spanish Fascism: The Women's Section of the Falange 1934–1959*. Routledge, 2003.

Robbins, Jill. "The (In)visible Lesbian: The Contradictory Representations of Female Homoeroticism in Contemporary Spain." *Journal of Lesbian Studies*, vol. 7, no. 3, 2003, pp. 107–31.

Robinson, Douglas. *The Translator's Turn*. Johns Hopkins UP, 1991.

Rodríguez del Pino, Juan Antonio. "A Farewell to the Iberian Spanish Macho? An Analysis of Masculinity in Spain. Conversations with Experts," *Revista Crítica de Ciências Sociais* [online], vol. 118, 2019, https://journals.openedition.org/rccs/8398.

Rodríguez Pérez, María Pilar. "Crítica lesbiana: lecturas de la narrativa española contemporánea." *Centro de estudios sobre la mujer*, vol. 1, 2003, pp. 87–102.

Romera, Magdalena. "Estereotipos para la mujer de hoy. La maternidad sexy en el discurso de las revistas españolas para mujeres." *Discurso & Sociedad*, vol. 14, no. 4, 2020, pp. 973–92.

Rubin Suleiman, Susan. "Writing and Motherhood." *Mother Reader: Essential Writings on Motherhood*, edited by Moyra Davey. Seven Stories Press, 2001, pp. 113–37.

Ryan, Lorraine. "All Turbulent on the Home Front: Unfulfilled Working Mothers in Almudena Grandes' *Altas de geografía humana*." *The Changing Spanish Family: Essays on New Views in Literature, Cinema and Theater*, edited by Tiffany Trotman. McFarland & Company, 2011, pp. 40–58.

— "Maternal Identities and Abject Equivalence in *Biutiful*." *MLN*, vol. 133, no. 2, 2018, pp. 388–410.

Ryan, Lorraine, and Ana Corbalán. *The Dynamics of Masculinity in Contemporary Spanish Culture*. Routledge, 2017.

Saavedra Macías, Javier, and Rafael Velez Núñez. "The Other Self: Psychopathology and Literature." *J Med Humanit*, vol. 32, no. 4, 2011, pp. 257–67.

Said, Edward W. *Beginnings: Intention and Method.* Basic Books, 1975.
Sartre, Jean-Paul. *The Words*, translated by Bernard Frechtman. George Braziller, 1964.
Schaffer, Talia. "'A Wilde Desire Took Me': The Homoerotic History of *Dracula*," *ELH* vol. 61, no. 2, 1994, pp. 381–425.
Schumm, Sandra J. *Mother and Myth in Spanish Novels: Rewriting the Maternal Archetype.* Bucknell UP, 2011.
Segado, Sagrario et al. "Adoption from Care in Spain." *Adoption from Care: International Perspectives on Children's Rights, Family Preservation and State Intervention*, edited by Tarja Pösö, Marit Skivenes, and June Thoburn, 2021, pp. 157–73.
Segalen, Martine. *Historical Anthropology of the Family.* Cambridge UP, 2010.
Selman, Peter. "The Rise and Fall of Intercountry Adoption in the 21st Century." *International Social Work*, vol. 52, no. 5, 2009, pp. 575–94.
Sempruch, Justyna. *Fantasies of Gender and the Witch in Feminist Theory and Literature.* Purdue UP, 2008.
Showalter, Elaine. "Critical Cross-Dressing; Male Feminists and the Woman of the Year." *Men in Feminism*, edited by Alice Jardine and Paul Smith. Methuen, 1987, pp. 116–32.
Sobol, Michael P., and Jeanette Cardiff. "A Sociopsychological Investigation of Adult Adoptees' Search for Birth Parents." *Family Relations*, vol. 32, no. 4, 1983, pp. 477–83.
Socolovsky, Jerome. "Spain's Pregnant Defense Minister Stirs Controversy." *NPR*, 16 April 2008, www.npr.org/2008/04/16/89676023/spains-pregnant-defense-minister-stirs-controversy. Accessed 23 Aug. 2022.
"Spain Sexual Assault: US Issues Security Alert over Rise in Reported Cases." *BBC News*, 5 Feb. 2020, www.bbc.com/news/world-europe-51384434. Accessed 11 Sept. 2021.
Stehle, Maria, and Beverly Weber. "The Politics of Touch in Contemporary Western European Cinema." *Commodified Intimacy in a Globalizing Europe.* Northwestern UP, 2020, pp. 93–122.
Suthrell, Charlotte. *Unzipping Gender: Sex, Cross-Dressing and Culture.* Berg, 2004.
Tiefer, Leonore. "In Pursuit of the Perfect Penis: The Medicalization of Male Sexuality." *Changing Men: New Directions in Research on Men and Masculinity*, edited by Michael S. Kimmel. Sage Publications, 1987, pp. 165–84.
Thomas, Sarah. *Inhabiting the In-Between: Childhood and Cinema in Spain's Long Transition.* U of Toronto P, 2019.
Thompson, Edward H., Jr. "What's Unique about Men's Caregiving?" *Men as Caregivers: Theory, Research, and Service Implications*, edited by Betty J. Kramer and Edward H. Thompson, Jr. Springer Publishing Company, 2002, pp. 20–47.

Todó, Lluís Maria. *El mal francés*. Egales, 2009.
Todo lo que tú quieras, directed by Achero Mañas. Bellatrix Films, 2010.
Triana-Toribio, Núria. "Spanish Cinema of the 2010s: Back to Punk and Other Lessons from the Crisis." *Hispanic Research Journal*, vol. 20, no. 1, 2019, pp. 10–25.
Trotman, Tiffany. *The Changing Spanish Family: Essays on New Views in Literature, Cinema and Theater*. McFarland & Company, 2011.
Tsuchiya, Akiko. *Marginal Subjects: Gender and Deviance in Fin-de-Siécle Spain*. U of Toronto P, 2011.
Tusquets, Esther. "Carta a la madre." *Correspondencia privada*. Anagrama, 2001.
– "Ser madre." *Ser mujer*, edited by Laura Freixas. Temas de hoy, 2000, pp. 81–101.
– *Varada tras el último naufragio*. Lumen, 1985.
Vardoulakis, Dimitris. *The Doppelgänger*. Fordham UP, 2010.
Vásquez, Mary S. "*The Sea of Becoming*: An Introduction to the Fiction of Esther Tusquets." *The Sea of Becoming: Approaches to the Fiction of Esther Tusquets*, edited by Mary S. Vásquez. Greenwood P, 1991, pp. 1–28.
Vega-Durán, Raquel. *Emigrant Dreams, Immigrant Borders: Migrants, Transnational Encounters, and Identity in Spain*. Bucknell UP, 2016.
Villarmea Requejo, Stella, and Francisca Fernández Guillén. "Fully Entitled Subjects: Birth as a Philosophical Topic." *Ontology Studies*, vol. 11, 2011, pp. 211–30.
Volver. Directed by Pedro Almodóvar, El Deseo, 2007.
Walsh, Fintan. *Male Trouble: Masculinity and the Performance of Crisis*. Palgrave Macmillan, 2010.
Warhol, Robyn R. "Double Gender, Double Genre in *Jane Eyre* and *Villete*." *Studies in English Literature, 1500–1900*, vol. 36, no. 4, 1996, pp. 857–75.
Warner, Michael. "Introduction: Fear of a Queer Planet." *Social Text*, vol. 29, 1991, pp. 3–17.
Watters, Wendell W. *Compulsory Parenthood: The Truth about Abortion*. M & S, 1976.
Webber, Andrew J. *The Doppelgänger: Double Visions in German Literature*. Claredon P, 1996.
Young, Iris Marion. *Throwing Like a Girl and Other Essays in Feminist Philosophy and Social Theory*. Oxford UP, 2005.
Zecchi, Barbara. "All about Mothers: Pronatalist Discources in Contemporary Spanish Cinema." *College Literature*, vol. 32, no. 1, 2005, pp. 146–64.
Zomeño, Fuencisla. "Feminism and Postmodernism in Paloma Díaz-Mas's 'The World According to Valdés' and 'In Search of a Portrait.'" *Studies in 20th & 21st CenturyLiterature*, vol. 26, no. 2, 2002, pp. 424–41.

Index

ableism, 23, 62, 66, 68–70, 73, 78, 84
abortion, 12, 64, 68, 70, 99, 196, 206n5, 212n1
adoption, 13, 38, 98, 100, 112, 123, 140, 142–7, 153, 213–14n2
affect, 12, 16, 25–6, 77, 110, 138, 140, 155, 174–9, 181–2, 185, 187–93, 200
affect alien, 26, 177, 195, 198–200. *See also* Ahmed, Sara
agency, 11–12, 16, 20, 23, 26, 64, 66, 82, 88, 99, 107, 122, 124–5, 128, 139, 145, 152, 156, 175, 182, 194, 196–8, 200–1, 210n2
Ahmed, Sara, 26, 177–8, 180–1, 183–4, 186–9, 195, 197–9. *See also* affect alien
AIDS, 86, 116, 178. *See also* HIV
Alberdi, Inés, 12–13, 143, 157
Almodóvar, Pedro, 3–4, 17, 179, 205n1
angel of the hearth, 7, 11, 63
anxiety, 17–18, 32–5, 39–41, 62, 128, 131, 186, 188, 198, 213n6; patriarchal, 33, 40
Aresti, Nerea, 7, 30, 91, 96, 208n4
Association for the Recovery of Historical Memory (ARHM), 4
autonomy, 7, 66, 77, 209–10n1

Barcelona, 13, 34, 36, 38, 46, 214n3
Baudrillard, Jean, 31, 33, 37, 40. *See also* simulacra

biography, 23, 29, 35, 47–50, 52
Botto, Juan Diego, 87
Bourland Ross, Catherine, 16, 18, 63, 157
Bugallo, Celso, 176
Burgos, Carmen de, 11
Butler, Judith, 24, 88, 145, 182; and performativity, 19–21, 106, 146, 202. *See also* gender performativity

Campoamor, Clara, 11
care recipient, 25, 119
caregiver, 8, 25–6, 98, 101, 108, 113, 119, 151, 156–8, 175–6, 180–4, 187, 200, 203
Carrero Blanco, Luis, 39
Catalan, 44, 208n1; authors, 28, 209n8, 209n10; culture, 54; people, 35
Catholic, 8, 30, 80, 113, 206n5; Catholic Church, 13, 211n5. *See also* National Catholicism
cine social, 87, 176, 217n1
colonialism, 195
community, 5, 13, 24–5, 65, 68, 87, 119–26, 129, 131, 134–9, 162, 203. *See also* motherhood, lesbian community of; motherhood community
compulsory able-bodiedness, 69. *See also* McRuer, Robert

compulsory hetero-parenting, 85, 88–90, 100, 102, 105, 117, 212n1
compulsory heterosexuality, 75, 89, 214n4. *See also* lesbian continuum; Rich, Adrienne
Connell, R.W., 24, 86, 88, 89, 93–4, 97, 104, 115, 117
Cooper, Sara, 7, 9, 15, 206n7
cross-dressing, 5, 24, 85–7, 102, 105–9, 114–15, 117
Cruz, Penelope, 3

death, 3, 10, 12, 14, 19, 39–40, 67, 72, 86–7, 92, 96, 100, 102, 113, 127, 138, 146, 176, 178–80, 188–94, 207n10, 213n1, 215–16n3. *See also* Sudden Infant Death Syndrome; suicide
dictatorship, 4–8, 10–11, 15, 30, 39, 63, 91–2, 95, 201, 205n4, 206n5, 207n8, 209–10n1, 216n5
disability, 23, 61, 64–70, 73, 210–11n3. *See also* pregnancy: and disability
disabled, 23, 62, 65, 68–70, 80–2; bodies, 5, 67–8, 70. *See also* pregnancy: and disability
divorce, 10–12, 30, 98, 207–8n12
DNA, 3–4, 36–7
domestic help, 5, 25, 178
domestic violence, 18, 179, 207n9. *See also* gender violence
don Juan, 41, 43–4, 132, 209n7
doppelgänger, 14, 25, 141, 164–8, 172–3, 203, 215n1, 216–17n8
dos Españas, 11
Dracula, 114, 213n6

economic crisis (Spain), 12, 91–2, 144, 176, 181, 206n6, 217n1
Engels, Friedrich, 29
erotic, 18, 74, 125, 136, 139, 171, 211n5, 213n6, 214n3, 216–17n8; eroticism, 74, 170

Escrivá, Josemaría, 39
European dream, 177, 198

failure, as queer art, 57. *See also* Halberstam, Jack; queer
Falange, 6, 8, 30
family: as decay, 14, 178–9, 187, 190, 193; as failure, 6, 201–2; under Franco, 4, 7–8, 10–12; heteronormative, 6, 16, 44, 54, 68, 100, 178; and immigration, 14, 18–19, 25, 93, 186; multicultural, 5, 14, 18, 27, 186, 188, 198; and nation, 4, 7, 30, 186–9; non-normative, 4, 25–6, 34, 86, 100–1, 103, 112–13, 115, 117, 131, 135–6, 141, 172, 174–6, 186–7, 197–8, 202–3; nuclear, 30, 90, 140, 178, 191; patriarchal, 6–7, 15–16, 30, 135, 151, 201–2; Republican, 3–4, 11; violent, 9. *See also* identity: familial; immigration; Second Republic; spectrum: of families
fascism, 4, 9, 38–9, 81, 91
fatherhood: absent or dead, 4, 15, 17, 138, 149–50, 158, 178–9; and authority, 7, 18, 29–30, 32, 40, 59; economic provider, 16–17, 71, 91, 97; as failure, 23, 29, 33–8, 47–8, 54–5, 57–60; gay literary father figures, 5, 22, 43–7; and masculinity, 17, 24, 30, 85, 88, 93, 95, 97, 113, 117; non-biological, 25, 101–2, 112, 114, 153; patriarchal father figure, 6–7, 23, 28–34, 37–40, 43–4, 47, 49, 57, 60, 72; sacrifice 91, 96, 113; violence, 18, 154; virility, 7. *See also* gay; identity: fatherhood; patriarchy; spectrum: of fatherhood
femininity, 74, 82, 106, 160, 171
feminism, 11–12, 174, 205n3, 216–17n8

Fernández, Lucía, 87
fetish mother, 64–5. *See also* Kukla, Rebecca
Franco, Francisco, 4, 6–12, 15, 29–30, 38–40, 47, 49, 57, 63, 80, 91–2, 140, 201, 206n5, 208n3, 208n4, 209–10n1, 216n5
Freud, Sigmund, 74, 80; and Oedipus complex, 29; and Schreber case, 36–7; and "Medusa's Head," 67; and *Interpretation of Dreams*, 29, 127. *See also* Oedipus

Garland Thomson, Rosemarie, 68, 70, 73
gay, 5, 12–13, 18, 28, 43–5, 51–2, 57, 89, 106, 144, 207–8n12, 209n8, 213n6. *See also* fatherhood: gay literary father figures
gay literature, 131, 214n3
gender, 6, 19–22, 66, 88–90, 106–7, 109–10, 145, 155, 157–8, 181–2, 195, 202–3, 216n7
gender equality, 11
gender identity, 19–20, 97. *See also* identity
gender performativity, 19–22, 88–9, 94, 97, 106–7, 110, 145–6. *See also* Butler, Judith: and performativity
gender roles, 5–7, 9–14, 16–17, 26, 29, 49, 71, 89–90, 93, 108, 140–1, 145, 159–60, 173, 201–2, 216n7
gender violence, 17, 92, 116, 207n10. *See also* domestic violence
Gide, André, 43–6, 58
Gilbert, Sandra M., 23, 31–3. *See also* Gubar, Susan; literary paternity
Granada, 3
Gubar, Susan, 23, 31–3. *See also* Gilbert, Sandra M.; literary paternity

Halberstam, Jack, 57, 59. *See also* failure, as queer art; queer
Hartson, Mary T., 91, 96, 111
herethics, 74–5, 77, 136. *See also* Kristeva, Julia
heteronormative, 4, 6, 16, 18, 20, 22–3, 26, 31, 35, 44, 46–7, 49, 54–5, 57–60, 64, 68, 70–1, 73, 76, 82, 90, 99, 106, 110–11, 114, 124–5, 129, 135, 138, 144–5, 151–2, 155–8, 164, 173–6, 178, 202, 212n3
heterosexuality, 21, 75, 89, 95, 104, 145, 150–1, 213n6
HIV, 86, 116. *See also* AIDS
home, 7–8, 11–12, 25–6, 30, 63, 86–7, 91–2, 96–100, 107–9, 113, 122, 147, 149, 157, 168, 172–3, 175, 177, 179, 182, 186, 188–9, 192–3, 196, 211n6, 218n5
homophobia, 88–9, 96, 114, 131; internalized, 25, 119, 131–4, 139
homosexuality, 22, 28, 34–5, 40, 44–6, 51–2, 104, 114, 130, 208n2, 213n6
hydrofeminism, 171–2. *See also* Neimanis, Astrida

Icarus, 72, 211n4
identity: cultural, 189; familial, 5; fatherhood, 23, 28, 33–4, 43–7, 50, 56–60; gender, 19–20, 88, 97, 145; and masculinity, 85, 92–3, 97, 102, 104, 114; motherhood, 8, 23, 61–2, 68, 75–8, 81, 84, 99, 107, 134, 162, 166, 174; national, 7, 19; parental, 20–2, 26, 92, 145, 156, 160, 164, 168, 202; performative, 6; sexual, 19, 21, 28, 40, 44–7, 51–2, 132, 202; women's, 11. *See also* family; fatherhood; gender identity; masculinity; motherhood; parenthood; spectrum: of identity

immigration, 5, 12–14, 17–19, 25–6, 93, 175–7, 181, 189–200; African, 18, 195; and care work, 180–2, 189; Latin America, 182–3, 186–8, 195. *See also* family: and immigration; masculinity: and immigration; motherhood: as caregiver; motherhood: immigrant
immortality, 14, 33, 49, 168
impotence, 24, 85–6, 104, 110–12, 115; emotional, 103, 113–14
incest, 14, 17, 25, 36, 41–2, 137, 141, 150–6, 165, 174, 178–9, 202–3, 208–9n6
individualism, 13, 91, 111, 143, 195
Irigaray, Luce, 75–6, 135
isolation, 14, 35, 78, 80, 166, 183

jouissance, 23, 74, 134, 211n5. *See also* Kristeva, Julia

Kent, Victoria, 11
Kimmel, Michael, 24, 35, 86, 88, 96–8, 158
Kristeva, Julia, 81–2, 136–7; "Stabat Mater," 23, 62, 74, 77, 82, 134. *See also* herethics; *jouissance*
Kukla, Rebecca, 23, 64–5, 136. *See also* fetish mother; unruly mother

Lacan, Jacques, 29, 36, 42
lesbian, 5, 24, 89, 119–20, 131–4, 136, 166, 213–14n2, 214–15n5, 217n9. *See also* motherhood: lesbian; motherhood: lesbian community of
lesbian continuum, 22, 136, 214n4. *See also* compulsory heterosexuality; Rich, Adrienne
lesbian literature, 131, 138, 214n3

Lévi-Strauss, Claude, 29
literary paternity, 23, 29, 31–4, 49–51, 54, 56, 60. *See also* Gilbert, Sandra M.; Gubar, Susan
loneliness, 13–14, 35, 161, 164, 178, 183
Lorde, Audre, 74, 214n4

Madres paralelas, 3–5
Madrid, 3, 13, 191, 199, 205n4, 214n3
magic, 42–3, 126–8, 130–6
magical realism, 24, 119, 130–4, 139
male gaze, 48, 119, 124–5, 139, 152, 154
masculinity, 14, 17–18, 24, 28–30, 35, 37, 40, 48, 85–6, 88–98, 101–6, 108–17, 145, 158, 171, 178, 202, 208n4, 212n2, 212n3; and crisis, 17, 92–3, 97, 110–11, 115; as failure, 92, 114–15; hegemonic, 16, 24, 29, 41, 85–6, 88–90, 92–8, 102–6, 108–17, 151, 156–7, 159; hypermasculinity, 116; and immigration, 17; as performance, 24, 85, 88, 92, 94–5, 103–6, 110, 112, 116–17; and violence, 86, 89, 95, 105, 109, 111, 115–17; and virility, 30, 91, 94, 101, 110–11. *See also* identity: and masculinity; immigration
McRuer, Robert, 69. *See also* compulsory able-bodiedness
medical community, 65, 124, 162, 210n2
mimesis, 14, 22–3, 28, 30, 32–3, 37, 40, 42–3, 46, 49–51, 60, 209n10
Moix, Terenci, 209n8
Mollá, Jordi, 86
Montserrat, Virgin of, 54
motherhood: as absent or dead mothers, 15, 24, 85, 87, 99, 102, 109, 120, 178; as caregiver, 25, 119, 182, 187, 203; and castration, 23,

32, 61–2, 67–8, 79–84; as failure, 169, 173; immigrant, 18–19, 217n3; lesbian, 16, 18, 25, 119, 135, 207–8n12, 214–15n5; lesbian community of, 24, 119, 129, 131, 134–9; as monstrous, 67–9, 73, 80–4, 126–7; non-biological, 25, 119, 121–3, 131, 134–5, 154, 174; Oedipal, 23, 62, 138–9; as patriotic duty, 8, 63; sacrifice, 7, 23, 61–3, 79–84, 99, 157, 161, 165, 182, 217n3; single, 3, 16, 216n5; traditional, 7–10, 21, 102, 122, 141, 157; working, 8, 14, 16, 91, 113. *See also* identity: motherhood; lesbian; parenthood: as performance; spectrum: of motherhood

motherhood community, 25, 119–20, 134, 137, 139

Mothering Queerly, 99, 123, 138–9. *See also* Park, Shelley M.; queer

Movida, la, 12, 205n4

Murray, N. Michelle, 181–2, 186–7, 189–90, 193

Nash, Mary, 11, 124, 209–10n1

National Catholicism, 4–5, 7–8, 63, 91, 140, 201. *See also* Catholic nationalism, 64, 209n10

Neimanis, Astrida, 171–2. *See also* hydrofeminism

Nelken, Margarita, 11

obstetric violence, 124, 210n2

Oedipus, 23, 62, 138. *See also* Freud, Sigmund

Opus Dei, 39, 55

orphan, 15, 142, 147–8, 150, 178

orphanage, 98, 103, 123

otherness, 26, 68–70, 73, 77, 82, 144, 166, 176, 198

parenthood: biological, 140; as failure, 143; gay, 5; heteronormative, 57, 89; non-biological, 5, 25, 27, 93, 140–8, 151, 155, 216n5; non-normative, 21–2, 24, 26, 60, 86, 110, 151, 155–6, 158, 160, 164, 201; as performance, 6, 9–10, 19–27, 29, 43, 49, 51–2, 60, 62–3, 69, 73, 76, 81, 84–6, 88–90, 94, 98–9, 103, 107, 110, 113, 117, 141, 143, 145–9, 155–9, 161, 165, 171, 173–4, 182, 186, 197–9, 201–4; and violence, 179. *See also* identity: parental; spectrum: of parenthood

Park, Shelley M., 99, 123, 138–9, 144–6. See also *Mothering Queerly*

patriarchy, 4, 8, 23–4, 28–33, 35–7, 40–1, 43, 47–9, 52, 54, 57–62, 64, 66–72, 74–5, 78–9, 81–4, 93, 97–8, 104, 106, 112, 114–15, 119, 124–6, 129, 135–6, 138, 151, 155–7, 171, 202, 207n9, 216n7. *See also* fatherhood: patriarchal father figure

Perriam, Chris, 7–8, 30, 207–8n12, 208n3

postcolonialism, 194–5

pregnancy, 3, 24, 26, 28, 35, 44–5, 51, 61, 72, 86, 94, 121–3, 135–7, 139, 142, 144, 159, 162, 175–7, 184–5, 188, 191, 196, 199, 207–8n12, 209–10n1, 212n1; and disability, 65–8, 81–2, 84, 124, 210–11n3; infantilization of pregnant individuals, 23, 64, 124, 210n2; pregnant man, 32, 208n5; sexualization of pregnant body, 25, 124–5, 210n2; and sexuality, 74, 119–20, 125–7, 129–30, 213–4n2. *See also* disability; disabled

pronatalist, 18, 140–1, 144

prostitute, 86, 94, 103–4, 160, 176, 179, 183, 217–18n4. *See also* sex worker

Proust, Marcel, 46
puzzle, 193–5, 197–8, 200

queer, 13, 27, 68, 131, 138, 144, 164; queer art of failure, 57; queer theory, 22, 155, 164, 214n4. *See also* failure, as queer art; Halberstam, Jack; *Mothering Queerly*

rape, 3, 5, 17, 83, 95, 116, 126, 162, 206n5
religion, 53, 55, 74, 211n6
repro-narrativity, 145
reprosexuality, 143, 145, 147, 162
Resines, Antonio, 86
Rich, Adrienne, 22, 78, 89, 136, 214n4. *See also* compulsory heterosexuality; lesbian continuum
Risueño, Ana, 87

Said, Edward, 31
Sartre, Jean-Paul, 37, 39
sea, 170–1, 188, 193–4, 197, 218n5
Sección Femenina, 8
Second Republic 3, 11. *See also* family, Republican
Sedgwick, Eve Kosofsky, 52
sex worker, 26, 175. *See also* prostitute
sexuality, 8–9, 19, 44–5, 55, 73–4, 94, 96, 114, 117, 132, 146, 171, 202, 211n6, 213n6; female, 76, 82, 104; male, 31; maternal, 119, 123–30, 139, 210n2, 213–14n2
Sibille, Pietro, 176
simulacra, 31, 33, 35, 40. *See also* Baudrillard, Jean

Smit, Milena, 3
Solier, Magaly, 176
Spanish Civil War, 4, 11, 90–1, 178, 206n8, 208n4
spectrum: of families, 4, 10, 25, 141, 143, 176, 187, 198, 200–4; of fatherhood, 51, 56–7, 60, 94; of identity, 50; of motherhood, 27; of parenthood, 6, 8, 19, 22–8, 49, 62, 81, 85, 90, 146, 155, 164, 172, 174; of sexuality, 19. *See also* family; fatherhood; identity; motherhood; parenthood
Sudden Infant Death Syndrome, 3. *See also* death
suffrage, 11
suicide, 169, 172–3. *See also* death

telepathy, 24, 120, 126, 129–32, 134–5
touch, 5, 8, 26, 74–8, 105, 112, 115–16, 121, 123, 131–3, 175, 180–6, 200, 202
Transition, 10, 12, 16, 63, 87, 91, 111, 143, 205n4, 206n5
Trotman, Tiffany, 7, 12, 16, 93, 207n9

uncanny, 67, 182
unruly mother, 64–5. *See also* Kukla, Rebecca

Verdú, Maribel, 86

Walsh, Fintan, 24, 86, 89, 97, 110–11, 116
witch, 67, 126, 130
womb, 63, 67, 120, 123, 127–8

Toronto Iberic

CO-EDITORS: Robert Davidson (Toronto) and Frederick A. de Armas (Chicago)

EDITORIAL BOARD: Josiah Blackmore (Harvard); Marina Brownlee (Princeton); Anthony J. Cascardi (Berkeley); Justin Crumbaugh (Mt Holyoke); Emily Francomano (Georgetown); Jordana Mendelson (NYU); Joan Ramon Resina (Stanford); Enrique García Santo-Tomás (U Michigan); H. Rosi Song (Durham); Kathleen Vernon (SUNY Stony Brook); William Viestenz (Minnesota)

1 Anthony J. Cascardi, *Cervantes, Literature, and the Discourse of Politics*
2 Jessica A. Boon, *The Mystical Science of the Soul: Medieval Cognition in Bernardino de Laredo's Recollection Method*
3 Susan Byrne, *Law and History in Cervantes'* Don Quixote
4 Mary E. Barnard and Frederick A. de Armas (eds.), *Objects of Culture in the Literature of Imperial Spain*
5 Nil Santiáñez, *Topographies of Fascism: Habitus, Space, and Writing in Twentieth-Century Spain*
6 Nelson R. Orringer, *Lorca in Tune with Falla: Literary and Musical Interludes*
7 Ana M. Gómez-Bravo, *Textual Agency: Writing Culture and Social Networks in Fifteenth-Century Spain*
8 Javier Irigoyen-García, *The Spanish Arcadia: Sheep Herding, Pastoral Discourse, and Ethnicity in Early Modern Spain*
9 Stephanie Sieburth, *Survival Songs: Conchita Piquer's* Coplas *and Franco's Regime of Terror*
10 Christine Arkinstall, *Spanish Female Writers and the Freethinking Press, 1879–1926*
11 Margaret E. Boyle, *Unruly Women: Performance, Penitence, and Punishment in Early Modern Spain*
12 Evelina Gužauskyt , *Christopher Columbus's Naming in the* diarios *of the Four Voyages (1492–1504): A Discourse of Negotiation*

13 Mary E. Barnard, *Garcilaso de la Vega and the Material Culture of Renaissance Europe*
14 William Viestenz, *By the Grace of God: Francoist Spain and the Sacred Roots of Political Imagination*
15 Michael Scham, *Lector Ludens: The Representation of Games and Play in Cervantes*
16 Stephen Rupp, *Heroic Forms: Cervantes and the Literature of War*
17 Enrique Fernandez, *Anxieties of Interiority and Dissection in Early Modern Spain*
18 Susan Byrne, *Ficino in Spain*
19 Patricia M. Keller, *Ghostly Landscapes: Film, Photography, and the Aesthetics of Haunting in Contemporary Spanish Culture*
20 Carolyn A. Nadeau, *Food Matters: Alonso Quijano's Diet and the Discourse of Food in Early Modern Spain*
21 Cristian Berco, *From Body to Community: Venereal Disease and Society in Baroque Spain*
22 Elizabeth R. Wright, *The Epic of Juan Latino: Dilemmas of Race and Religion in Renaissance Spain*
23 Ryan D. Giles, *Inscribed Power: Amulets and Magic in Early Spanish Literature*
24 Jorge Pérez, *Confessional Cinema: Religion, Film, and Modernity in Spain's Development Years, 1960–1975*
25 Joan Ramon Resina, *Josep Pla: Seeing the World in the Form of Articles*
26 Javier Irigoyen-García, *"Moors Dressed as Moors": Clothing, Social Distinction, and Ethnicity in Early Modern Iberia*
27 Jean Dangler, *Edging toward Iberia*
28 Ryan D. Giles and Steven Wagschal (eds.), *Beyond Sight: Engaging the Senses in Iberian Literatures and Cultures, 1200–1750*
29 Silvia Bermúdez, *Rocking the Boat: Migration and Race in Contemporary Spanish Music*
30 Hilaire Kallendorf, *Ambiguous Antidotes: Virtue as Vaccine for Vice in Early Modern Spain*
31 Leslie J. Harkema, *Spanish Modernism and the Poetics of Youth: From Miguel de Unamuno to* La Joven Literatura
32 Benjamin Fraser, *Cognitive Disability Aesthetics: Visual Culture, Disability Representations, and the (In)Visibility of Cognitive Difference*
33 Robert Patrick Newcomb, *Iberianism and Crisis: Spain and Portugal at the Turn of the Twentieth Century*
34 Sara J. Brenneis, *Spaniards in Mauthausen: Representations of a Nazi Concentration Camp, 1940–2015*
35 Silvia Bermúdez and Roberta Johnson (eds.), *A New History of Iberian Feminisms*
36 Steven Wagschal, *Minding Animals in the Old and New Worlds: A Cognitive Historical Analysis*

37 Heather Bamford, *Cultures of the Fragment: Uses of the Iberian Manuscript, 1100–1600*
38 Enrique García Santo-Tomás (ed.), *Science on Stage in Early Modern Spain*
39 Marina S. Brownlee (ed.), *Cervantes' Persiles and the Travails of Romance*
40 Sarah Thomas, *Inhabiting the In-Between: Childhood and Cinema in Spain's Long Transition*
41 David A. Wacks, *Medieval Iberian Crusade Fiction and the Mediterranean World*
42 Rosilie Hernández, *Immaculate Conceptions: The Power of the Religious Imagination in Early Modern Spain*
43 Mary L. Coffey and Margot Versteeg (eds.), *Imagined Truths: Realism in Modern Spanish Literature and Culture*
44 Diana Aramburu, *Resisting Invisibility: Detecting the Female Body in Spanish Crime Fiction*
45 Samuel Amago and Matthew J. Marr (eds.), *Consequential Art: Comics Culture in Contemporary Spain*
46 Richard P. Kinkade, *Dawn of a Dynasty: The Life and Times of Infante Manuel of Castile*
47 Jill Robbins, *Poetry and Crisis: Cultural Politics and Citizenship in the Wake of the Madrid Bombings*
48 Ana María Laguna and John Beusterien (eds.), *Goodbye Eros: Recasting Forms and Norms of Love in the Age of Cervantes*
49 Sara J. Brenneis and Gina Herrmann (eds.), *Spain, the Second World War, and the Holocaust: History and Representation*
50 Francisco Fernández de Alba, *Sex, Drugs, and Fashion in 1970s Madrid*
51 Daniel Aguirre-Oteiza, *This Ghostly Poetry: History and Memory of Exiled Spanish Republican Poets*
52 Lara Anderson, *Control and Resistance: Food Discourse in Franco Spain*
53 Faith S. Harden, *Arms and Letters: Military Life Writing in Early Modern Spain*
54 Erin Alice Cowling, Tania de Miguel Magro, Mina García Jordán, and Glenda Y. Nieto-Cuebas (eds.), *Social Justice in Spanish Golden Age Theatre*
55 Paul Michael Johnson, *Affective Geographies: Cervantes, Emotion, and the Literary Mediterranean*
56 Justin Crumbaugh and Nil Santiáñez (eds.), *Spanish Fascist Writing: An Anthology*
57 Margaret E. Boyle and Sarah E. Owens (eds.), *Health and Healing in the Early Modern Iberian World: A Gendered Perspective*
58 Leticia Álvarez-Recio (ed.), *Iberian Chivalric Romance: Translations and Cultural Transmission in Early Modern England*
59 Henry Berlin, *Alone Together: Poetics of the Passions in Late Medieval Iberia*
60 Adrian Shubert, *The Sword of Luchana: Baldomero Espartero and the Making of Modern Spain, 1793–1879*
61 Jorge Pérez, *Fashioning Spanish Cinema: Costume, Identity, and Stardom*

62　Enriqueta Zafra, *Lazarillo de Tormes: A Graphic Novel*
63　Erin Alice Cowling, *Chocolate: How a New World Commodity Conquered Spanish Literature*
64　Mary E. Barnard, *A Poetry of Things: The Material Lyric in Habsburg Spain*
65　Frederick A. de Armas and James Mandrell (eds.), *The Gastronomical Arts in Spain: Food and Etiquette*
66　Catherine Infante, *The Arts of Encounter: Christians, Muslims, and the Power of Images in Early Modern Spain*
67　Robert Richmond Ellis, *Bibliophiles, Murderous Bookmen, and Mad Librarians: The Story of Books in Modern Spain*
68　Beatriz de Alba-Koch (ed.), *The Ibero-American Baroque*
69　Deborah R. Forteza, *The English Reformation in the Spanish Imagination: Rewriting Nero, Jezebel, and the Dragon*
70　Olga Sendra Ferrer, *Barcelona, City of Margins*
71　Dale Shuger, *God Made Word: An Archaeology of Mystic Discourse in Early Modern Spain*
72　Xosé M. Núñez Seixas, *The Spanish Blue Division on the Eastern Front, 1941–1945: War, Occupation, Memory*
73　Julia Domínguez, *Quixotic Memories: Cervantes and Memory in Early Modern Spain*
74　Anna Casas Aguilar, *Bilingual Legacies: Father Figures in Self-Writing from Barcelona*
75　Julia H. Chang, *Blood Novels: Gender, Caste, and Race in Spanish Realism*
76　Frederick A. de Armas, *Cervantes' Architectures: The Dangers Outside*
77　Michael Iarocci, *The Art of Witnessing: Francisco de Goya's* Disasters of War
78　Esther Fernández and Adrienne L. Martín (eds.), *Drawing the Curtain: Cervantes's Theatrical Revelations*
79　Emiro Martínez-Osorio and Mercedes Blanco (eds.), *The War Trumpet: Iberian Epic Poetry, 1543–1639*
80　Christine Arkinstall, *Women on War in Spain's Long Nineteenth Century: Virtue, Patriotism, Citizenship*
81　Ignacio Infante, *A Planetary Avant-Garde: Experimental Literature Networks and the Legacy of Iberian Colonialism*
82　Enrique Fernández, *The Image of Celestina: Illustrations, Paintings, and Advertisements*
83　Maryanne L. Leone and Shanna Lino (eds.), *Beyond Human: Decentring the Anthropocene in Spanish Ecocriticism*
84　Jennifer Nagtegaal, *Politically Animated: Non-fiction Animation from the Hispanic World*
85　Anton Pujol and Jaume Martí-Olivella (eds.), *Catalan Cinema: The Barcelona Film School and the New Avant-Garde*
86　Matthew Bailey, *Speaking Truth to Power: The Legacy of the Young Cid*

87 Hilaire Kallendorf, *Perilous Passions: Ethics and Emotion in Early Modern Spain*
88 Anita Savo, *Portraying Authorship: Juan Manuel and the Rhetoric of Authority*
89 Robin M. Bower, *In the Doorway of All Worlds: Gonzalo de Berceo's Translation of the Saints*
90 Daniel Holcombe and Frederick A. de Armas (eds.), *Bodies Beyond Labels: Finding Joy in the Shadows of Imperial Spain*
91 Susan Larson (ed.), *Comfort and Domestic Space in Modern Spain*
92 Heather Jerónimo, *Performing Parenthood: Non-Normative Fathers and Mothers in Spanish Narrative and Film*

Milton Keynes UK
Ingram Content Group UK Ltd.
UKHW021850070724
445128UK00003B/13/J